LOCATING BOURDIEU

NEW ANTHROPOLOGIES OF EUROPE

Daphne Berdahl, Matti Bunzl, and Michael Herzfeld

Locating Bourdieu

DEBORAH REED-DANAHAY

Indiana University Press
Bloomington and Indianapolis

This book is a publication of

Indiana University Press
601 North Morton Street
Bloomington, IN 47404-3797 USA

http://iupress.indiana.edu

Telephone orders   800-842-6796
Fax orders   812-855-7931
Orders by e-mail   iuporder@indiana.edu

The paper used in this publication meets the minimum requirements
of American National Standard for Information Sciences—
Permanence of Paper for Printed Library Materials, ANSI Z39.48-
1984.

Manufactured in the United States of America

Library of Congress Cataloging-in-Publication Data

Reed-Danahay, Deborah.
    Locating Bourdieu / Deborah Reed-Danahay.
      p.   cm. — (New anthropologies of Europe)
    Includes bibliographical references and index.
    ISBN 0-253-34508-1 (cloth : alk. paper) — ISBN 0-253-21732-6
(pbk. : alk. paper)
    1. Bourdieu, Pierre. 2. Sociologists—France—Biography.
3. Anthropologists—France—Biography. 4. Sociology.
5. Anthropology. 6. Educational sociology. I. Title. II. Series.
    HM479.B68R44 2004
    301'.092—dc22

                                                                    2004009429

1 2 3 4 5 10 09 08 07 06 05

To my children, Emily and Ian

So the little boy's mind began to focus on the idea of surviving
the hardships of school.
Surviving.
Getting through it.
And that, he could tell, was estranging himself from his family
by opening pockets of solitude in the core of his being.

Patrick Chamoiseau, *School Days* (1997 [1994])

CONTENTS

ACKNOWLEDGMENTS

My interest in the work of Pierre Bourdieu goes back many years, and this book draws on numerous experiences and the help of many institutions and individuals over the years. I would like to thank Michael Apple for encouraging me to write a book on Bourdieu over a decade ago—a project that was interrupted by various happenstances. I also would like to thank Michael Herzfeld for encouraging me more recently to write this book. Thanks also go to the graduate students in seminars dealing with some of the issues I raise in this book that I have taught at the Department of Educational Policy Studies at the University of Wisconsin and in the Anthropology and Humanities Programs at the University of Texas at Arlington (UTA). I have been privileged to work with some excellent students who helped push my thinking in important ways. I would like to thank UTA for granting me a leave during the fall of 2003, which was invaluable as I completed this book. I also am grateful to former interim Dean Richard Cole in the College of Liberal Arts at UTA for providing funds for a graduate research assistant. Jason Rodriguez, who served as my excellent research assistant, was more than helpful in locating sources. I am indebted to the following colleagues who have read and commented on this manuscript or portions of it: Kathryn M. Anderson-Levitt, Jill Dubisch, Jane Goodman, Bradley Levinson, and Susan Carol Rogers. Their guidance and feedback were indispensable, and I hope they will excuse any remaining oversights that are entirely my fault. Rebecca Tolen at Indiana University Press has been supportive of this project from the beginning; her interest, encouragement, and intelligent advice were invaluable to me as I worked on this book.

The time that I have been able to spend in Paris and the time I have been able to spend in a dairy farming community in Auvergne have both added insights for me to the context of Bourdieu's life and work. Although I did not receive specific funding for this project on Bourdieu, the grants and fellowships that have enabled me to travel to France over the years have been crucial. I would like to thank the National Science Foundation, the National Endowment for the Humanities, Fulbright, the French Ministry of Culture (Bourse Chateaubriand) and the French Ministry of Education (Institut National de Recherche Pédagoqique), and UTA for these travel funds. I also am indebted to countless colleagues in France who helped explain the ways of academia there, as well as to my research participants and informants who explained the ways of French rural life and education to me. I especially would like to thank Colette Valleix Kosinski for friendship and ethnographic insights over many years of my fieldwork in her natal village. Pierre Bourdieu also must be thanked for taking the time to meet occasionally over the years to discuss French rural ethnography and educational narratives with a little-known American anthropologist. I hope he would not now regret having done so. I do not know how this book might have been written differently were he still alive, but I hope he would not object too strongly to it.

My family has, as always, been a significant basis of love and support for me as I worked on this project. I am grateful to my husband Martin Danahay, and children Emily and Ian, for their encouragement and understanding of long hours spent writing. Martin did more than his share of domestic duty, even while he worked on his own book on Victorian masculinity and labor. And I must apologize to Ian for missing so many of his soccer games while I wrote this book (of which I am sure Bourdieu would not have approved, given his love of field sport and rugby!).

LOCATING BOURDIEU

Introduction

Nothing is more false, in my view, than the maxim almost universally accepted in the social sciences according to which the researcher must put nothing of himself into his research.

—*Participant Objectivation* (2003)

Pierre Bourdieu was, as a writer, a *provocateur*, who seemed to enjoy the challenge and riposte of academic discourse as he attacked his opponents and was defensive in responses to critics. In anthropology, he attacked structuralism (for ignoring subjectivity), interpretive anthropology (for imposing a "scholastic" view on informants), ethnomethodology (for putting too much emphasis on subjectivity), and postmodernism (for being unscientific and relativist). Bourdieu attacked philosophy for its disdain of empirical research, economics for its theory of rational action, and he attacked his own chosen discipline of sociology for its survey methods that were too objectivist.[1] He was, in turn, criticized by others for being too deterministic in his theories of habitus, and in France, especially for depending too much on his social origins to lend authority to his research ("the neurosis of class").[2] He viewed the academic field, as other fields, as a game in which conflict and struggle over symbolic capital were *de rigueur*. At the same time, he was uneasy with his existence as an intellectual, and wrote in the introduction to *Pascalian Meditations:* "I do not like the intellectual in myself, and what may sound, in my writing, like anti-intellectualism is chiefly directed against the intellectualism of intellectuality that remains in me, despite all my efforts, such as the difficulty, so typical of intellectuals, I have in accepting that my freedom has its limits" (2000b: 7).[3] In a book published in France after his death (Bourdieu 2004: 135), Bourdieu wrote, "The intellectual world, which believes itself so profoundly liberated from conformity and convention, has always seemed to me as inhabited by profound conformities, that acted upon me as repulsive forces." He continued in that passage to speak of a "double distance" that he felt from the world of intellectuals—his distance from the intellectual games in France and from the "grand role" of the professor, and his distance from both the elitism and populism of culture in France.

Bourdieu was born in 1930 in a village near the Pyrenees in southwestern France, and died of cancer in 2002, not long after retiring from his position as Chair of Sociology at the Collège de France. His grandfather was a sharecropper and his childhood was spent in a rural milieu. He attended the elite École Normale Supérieure (ENS) in Paris during the 1950s, with early training in philosophy—which was in France at the time the most the prestigious of intellectual pursuits. In what sounds much like a "conversion narrative" or "epiphanal moment" (Denzin 1989), Bourdieu has written that his conscription to military service and assignment to Algeria in the early 1950s turned him toward the social sciences of ethnology and later sociology, and away from philosophy. He stayed on to teach in Algiers and to conduct research in villages and resettlement centers in late colonial Algeria, eventually forced to leave because of his opposition to the French war policy.[4] Bourdieu also has written that fieldwork he undertook in his native region of Béarn in 1959–60 had the same "conversion" effect, drawing him away from philosophy and toward the social sciences. Bourdieu rose through the ranks of academia in France, built a strong research center and team of collaborators at the École des Hautes Études en Sciences Sociales, established his own journal and eventually a publishing house, often took public political stances that were highly controversial in France, and was, to say the least, a prolific writer.

Bourdieu's research and writings touched on the fields of philosophy, anthropology, sociology, education, literary criticism, art history, and science. His two most cited books are *Outline of a Theory of Practice,* which was both an ethnography of the Kabyles in Algeria and a critique of Lévi-Straussian structuralism, and *Distinction,* an ethnography of France, linking social class position to aesthetic tastes and judgments of value that took Bourdieu's work to a wider audience, engaging those in cultural studies, literary criticism, and art history. Bourdieu's work on French education, especially his early book *Reproduction in Education, Culture, and Society,* coauthored with Jean-Claude Passeron, has been highly influential in debates on social class reproduction through schooling. Much of Bourdieu's work was concerned with articulating the ways in which a person's social position (and the "cultural capital," or values and resources connected to this) affects the choices he or she makes in life—from that of choosing a suitable marriage partner, to educational and career decisions, to deciding how much time should elapse before repaying a gift. For Bourdieu, these were not wholly conscious decisions or calculated strategies, but, rather, products of the habitus—embodied feelings and thoughts connected to commonsense understandings of the world (what he called the *doxa*) and arising from particular social positions, including those of class, gender, nationality, and ethnicity.

Bourdieu seemed to prefer being in a position of marginality, adopting the stance of the "professional stranger" (Agar 1980) or "familiar stranger," which he would undoubtedly have argued was a "virtue made of necessity," because his own social background in rural France denied him the automatic inheritance of social class privilege. In later writings (2004: 130), Bourdieu spoke of his *habitus clivé* (split habitus), which resulted from his elevated social position in academia and his low social origins. Bourdieu went outside of his own disciplines to literary and art criticism to offer critiques of sociology and anthropology, and to sociology to critique ethnology; he left his original discipline of philosophy, yet continued to criticize its assumptions and its institutional position in France throughout his career. Even though his political leanings were to the left, he remained outside of the organized political parties and factions in France so as to criticize the left on many counts. By continuing to evoke his social origins, right up until his last writings, and by continuing to criticize all manner of scholarship from a position that he felt was somewhat apart because of those social origins as well as his crossovers from ethnology in Algeria to sociology in France, Bourdieu maintained a posture of marginality.[5]

Different readers of Bourdieu enter his work from different positions or "points of view" depending on, to use his own phrasing, the field in which they are operating. In this book, I write from the perspective of a Europeanist anthropologist, a specialist in French ethnology, who has worked with and sometimes against Bourdieu's theoretical concepts for several years. My approach is ethnographic and biographical, both as methods and in terms of those aspects of his work that are of most interest to me. I do not intend a psychological or even very personal study of Bourdieu, although he as a person does appear quite often. I do not believe that it is desirable or helpful to separate Bourdieu the person from Bourdieu the sociologist and anthropologist or from his work itself, and understanding something of his background and motivations is useful in an analysis of his contributions to scholarship. But I agree with Geertz (1973) that one can really only approach the public meanings and interpretations of one's informants.

The ethnographic gaze is predicated on some mixture of distance from and familiarity with one's object. Bourdieu advocated a method of "reflexive sociology" or "participant objectivation" in order to balance subjectivity and objectivity in research, and increasingly turned to the "socioanalysis" (recalling the methods of psychoanalysis) of sociology and anthropology in his later years. In this book, I employ several of Bourdieu's own methodologies in order to interrogate his work and to place, or locate him in the social space of European ethnology. In this, I am conscious of my own familiarity and distance from these social spaces, as an American anthropologist who has acquired cultural knowledge of many aspects of French society as participant and observer. At the same time, I am aware that distance and familiarity (as are exotic and domestic or insider/outsider) are themselves tropes in ethnographic inquiry that have certain origins and consequences in European and postcolonial contexts. Bourdieu himself employed the concepts of familiarity and distance, native and outsider, quite often in his own work. This book is partly about this construction and the ways it operates in Bourdieu's work.

This book is also about relationships between autobiography and anthropology, or what I have called autoethnography.[6] Bourdieu was himself concerned with "reflexivity" and what he later called "auto-analysis"—but in a fairly circumscribed way that was connected to his sociological method. I have in mind here a view of his work that goes beyond that methodology. Bourdieu's work was, I will argue, to a large extent a form of autoethnography in the double sense of being self-referential (referring back to his own origins and cultural preoccupations), and of constituting a description and analysis of his own sociocultural milieu in France and its former colony in Algeria. This book is not in itself a biography of Bourdieu, although it shares kinship with "ethnographic biography" (Herzfeld 1987); rather, it locates Bourdieu's own uses of his biography within his work. I take Bourdieu as my main informant in this task. I employ the standard ethnographic and literary device of not assuming that Bourdieu is always, however, a "reliable narrator" about himself, and have looked for slippages, silences, and eruptions in his work that contradict some of his own interpretations. Bourdieu produced many statements, or metacommentaries, about his work and his biography that are useful in understanding his modes of self-presentation. This book relies primarily on Bourdieu's published work and public proclamations in published interviews about his work, with reference to the critical literature on his work that increasingly surrounded it. Although I knew Bourdieu, I never interviewed him.

Bourdieu made use of life narrative quite a bit in his work, starting with the narratives of displaced Algerian workers in the early 1960s and culminating in the collection of personal stories published in *The Weight of the World,* and much of his statistical work is offset by first-person accounts of experience. I am interested in the ways that he employed these narratives in his sociological and anthropological approaches to the articulation of habitus and field. The one area to which he did not apply the narrative approach, however, was that of education—with the exception of *The Weight of World,* which includes some interviews on education. This neglect is one that derives, I believe, from his need earlier in his career to distance himself from his own feelings about becoming educated—feelings that he confronted and wrote about during the last decade of his life. Although Bourdieu had written about his own educational experiences, in a somewhat veiled form, in *Homo Academicus* (1984a), he did not explicitly recount those experiences in the first person until 1997 (in *Pascalian Meditations*), and even then he did so in the form of what he called an "impersonal confession." Toward the end of his life, Bourdieu became more explicit about his educational autobiography—in both his final lectures at the Collège de France (2001a) and in a later, posthumously published, revision of one of these (2004 [2002g]).

ENCOUNTERS WITH BOURDIEU
AND FRENCH ACADEMIA

My interest in writing this book arose in part from the myriad ways in which I have, often by chance, come across Bourdieu's writing in a variety of contexts and also in my early encounter with Bourdieu himself during my first fieldwork in France. There are both arbitrary and inevitable aspects to my familiarity with Bourdieu's work. Inevitable, perhaps, because I am an ethnographer of rural France and have studied French education, so Bourdieu's work on peasant societies and education would invariably cross my path and be crucial to my work. As my training was in political anthropology, I was drawn to his analyses of education and power and intrigued by the concept of cultural capital. When I first set off for fieldwork in France, however, I must confess that I had read few of his educational writings and was not at all aware of his work on rural France—and found his writings on education too focused on secondary schooling and too mechanistic to have any relevance to my ethnographic fieldwork among living and breathing and acting informants. I had not read *Outline of a Theory of Practice* but I had read his early articles on the Kabyles.

I was not taught by Europeanists in my anthropological studies, or specialists in educational anthropology, so I am by necessity a bit of an autodidact in these fields, as Bourdieu claimed he was in ethnology (having been trained in philosophy). I offer this as an excuse for my framing of having "stumbled on" Bourdieu's work at various points. My introduction to Bourdieu's work was in an anthropology class on "Peasants" that I took in graduate school at Brandeis University, and in which I read his essay on time in Algeria. I liked his Algerian ethnography and especially his symbolic analyses of issues of honor and concepts of time. A little later in my graduate studies, I embarked on a thesis project on education and France, and quickly learned that Bourdieu was a major figure in debates about education and social reproduction. At first, I was not sure if this was the same person who had written so eloquently and descriptively about Algerian peasant society—this sociologist who I thought (at first, I must admit) dryly used statistics and cumbersome phrasings to advance a thesis about social class reproduction. I had already read Laurence Wylie's *Village in the Vaucluse* (1975 [1957]) as I attempted to read any and all of the ethnography of France that had been published up until that time—and there was little of it. Wylie and Bourdieu were saying very different things about education. I was critical of Wylie for being too much of a functionalist, and hoped to integrate more of an ethnographic perspective on education with the theoretical ideas espoused by Bourdieu. I had read Bourdieu's article on cultural and symbolic reproduction reprinted in Karabel and Halsey's *Power and Ideology in Education* (1977), and it was my introduction to a new way of looking at education that standard anthropological literature at the time ignored in its emphases on ethnic and cultural difference—the issue of social class. But this essay spoke of laws (phrases in it included "it becomes necessary to study the laws that determine the tendency of structures . . .") and institutions, and was peppered with statistics: it lacked any ethnographic details of lived experience. At the time, I found historical studies of French education more helpful and interesting than this type of analysis (and there were no ethnographies of education in France, apart from Wylie's study). I received dissertation funding for a proposal to look at local-level influences on the seemingly monolithic centralized French educational system, as a way to challenge its own mythic view of itself, and see if I could find evidence of local interpretations and uses of the national institution.[7] I set off for France in the fall of 1980, and spent one month in Paris to do background research and start to locate a fieldsite—eventually settling in the region of Auvergne in central France.

I had still not read much beyond the translated essays on Algeria and the early books and some essays in French on education by Bourdieu when I met him in Paris. I had received one of my dissertation grants from the French Ministry of Culture, a Bourse Chateaubriand, and through this was assigned to the eminent French historian François Furet as my mentor/contact. My introduction to Bourdieu is part of the story of my introduction to the French university system and its system of patronage, its styles of interaction and deference, and its formal relationships between students and their professors. As I would later read more of Bourdieu's writings on this system, in *Homo Academicus* and *La noblesse d'état,* I experienced an immediate recognition of what he described. I had arrived in France a fairly naïve young woman (a familiar ethnographic trope) with regard to this French university system and its culture, even though I had done thorough background research on rural France and primary schooling. I confess that I was, thus, not at all aware of the impending naming of Bourdieu to the Chair of Sociology at the Collège de France or of the enormity of his reputation and growing stature in French academia. I did know of Furet's reputation as an historian, however, and was quite in awe of having been assigned to his mentorship through the grant. I arrived one day at his office, having gotten up the courage to meet with him, and knocked on his door (a significant *faux pas* as one of my French student friends later scolded me, as the protocol requires calling the secretary first for an appointment). Furet was there, and despite my bad manners, or perhaps because I was American and not expected to have any manners, he graciously welcomed me to his office and offered his assistance right there and then. After I had described what I intended to do through my field research, he told me that I needed to go and see three people: Isac Chiva, Henri Mendras, and Pierre Bourdieu. He suggested that I contact them on his behalf (*de ma part,* as the French put it). The name of Furet and the fact that I had a Ministry of Culture grant was like a key opening doors for me, and I was quickly able to meet with each of these scholars, who warmly welcomed me to their offices during our first appointments. One of my new French student friends, who was from the provinces, remarked with a tinge of jealousy about how easy it had been for me as an outsider to penetrate the elite offices of French academics, in comparison with the competition and "games" in which French students needed to engage in order to gain the favor and attention of professors. As this example shows, I learned about French academia both through my contacts with these professors and through the commentaries on these contacts that I received from French students I had met. They helped me to see the special status I had as outsider to this system, and that I could not take my own experiences as standard or normal.

I remember meeting Isac Chiva first, who asked that I meet him at his offices in the Collège de France, where he was Associate Director of the Laboratory of Social Anthropology and colleague of Claude Lévi-Strauss, who had recently retired. Chiva was a courtly gentleman, nicely dressed in formal suit (luckily I had received sufficient good advice from one of my thesis advisors to buy a suit and wear that in Paris). We met for the first time in the library of the laboratory. As we were chatting, a much older gentleman arrived in the room and was looking in the stacks. I did not recognize him, so Chiva cleared his throat a bit and asked me if I knew Professor Lévi-Strauss. As a young graduate student at the time, I was completely shocked to learn that this was Lévi-Strauss, already a legendary figure in anthropology. I was introduced, and mentioned that one of my advisors (Pierre-Yves Jacopin, a South Americanist) had taken some classes with him and he immediately recognized the name and said a few kind words. He went back to his research, while Chiva and I continued our discussion. In subsequent meetings, Chiva and I would meet in Lévi-Strauss's office, where I still remember seeing an ironic photograph on the wall of an Amazonian Indian reading one of Lévi-Strauss's books.

In addition to my meetings with Chiva, who was instrumental in leading me to the contacts through which I would locate my fieldsite in Auvergne, I found a welcome reception by Henri Mendras and the group of rural sociologists at Nanterre. I was invited to attend a meeting of the Association of Rural Sociologists in the Vendée, and made many contacts there with interesting students and scholars. At this time, there was precious little French ethnography undertaken by French anthropologists, most of whom had not yet "discovered" France as a terrain of fieldwork. It was among rural sociologists that most rural ethnography was being conducted. I did also, however, meet with the anthropologist Françoise Zonabend at the Collège de France, who was part of the "new wave" of anthropology "at home" and had worked on a collaborative project (Minot) in Burgundy. She had studied childhood, and gave me good suggestions for fieldwork questions.

It seems in retrospect that when I finally met with Bourdieu, I was able to mention my encounter with Chiva and Lévi-Strauss, and that it helped that I'd made this connection at the Collège de France already. I had by that time the recommendations of Chiva, as well as Furet, as introductions to Bourdieu. Bourdieu and I met in his offices at the École des Hautes Études en Sciences Sociales on Boulevard Raspail. He seemed to me the younger, kinder, and more informal of the three scholars to whom I had been referred by Furet. Bourdieu took an avid interest in my project and invited me to meet with him again after I'd conducted some of my fieldwork. Our discussions when I would return to visit Paris during my fieldwork were highly important to me and helped reinforce that I was on the "right track" in my analyses. I have to add here that I was working on social practice, family strategies, and resistances of parents and children to the school. Bourdieu was supportive, even though I was not interested in doing the type of project conducted among his team. I clearly remember resisting one of his suggestions, which was that I collect teacher comments about the children in the school. He told me that if I did that and could place those comments under photos of the children, and write an article about it, he would publish that in his journal *Actes de la Recherche en Sciences Sociales*. I was appalled at the idea of exposing either the teachers or children in that way! Nevertheless, of all the scholars in France with whom I discussed my fieldwork, I felt that he was the one who "got it" the most, and I realize now more than ever that this was because of his own primary experiences growing up in a rural milieu. So many of the other scholars, many of whom I have not named here and certainly not all that I have named, were the product of bourgeois backgrounds, and had quite distant and stereotyped views of rural society in my mind even if they had worked in rural areas.

Over the subsequent years, as I turned my field research into a dissertation and then a few years later rewrote and updated it into a book, I read more of Bourdieu's work and continued to enter into a dialogue with his theories. I have been critical in my work of his overreliance on a view of habitus that struggles to deal with resistance or change, and I continue to feel that he did not lend enough attention to lived practice and social agency in his work. My writings on rural France contain criticisms of his theories, perhaps most forcibly in my article (Reed-Danahay 1995) charging him with Occidentalism in his approach to French education. But I also have found other parts of his work useful and interesting "to think with" in other areas of my research—for instance, his concepts of distinction helped me analyze a scatological wedding ritual (Reed-Danahay 1996b), and his more recent use of *lieu* as physical location helped me analyze material from ethnography in an American nursing home (Reed-Danahay 2001a). I kept in intermittent contact with Bourdieu over the years but never entered into his "circle" of close associates or colleagues. Twice I tried to get him to speak as Distinguished Lecturer for the Society for the Anthropology of Europe at the American Anthropological Association meetings, which he declined—both times saying he was "*trop fatigué.*" I last saw him during the summer of 1996, when I was in Paris doing research on published schooling narratives. I had discovered his work on the "Biographical Illusion" and on literary figures such as Flaubert by that time, and was intrigued by their implications for my studies of narratives. We met at a café near the Bastille and had a very lively discussion about the meaning of schooling for peasants and the implications of becoming educated for those who left that milieu. I had not at that time read (or if I did read, had not paid close attention to those bits), the interviews in which he mentioned his own experiences with schooling. It has been more recently, as I undertook research for this book, that I have come to better understand why he was so interested in my own work and enjoyed talking about it—it was very close to home for him and by that time he had come to terms with his own background and trajectory.

Although I cannot claim to have known Bourdieu extremely well, and would never want to trade on such an impression, I was able to gain a sense of him in person that is quite different from what one encounters in his (often difficult) writings alone. He was ironic, amused, and amusing, and much less dogmatic when speaking than comes across in his writing style. He also struck me as perceptive and interested in the minutia of daily life. For instance, he often shared various folk and idiomatic expressions with me and obviously enjoyed the wordplay of language. He also made a statement to me during my early first fieldwork that really struck a chord with me and summed up a crucial difference between French and American attitudes toward education—he told me that French peasants would much prefer to talk to you about their sex lives than about their educational experiences. And, of course, they are reticent to speak about their sex lives! This statement sums up the heavy weight given to education in that society and helps to explain his own preoccupation with education in his work. My position vis-à-vis Bourdieu and his academic milieu is one of both distance and familiarity, the common situation of the ethnographer. I must admit that I know much more about how a dairy farm operates in France, or of what goes on in a rural primary classroom, than I do about French academia, to which I have remained, sometimes by choice, somewhat distant over the years.

I did have the opportunity in the summers of both 2001 and 2002, however, to change that. I spent the first summer attached to the Anthropology Laboratory at the Université Blaise Pascale in Clermont-Ferrand, thanks to a Fulbright Research Award, and although most of my own research that summer took me out of the city and back to the countryside, I was able to get a glimpse of daily life and exchanges in such a setting—and a view from the provinces that has helped complement my previous experiences in Parisian academic institutions. While there I was struck, however, by the lack of attention paid to the rural milieu surrounding their laboratory among ethnographers there, most of whom were specialists of non-French societies. My work in the countryside of Auvergne appeared to some of them as both exotic and too familiar and, although they were happy to be "relativists" when it came to strange practices elsewhere, they were somewhat condescending to the "hicks" (in their minds) that I studied and even liked to be with! This experience illustrates the attitudes of some French academics (even ethnographers) toward the countryside (which is both romanticized and put down), attitudes that Bourdieu had to deal with in terms of his own social origins.[8] I was invited to spend the summer of 2002 at the Institute of Pedagogical Research (INRP) in Paris, which is the research arm of the Ministry of Education (and has since moved to Lyon), and this afforded me a view of both the insides of the bureaucracy of the system as well a chance to get to know researchers working there and to collaborate with them. While there, I was privy to insider critiques of and remarks about Bourdieu from educational researchers that, although I can't quote them here as I did not get permission from anyone to do so and all of this was unofficial research, have helped enormously in my ability to place Bourdieu in his milieu. This brief history is not in any way an exhaustive survey of my contacts with French academics, of which there have been many, but simply suggestive of the experiences on which I drew in writing this book. The other sources of experience from which I draw in this study of Bourdieu's work are my more recent work on education and European identity in France (Reed-Danahay 2003), and my long-term ethnographic fieldwork in rural Auvergne, about which I have written at length elsewhere (i.e., Reed-Danahay 1996a).

ON THE CONCEPT OF POINT OF VIEW

Bourdieu increasingly emphasized the concept of "point of view" in the latter part of his career, as a way to position the habitus within the social and spatial fields. For Bourdieu, social fields (*champs*) are sites of struggle over "symbolic capital" that are organized around interests such as education, art, politics, and literature. Social agents (Bourdieu's term for individuals) interact within social fields through their habitus (inculcated dispositions and cultural capital—including values, beliefs, tastes, etc.). The theoretical constructs of habitus and field will be explored in greater detail in the following chapters, but here I will introduce this important notion of point of view with respect to Bourdieu's analysis of the nineteenth-century French novelist Gustave Flaubert, in the 1988 article "Flaubert's Point of View." In his analysis of Flaubert, Bourdieu described his position in the artistic field, and the "position-takings" that he took within this field, all within the context of his social background as the son of a provincial doctor. Bourdieu's analysis of Flaubert's point of view is particularly interesting because there are autobiographical undertones to this analysis. In analyzing Flaubert's point of view, Bourdieu was also articulating, I suggest, some aspects of his own. At the same time, however, Bourdieu underscored the autobiographical elements to Flaubert's work as, for example, when he wrote that "the work of formalization gave the writer the opportunity to work on himself and thereby allowed him to objectify not only the positions in the field and their occupants he opposed, but also, through the space that included him, his own position" (1988c: 559). This was part of Bourdieu's own project as well, to analyze the spaces he occupied, as with his critique of academia in *Homo Academicus.*

Bourdieu described Flaubert, whose most famous novels are *Madame Bovary* and *Sentimental Education,* as rejecting both romanticism and realism. He wrote within a literary field whose dominant genre was "romantic" bourgeois art and whose most dominated form was the realism of writers such as George Sand. Flaubert, who championed "art for art's sake," was located in the middle position. He scorned other artists, and rejected political positions. There are parallels to his own life when Bourdieu notes that Flaubert wrote in a genre that was subordinate in the field of art—the novel, as Bourdieu also noted elsewhere in his writings that sociology was subordinate in the academic field in France. Both men had chosen subordinate genres within the fields of possibilities open to them. Another parallel is that Bourdieu notes that Flaubert wanted to present himself as unclassifiable, which also was a trait of Bourdieu. Bourdieu seemed to identify with Flaubert's writing as a form of reflexivity. In a passage in which he could be writing about himself, Bourdieu said of Flaubert:

The familiar world keeps us from understanding, among other things, the extraordinary effort that he had to make, the exceptional resistance that he had to surmount, beginning within himself, in order to produce and impose that which, largely because of him, we now take for granted. (1988c: 558)

The two major objectives of Bourdieu's analysis were, first, to argue that Flaubert was not "unique" in that others of his cohort who had similar social trajectories took similar positions within the field of art; and, second, that Flaubert was not conscious of his own "strategies of distinction" within that field. Here, Bourdieu's theory of habitus was articulated in the specific case of a life history that illustrates wider social structures at work. This work on Flaubert also shows Bourdieu's interest in artists as models for social science—which he would again use in the cases of Manet and Virginia Woolf, among other artists, and of his identification with the artistic sensibility even as he championed the scientific study of sociology.

The phrase "point of view" that Bourdieu used in relationship to Flaubert has particular resonance in the field of anthropology, where the notion of gaining the "native's point of view" as a supreme goal of ethnographic fieldwork was introduced by Bronislaw Malinowski (1961 [1922]) in his *Argonauts of the Western Pacific*. Anthropologists have struggled ever since with what that really means and whether that is truly even possible or desirable. Bourdieu himself entered the debate in *Outline of a Theory of Practice* with his warning that "native theories are dangerous" (because misleading for the anthropologist who takes them at face value). This idea of native point of view was in turn critiqued by Clifford Geertz (1973) in his essay "From the Native's Point of View." By that time, Malinowski's diaries had been published, and revealed his relationship to "the natives" as a bit more complicated than he had let on in his monograph. Geertz introduced (following Kohut) the distinction between "experience-near" and "experience-far" concepts, with the first being those that Bourdieu referred to as "commonsense" understandings of the world (the *doxa*)—those concepts that seemed "natural" to informants, and the latter as those of the analyst or specialist—such as the term "habitus."[9] For Geertz, the anthropologist's goal is to combine both, rather than to depend on one or the other of these concepts. He argued against the possibility of empathic understanding, which would impose Western notions of selfhood on informants (in his case, in Morocco or Bali), and for the analysis of the parts and whole of symbolic systems. Bourdieu's perspective was different from that of Geertz, although he shared the view that the goal of research was to synthesize what Bourdieu termed the subjectivist ("experience-near") versus objectivist ("experience-far") perspective. Bourdieu also shared the view that empathy was not the answer. He wrote that the ethnographer should place herself "in the thought of agents (not through intuition or 'emotional participation' but through theoretical and empirical effort)" (2000b: 55), in order to see the logic of their practices.

For Bourdieu, who had a more materialist approach than that of Geertz, the point of view was not something to be understood through symbolic analysis but through an analysis of the economic and social fields and the positions of various social agents within these. Point of view is thus a form of "position-taking" in a social field. Bourdieu distinguished between what he called differentiated and undifferentiated societies in his thinking about point of view. In societies that were undifferentiated (similar to Durkheim's model of mechanical solidarity) people were in fixed positions and had no options about their point of view. It derived from the habitus that they all shared, except for gender differences between men and women. Thus, in traditional Kabyle society in Algeria, all men would have the same point of view. In so-called differentiated societies, according to Bourdieu, there are multiple fields and a range of possibilities for position-taking within each one.

Another aspect of Bourdieu's thought on point of view, which he increasingly developed in the 1990s, was his concept of "the scholastic point of view" or "scholastic fallacy" (following Austin; Bourdieu 1990c; 2000b).[10] This "academic vision" (1990c: 380) is the experience-far (to use Geertz's terms) point of view which seems "natural" and commonsensical to the analyst or ethnographer, and is inculcated in formal institutions of higher education—which Bourdieu referred to with the generic term *skholè*. Forms of "common sense" (as opposed to "scholastic reason") are also, however, inculcated through education but at lower levels. Bourdieu wrote that this produces nationalism, and that schools "construct the nation as a population endowed with the same categories and therefore the same commonsense" (2000b: 98). Scholastic reason (as distinguished from "practical reason") is most accessible to those higher in the social system. It is this form of cognition that sets up the distinctions between distance and familiarity, experience-near and experience-far, objective and subjective. Bourdieu (2000b: 17) believed that those lower in the social hierarchy have less time for thought and have more strictly defined social positions in comparison with those higher in social status, who have "less strictly defined positions" and more room for maneuver. They have a "detached, distant disposition" that permits them to experience "role distance" (here Bourdieu evokes Goffman), because their lives are free of necessity and they are, thus, able to participate in various "mental spaces" (after Gilles Fauconnier) simultaneously. The "scholastic point of view" is that distant, "lofty gaze" of the ethnographer or any analyst that divorces intellect and body, economic and symbolic worlds (23). For Bourdieu, it was opposed to "the logic of practice" or "practical reason," and needed to be made more conscious in the minds of ethnographers so that they could "take a theoretical view on [their] own theoretical point of view" (2000b: 54). Bourdieu was not, however, opposed to scholastic reason in and of itself. Although he accused Geertz, among others, of applying the "scholastic fallacy" in his work, imposing his own reasoning onto his informants (2000b: 53), Bourdieu viewed the dominated classes as "confined" to commonsense because they did not have access to scholastic reason. He noted (2000b: 60) that in the collaborative project *The Weight of the World*, in which he and his team interviewed many people from lower social classes, part of the aim was to help people who did not normally have access to the scholastic point of view, and who could not thus take a distant or "objective" view of their own position, to realize a form of self-understanding through access to a "quasi-theoretical" discourse.

BOURDIEU AND LATE-TWENTIETH CENTURY SOCIAL THEORY: STRUCTURE, PRACTICE, AGENCY

There have already been several very sophisticated discussions of Bourdieu in relationship to contemporary social theory,[11] and this book intends to complement those with an ethnographic perspective on his work. Although I will continue to discuss and elaborate on Bourdieu's theoretical frameworks throughout this book, brief mention of the influences on his work, and of his locations within social theory debates during his lifetime, are helpful to have here at hand at the outset. The major historical influences on Bourdieu's thought were Emile Durkheim, Max Weber, and Karl Marx. Other figures in his intellectual genealogy include Norbert Elias, Georges Bachelard, and Erving Goffman. But it must be emphasized that Bourdieu's own intellectual heritage in France was most directly shaped during the 1950s in the context of an academic world dominated by Jean-Paul Sartre and Claude Lévi-Strauss, and he worked out his methods, practice, and theory largely in response to the paradigms they had established. In his later autobiographical writings, Bourdieu would discuss these influences in terms of the "space of possibilities" available to him.

Bourdieu came of age in a period of European history that marked the beginning of the end of colonialism, and was experiencing the aftermath of World War II. This was a time of economic expansion, urbanization, and social dislocation. Issues of freedom and of self-determination were highly contested in these circumstances, and there were several theoretical responses to these concerns. Movements such as the Frankfurt School responded to the wake of totalitarian fascist regimes with a theory of historical materialism influenced by Marx and a critical theory that analyzed capitalism, consumer culture, and the mass media. Figures in that movement such as Adorno, Marcuse, Benjamin, and Habermas theorized human freedom and constraint within both communist and capitalist economic systems. Another response to twentieth-century upheavals was that of phenomenology, associated with Heidegger, Husserl, Merleau-Ponty, and Sartre. This was a philosophy of subjectivity, of human consciousness and intentionality. Merleau-Ponty's work on the embodied nature of consciousness was particularly influential on Bourdieu. Yet, another philosophical response to uncertainties in the modern world—in many ways a mirror image of the Frankfurt School's emphasis on constraints on freedom—was existentialism, a theory of individual choice and autonomy, in which each person was believed responsible for his or her own destiny. This was most closely associated with Sartre and, later, Albert Camus.

Although neither Bourdieu nor Lévi-Strauss claimed affiliation with the Frankfurt School, they both rejected the existentialist views of Sartre and viewed human freedom as limited by culture and society. Lévi-Strauss, influenced by Durkheim, Marx, and Freud as well as by structural linguistics, developed a theory of structuralism in anthropology that focused on underlying, unconscious systems of classification in language, kinship, and myth. For Lévi-Strauss, humans were constrained by these underlying structures and the rules of classification they entailed. Bourdieu's own project was initially to study traditional societies such as Kabylia and rural France, and modern institutions such as the French educational system, in order to develop a theory of human social practice that located constraints on freedom not in the structures of the mind but in a particular historical constellation of socioeconomic structures that were then inculcated in each person through the habitus. Bourdieu incorporated a theory of power into his discussions of society, whereas Lévi-Strauss viewed the unconscious structures of the mind as politically neutral and "naturally" occurring. He also incorporated a theory of human action that was lacking in structuralism, which had relied primarily on classifications rather than behaviors—which were seen as secondary to these and not terribly important theoretically. Bourdieu argued for the arbitrariness of values and classifications (or distinctions) in society, concurring with Marx that the most highly valued things and beliefs in society are those of the dominant classes. Because I will discuss Bourdieu's theories in greater detail in other chapters, I will not elaborate on these points here. I do want to emphasize here, however, that Bourdieu rejected categorically a rational actor theory of human behavior, and did not view people as autonomous individuals but as bearers of shared habituses. There are ambiguities in Bourdieu's work about the relative degree of freedom and constraint on human agency, as evident in the gap between readings of his work on education (viewed in its earliest forms as a theory of reproduction with no possibility of human agency) and his work on the Kabyles in *Outline* (viewed as a form of emergent practice theory exploring human agency).

The implications of Bourdieu's thought for late-twentieth-century anthropological theory, particularly in Anglo-American contexts, is an issue to which I will now turn with a discussion of three key texts of this period. Sherry Ortner (1984) identified a growing emphasis on "practice" in anthropological theory beginning in the 1960s, which she associated with a wider trend toward a shift "from static, synchronic analyses to diachronic, processual ones" (158). This approach illustrated, she suggested, the ways in which people make history, and in some versions "make themselves." Ortner thereby linked a process-oriented approach to an actor-centered approach (which, I would argue, is not helpful in the case of Bourdieu). Marcus and Fischer (1986) defined the 1980s as a period of experiment in anthropology, prompted by a "crisis of representation" related to postcolonialism and new concerns about power in relationships between peoples and nations. One trend that they identified was a new emphasis in political economy approaches that focuses on local-level responses to macrohistorical processes. They saw in Bourdieu's work a synthesis of cultural and political economy approaches, and an emphasis on cultural production as a form of practice. In a more recent overview of "the state" of anthropological theory, Michael Herzfeld (2001: 53–54) points out that the greatest virtue of a practice approach is that it calls into question static views of culture that deny tensions and transience. In the spirit of critique and self-consciousness about the anthropological enterprise that Marcus and Fischer identified as a new development in the 1980s, which has now become more commonplace by the early twenty-first century, Herzfeld suggests that concerns with human agency and practice leads us away from master narratives to "the rich play of multiple histories." Bourdieu viewed the habitus as a form of collective, shared history among people in the same social position. The possibilities for human agency and constraints on it were issues that he first addressed in a particular historical moment in postwar France but sought to clarify over the course of his career. Even his former rival in France, Alain Touraine (2002: 103; my translation), wrote in an essay assessing Bourdieu's work after his death that his strongest thesis, that of the habitus, "was on one of the great questions of philosophy and sociology: how can an individual have freedom while captured in multiple constraints and determinisms?"

ON SOCIOLOGY AS A "MARTIAL ART"[12]

Bourdieu was a combative and defensive scholar. Clifford Geertz's observation about Wittgenstein that "he did not much like to think he was agreed with or understood" (2000: xii) is aptly applied to Bourdieu as well. Many of Bourdieu's later self-reflexive writings (2000b; 2001a; 2004) were responses to his critics as much as they were aimed at explaining his motivations and "point of view" for his followers. Let me give three examples. Bourdieu often reproached those who sought the origins of the concept of habitus in order to accuse him of not being original or of altering the intent of another person who used the term. Although Bourdieu never devoted much space on the page to the genealogy of this term or the distinctions between his uses of the term and that of his predecessors, he claimed that his use of the term was calling attention to the uses of predecessors in interesting ways. In a footnote in the *Rules of Art,* Bourdieu wrote: "someone who (like so many other 'genealogists') would never have paid the least attention to the notion of habitus or to the uses made of it by Husserl, if I had not used it, rushes to exhume the Husserlian usages in order to reproach me, as if in passing, for having betrayed the magisterial thought— in which the same person wants nevertheless to discover a destructive anticipation" (1996c: 375, fn. 5).

Bourdieu was also combative about uses of his work made by others. He bitingly attacked the "unauthorized" Internet bibliography Hyper-Bourdieu during his published interview with Yvette Delsaut (one of his "authorized" bibliographers), when the topic was raised by Delsaut. In responding to her criticism of "tentacled" postmodern Internet sites surrounding his work, including HyperBourdieu, which she noted was Austrian, Bourdieu said, "Yes, I saw that. I saw that they even put a copyright on their bibliography, and I have trouble understanding that, what is this self-proclaimed property right on work that comes from other sites (which in another level of their work, they have declared)?" (Bourdieu and Delsaut 2002f: 185). They also discussed the citing of his unpublished works on that site, particularly his unfinished thesis. Bourdieu appeared outraged by what he saw as an appropriation of his work outside of his control. It has been very clear that Bourdieu wanted to have some control over the understandings and uses of his work, however futile such an aim is, and the case of HyperBourdieu is but one example of this.

A final example is Bourdieu's outrage at those who did not understand that his theories could be liberating for those who seriously listened to them. He felt he had been misunderstood (by what he called "fast readings" of his work) to imply that resistance was impossible and that social life is determined by the structures of domination; at the same time, he felt misunderstood by those, alternatively, who thought his work implied a theory of rational action, to which he was adamantly opposed. He also felt that he was attacked because his research threatened those in power. In his study of French higher education, *The State Nobility,* Bourdieu spoke of the "suffering that scientific unveiling sometimes causes, in spite of its undoubtedly liberating nature" (1996a: 5). He noted in a footnote to that book that he agreed with Deleuze that freedom is a form of "expansion of the consciousness," and followed with: "Paradoxically, there are those who would stigmatize as 'deterministic' analyses that, by working to enlarge the space open to consciousness and clarification, offer those being studied the possibility of liberation (teachers in the present case, for example)" (1996a: 395, fn. 5).

ON SILENCES

One of the underlying themes of this book is that of silences and ellipses both in Bourdieu's work and in the literature on his work. In part, the silences in Bourdieu's work are due to his own "commonsense" understandings of the world, I will argue, that caused him to take for granted certain aspects of social life. I will, for example, discuss his relative silence on issues of religion and education in France in Chapter 2. He also neglected the role of Islam in his studies of Algeria. Despite his autobiographical reflections on fieldwork experiences and his social origins, Bourdieu wrote little about his experiences as a soldier in Algeria until the last years of his life (Bourdieu 2004; see also Yacine 2003). He rarely addressed the influences of World War II on either his own youth or on his natal region of Béarn. In Chapter 3, I will address the silences in his work on Algeria in *Outline* regarding both the disruption of the war and the presence of educational institutions in "traditional" Kabylia. Chapters 4 and 5 deal with silences in the critical literature on Bourdieu, and on topics that were not foregrounded in his own discussions of his work. Because so much of the emphasis in the critical literature on Bourdieu's work has been on issues of agency and structure, particularly among English-speaking readers of his work, other aspects have been overlooked. The implication of his theory of habitus and dispositions for the study of emotions is one of those themes. The other is the uses of personal narrative in his work and his own autobiographical reflections.

ON LOCATION

Bourdieu's "locations" (Gupta and Ferguson 1997) are telling for an understanding of the constructions of fields of study in the late twentieth century. Bourdieu's work is of interest not only for its contributions to knowledge and theory in the social sciences but for its implications for the doing of anthropology and sociology. Bourdieu made sense of the locations or sites in which he did his research through the lens of his own "point of view"—which was French, European, and of the postwar period, and that reflected his origins in rural France and eventual ascent to the

Chair in Sociology at the Collège de France. Bourdieu was unique in having worked ethnographically both on the metropole of France and on the French colonial milieu of Algeria.[13] He moved back and forth between France and Algeria in his theoretical formulations, and, for France, researched topics at both its margins and centers. An analysis of this feature of his work can illuminate for us the relationships between these sites in a European framework, and the cultural assumptions underlying the trajectory that led him to these particular locations.

Although this book is entitled "Locating Bourdieu," the notion of locating him in the sense of "fixing" him to a particular location also seems a bit futile given his mobility—his scholarly mobility across disciplinary boundaries, and his spatial mobility of travel and research. Bourdieu remains a "moving target" as a subject for research, despite his death, because of the sheer amount of writing he did and the nuanced changes in the casting of his ideas that he made over time. It may, sadly, be a bit easier now that he has passed away and stopped writing to take stock of his contributions. However, even though this book was begun after his death, publications of his work have continued to appear. And I expect more of his unpublished manuscripts will be edited and published. Not only was Bourdieu a prolific writer, but there is a growing production of works, in different media, about him. Bourdieu was an enormously famous figure, especially in France, at the end of his life. He was the subject of a documentary that appeared in movie houses across France, *La sociologie est un sport de combat* (Carles 2001), and the subject of a novel in which a sociologist patterned after him is the protagonist, *La teinturerie* (Guillais 2002). He was also the subject of a bitingly critical book, subtitled "against the sociological terrorism of Pierre Bourdieu" (Verdes-Leroux 2001 [1998]).[14] Several plays were produced in France following the publication of the popular book *La misère du monde*. Bourdieu's son Emmanuel has made a film based on the story of an ethnographer who goes to study bachelors in his native region of Béarn, which is a fictionalized portrayal of Bourdieu's own research experiences. This film, released in both television and movie house versions in early 2004, is called *Le vert paradis*. Three examples of homage paid to him already in France include a special issue of the popular social science magazine *Sciences Humaines* dedicated to a retrospective of his work (2002); a recent volume of writings by colleagues and admirers (Encrevé and Lagrave 2003); and a special issue of the journal *Actes de la Recherche en Sciences Sociales*, edited by Bourdieu's son Jérome and others (Bourdieu, Champagne, and Poupeau 2003). Bourdieu is also very present in cyberspace: there are numerous Web sites devoted to his work, from a variety of perspectives, and an Internet discussion group about him. Not to mention the scores of books and articles that have been published about him in the scholarly literature!

My intention in this book is to draw upon Bourdieu's own understandings of location and its importance in social analysis. In his Huxley lecture on "Participant Objectivation," Bourdieu outlined a blueprint for this type of study that would locate an anthropologist's "particular position within the microcosm of anthropologists." He wrote that the anthropologist's

> most decisive choices (of topic, method, theory, etc.) depend very closely on the *location* she (or he) occupies within her professional universe, what I call the "anthropological field" with its national traditions and peculiarities, its habits of thought, its mandatory problematics, its shared beliefs and commonplaces, its rituals, values, and consecrations, its constraints in matters of publication and findings, its specific censorships, and, by the same token, the biases embedded in the organizational structure of the discipline, that is, in the collective history of the specialism, and all the unconscious presuppositions built into the (national) categories of scholarly understanding. (2003c: 283; my emphasis)

Bourdieu increasingly emphasized social and physical space as important elements in sociological analysis, and was critical of postmodern views of the "rootless and free-floating" subject (an idea Bourdieu attributed to Mannheim), and wrote that this perspective entailed a desire to escape localization and the "fixed viewpoint of a motionless spectator, every objectivist perspective" (2000b: 108). For Bourdieu, a politically engaged sociology that would effectively critique the state and its policies of neoliberalism could not adopt such a theory. For Bourdieu, the charge of social analysis was to show how each social agent is situated in a physical and social space that has a ranked order to it and is defined by exclusions or distinctions. My own perspective, however, will lend Bourdieu a bit more social agency than he admits.

NOTE ON THE TEXTS

A full bibliography of the references cited to Bourdieu's work is included at the end of this book. In the bibliography, I follow Bourdieu's own citation style by including his coauthored writings alongside his single-authored works. Whenever possible, I quote from the English translations of Bourdieu's work for the convenience of English speakers, but sometimes I do refer to the original French. All translations of work not previously translated are by me. Several major texts will be referred to repeatedly in my analysis, and so I list them here (with their English titles—if translated), and in order of publication in France—with the date of the original French edition indicated first and the date of the English translation (if any) appearing in parentheses. I list these books in order of publication in French so as to provide a context for the historical development of Bourdieu's thought, which is not always obvious from the dates of English translations of his work or in standard bibliographic formats. I will sometimes use a shorter version for these titles, such as *Outline* for *Outline of a Theory of Practice* and *Reproduction* for *Reproduction in Education, Society and Culture.*

Travail et travailleurs en Algérie, 1963

Photography: A Middle-Brow Art, 1965 (1990)

Reproduction in Education, Society, and Culture, 1970 (1977)

Outline of a Theory of Practice, 1972 (1977)

Distinction, 1979 (1984)

The Logic of Practice, 1980 (1990)

Language and Symbolic Power, 1982 (1991)

Homo Academicus, 1984 (1988)

The Field of Cultural Production, collected essays from 1968–87 (1993)

In Other Words, 1987 (1990)

The State Nobility, 1989 (1996)

The Rules of Art: Genesis and Structure of the Literary Field, 1992 (1996)

An Invitation to Reflexive Sociology, 1992

The Weight of the World: Social Suffering in Contemporary Society, 1993 (1999)

Practical Reason, 1994 (1998)

Pascalian Meditations, 1997 (2000)

Masculine Domination, 1998 (2001)

Science de la science et réflexivité: Cours du Collège de France, 2000–2001, 2001

Le bal des célibataires: Crise de la société paysanne en Béarn, 2002

Images d'Algérie, 2003

Esquisse pour une auto-analyse, 2004

ONE

Bourdieu's Point of View

> I think that I could create two intellectual biographies for myself
> that were completely different—one which made all my
> successive choices appear to be the product of a project directed
> in a methodical way, since the beginning; the other, also
> completely accurate, that described a chain of chance, of more or
> less fortuitous encounters, happy or unhappy.
>
> —*Interview between Pierre Bourdieu*
> *and Yvette Delsaut* (2002)

For Bourdieu, people did not live their lives according to freely made choices or strategies but, rather, under the constraints of the habitus and the objective conditions of social fields. He wrote in *Reproduction* that "at every moment of an educational or intellectual biography," the habitus "tends to reproduce the system of objective conditions of which it is the product" (Bourdieu and Passeron 1990: 161). In his essay "L'illusion biographique" (1986a), Bourdieu was critical of most approaches to life history or biography, which adopted the notion of a unified self whose life follows a linear trajectory—often portrayed through terms such as voyage or passage. He argued that although the state constructs us as individuals, through its "rites of institution" (through the practice of identity cards, legal names, and signatures, etc.), we must seek another way of looking at the life history. While not adopting a postmodern view of the fragmented self as a way out of this state-constructed illusion, preferring his notions of the habitus (as an underlying set of dispositions common to the class and the individual) and the field (*champ*) as both "objective" facts, Bourdieu proposed an understanding that took into account the various fields in which the social agent operated.[1] He criticized most life histories by comparing them to a description of a trip in the metro that did not take into account the "structure of the network, that is, the matrix of objective relations between the different stations" (1986a: 71). In its place, Bourdieu argued for a view of life trajectory that sees it in terms of "a series of positions successively occupied by the same agent (or same group) in a space itself in flux and undergoing incessant transformations" (1986a: 71).

According to Bourdieu, the life trajectory comes about not as a result of some inherent unity or identity of the individual who follows a particular path but, rather, as an outcome of the various social fields and their attendant value in the overall economy of symbolic exchanges, in which the person operated. A consideration of Bourdieu's autobiographical reflections is instructive in understanding his theory of habitus and the ways in which it both determines social trajectories and presents possibilities that a social agent can manipulate or take advantage of in various social fields. Given his theory, he could not write an autobiography in which he was the heroic, unique, individual; but, at the same time, in order to lend authority to himself and his work, he needed to put some of his background into the picture. Bourdieu himself was aware of this. Toward the end of his life, he expanded one of the lectures he had given at the Collège de France, entitled "Esquisse pour une auto-analyse" ("Outline for an Auto-Analysis") into a book-length essay. This intellectual memoir was first published in Germany and, after his death, was published in France. The French version (Bourdieu 2004) has as its epigraph, "This is not an autobiography" (*Ceci n'est pas une autobiographie*).

For the most part in his writings, Bourdieu eschewed autobiographical reflection upon his own educational trajectory or career, and adopted an "objective" and "scientific" voice in order to lend authority to his research. He was more apt to reveal details of his own background either elliptically in these writings, or in the interview format that he came to favor during the second half of his career. Bourdieu's position on self-reflexivity was complex and contradictory, as many examples in this book illustrate. And, yet, his biographical details are compelling. Bourdieu was a sociologist of education whose work demonstrates that educational systems reproduce social class, and that the children of working-class parents, through their inculcated habitus and its associated dispositions, generally fail to succeed in the French educational system. He and his colleagues (especially Jean-Claude Passeron) argued that the children of the French bourgeoisie (the heirs) were those most apt to acquire educational credentials in elite institutions of higher education. Bourdieu himself, however, was a striking exception to this. He was from the provinces, and of modest background. He succeeded in the French educational system in spite of this, but he revealed very little in his interviews or other writings about how this occurred or of what factors led him to eventually become the Chair of Sociology at the Collège de France.

Bourdieu made a strong statement regarding his stance toward reflexivity and postmodernism in his 2002 Huxley Memorial Lecture delivered in 2000 (Bourdieu 2003c). He rejected any form of what he disparagingly referred to (following Geertz and Barthes) as the "diary disease," and advocated instead the reflexivity of what he called the "knowing subject." Promoting a stance he called "participant objectivation," he wrote that "one does not have to choose between participant observation, a necessarily fictitious immersion in a foreign milieu, and the objectivism of the 'gaze from afar' of an observer who remains as remote from himself as from his object" (2003c: 282). Bourdieu distanced himself in this lecture from his own autobiographical reflections, thereby lending them the aura (and legitimacy) of scientific authority. He made a similar move in earlier statements, notably in the interview contained in "Fieldwork in Philosophy," where he stated in reference to an autobiographical reflection, "I'm not telling my life history here: I am trying to make a contribution to the sociology of science" (1990b: 8). Bourdieu continued to use this type of disclaimer, about the refusal of autobiography, even in writings that were confessional and quite self-referential, as in his posthumously published intellectual memoir (2004).

Bourdieu's approach to autoethnography was, in short, contradictory. On the one hand, he frequently mentioned his own social origins (increasingly as the years went by) in order to lend legitimacy to his work and to stress his own "authentic" roots as distinct from bourgeois academics who were themselves part of the dominant and dominating class. On the other hand, he denied that his references to his own life story were in any way "naval gazing" enterprises or self indulgent; rather, they constituted the scientific version of self-reflexivity. Bourdieu asserted his ethnographic authority in education by positioning himself as the "outsider" in academia and "outsider" to the realms of the powerful, so that he was able to challenge academia's assumptions and understand power relations in ways that were less accessible to either other academics or to the working classes who had not gained social scientific training as had he. He asserted his ethnographic authority by positioning himself as a "quasi-native" in Algeria, because of his rural French roots, and as an "objective intimate" (my term, not his) in his fieldwork in rural France.

IMPERSONAL CONFESSIONS

Bourdieu wrote a short intellectual autobiography, in his own fashion, in earnest in *Pascalian Meditations* (2000b [1997]) and also discussed his career trajectory in his final lectures at the Collège de France (2001a) and in *Esquisse pour une auto-analyse* (2004). *Meditations,* as I will refer to it by shorthand here, is Bourdieu's version of Clifford Geertz's *After the Fact* (1995) or *Available Light* (2000). It contains one essay, in the form of a postscript to a chapter, which offers autobiographical reflections on Bourdieu's experiences while studying philosophy. The rest of the book is a sort of recapping of the major themes in Bourdieu's work thus far, with particular emphasis on his relationship to philosophy. Geertz referred to intellectual autobiography, with characteristic irony, as a form of "auto-obituary" in an essay appearing in *Available Light,* and I think both books represented a way for the authors, toward the end of their careers, to explain themselves and answer critics. Bourdieu expressed the feeling that he had "been rather ill-understood" (2000b: 7). He titled his own version of intellectual autobiography, in the essay that appears in *Meditations,* an "impersonal confession"—both distancing himself in this way from the French autobiographical tradition of confession as incarnated in Rousseau, and by evoking that trope, placing himself within the lineage. He wrote that he would speak little of himself ("the singular self"), and was critical of the "self-indulgence of nostalgic evocations" (2000b: 34). For Bourdieu, life trajectories reflect collective histories, not singular ones, and he wanted to downplay the unique aspects of his own experiences—seeing them as common to anyone else who had come from a similar background.

Nevertheless, in his later essay *Esquisse pour une auto-analyse* (2004), Bourdieu stated that he had written it partly to trump his future biographers. In *Esquisse,* he revealed details of his personal life, if in somewhat veiled form, that are confessional and idiosyncratic—particularly in passages in which he revealed that he suffered from depression and alluded to difficulties in his relationship with his father. *Esquisse* is ostensibly an attempt to employ the theory of habitus and its method of interrogation of a life trajectory back upon Bourdieu himself, and to explain his life in terms of habitus, point of view, and position-takings. It is the most intimate and personal of his writings, however, and in this essay he writes more than before about topics such as his childhood, his early educational experiences at boarding school, and his experiences in military service in Algeria. Much more so than *Pascalian Meditations, Esquisse* displays a Bourdieu writing about his private, inner self, and justifying his public persona and its contradictions. It is evident that Bourdieu viewed the habitus in terms of personality characteristics as well as life trajectories. The main influences on his life that he narrated in all of the self-reflective writings are: his childhood in Béarn, his boarding school experiences, his education at ENS, and his experiences as a soldier and ethnologist in Algeria. These are the touchpoints to which he returned time and again.

In order to understand the specifically French aspects of Bourdieu's life, it is instructive to compare a few points with Geertz's own story. Although Geertz was born a few years earlier than Bourdieu, they were both part of the postwar generation of college students in their countries. Geertz, however, attended university thanks to the GI Bill and after having served in the military, and was, he admits, part of a wave of students who arrived during a time of high funding, plentiful resources, and jobs in academia.

He notes that he was from a small out-of-the-way place initially and had not expected to attend college. He wrote: "Having grown up rural in the Great Depression, I had not supposed I would be going to college, so that when the possibility suddenly presented itself, I had no idea how to respond to it" (2000: 4). Geertz wound up in graduate school at Harvard and later found his academic home at Princeton. This is quite a different situation from France where, if a student has not trained for the elite institutions of higher education from an early age, attending the preparatory classes, passing the exams, and so on, there is no hope of doing so later in life. For a soldier returning from the war in France who had not been on the "right track" before leaving, it would not have been possible to switch gears and suddenly (at least as Geertz describes his own educational trajectory), go on to college and graduate school. In Bourdieu's case, the "decision" to go on in education was one that had to be made very early on. The hierarchy and centralization of the French educational system deeply marked Bourdieu's experience, his attitudes toward education and its place in society, and his ambivalence about having become an intellectual. Bourdieu described his educational trajectory in terms of a long "apprenticeship" in philosophy, starting in high school and continuing in the preparatory class for ENS.

Despite the differences related to national location for these two scholars, and, although I won't get into it here, their differences of theoretical approach, there are interesting similarities in their ways of telling their stories. Both *Meditations* and *Available Light* highlight the authors' early training and interest in philosophy, with a later turn toward anthropology: both are cast as meditations (Bourdieu) or reflections (Geertz) on the relationship between philosophy and anthropology/sociology. Neither author casts himself as the "scholar as hero," in the autobiographical genre of showing an individual who triumphs over adversity and designs his own life (and I use the masculine pronoun here deliberately). Bourdieu wrote that he did "not intend to deliver the kind of so-called 'personal' memories that provide the dismal backdrop for academic autobiographies—awestruck encounters with eminent masters, intellectual choices interlaced with career choices" (2000b: 33). Both Bourdieu and Geertz show themselves to be somewhat reluctant and at times almost accidental narrators of their careers. Geertz even titles his essay "Passage and Accident" to highlight this. Bourdieu wrote that "the distance I have progressively taken from philosophy no doubt owes a lot to what are called the chance events of existence, in particular a forced stay in Algeria, which one could say, without looking further, was at the origins of my 'vocation' as an ethnologist and then as a sociologist" (2000b: 42). He continued to add, however, that he was probably receptive to such a conversion because he was already dissatisfied with philosophy. Although he arrived at ENS with the "be-dazzlement" of the new student, he soon became disenchanted and took what he referred to as an "objective distance" from it. This posture permitted him, he suggested, to be a good informant on the system. Here Bourdieu again lent authority to his ethnographic perspectives based on his own social origins and personal experiences.

Bourdieu frequently made reference to the veiled autobiographical nature of his other study of French academia, *Homo Academicus,* a study of social class and educational trajectories among professors. Bourdieu showed how the social class origins or habitus of an academic played a large role in the type of education they received and in their ultimate position within the academic hierarchy. That book did not contain explicit autobiographical details from Bourdieu's life. At the end of the Preface to the English edition of *Homo Academicus,* Bourdieu did, however, write of his motivations to explore this theme of educational trajectory and their roots in his own experience:

> The special place held in my work by a somewhat singular sociology of the university institution is no doubt explained by the peculiar force with which I felt the need to gain rational control over the disappointment felt by an "oblate" faced with the annihilation of the truths and values of which he was destined and dedicated rather than take refuge in the feelings of self-destructive resentment. (1988b: xxvi)

Critics of Bourdieu have pointed to his seemingly arrogant privileging of his background and his scientific approach as the only way of understanding educational processes in France. He himself has made reference to the distinction between his approach and that of academics of bourgeois origin, as in "I didn't have any accounts to settle with the bourgeois family" (1990b: 4). In a book critiquing what they label as the "anti-humanist philosophies" surrounding the May '68 movement, the philosophers Luc Ferry and Alain Renaut launched a stinging attack on Bourdieu's claims to legitimacy: "The moral of the story is clear: Unless one has been a mountain peasant, preferably socially indigenous, one is in grave danger of being a bad sociologist" (1990 [1985]: 167). Ferry, I might add here, served briefly as the French Minister of Education (2002–2004). I think it would be more accurate to say that Bourdieu had "accounts to settle" with the educational system rather than with the bourgeois family.

Bourdieu's description of his apprenticeship in philosophy in "Impersonal Confessions" shows the veiled autobiographical nature of *The State Nobility,* or perhaps, in his terms, the collective experience of his own apprenticeship. *The State Nobility* is a sociological and ethnographic study of the ritual and symbolic "rites of institution" at his own alma mater,

ENS. Although he described this institution from an "objective" point of view in *The State Nobility*, he offered a more personal and overtly subjective perspective several years later in "Impersonal Confessions," and even more so in *Esquisse pour une auto-analyse* (2004). This reflects the standard anthropological practice of dividing writing about fieldwork into scholarly monographs and memoirs or diaries, but in Bourdieu's case, the fieldwork and other research was itself largely drawing on his own personal past experiences in a form of autoethnography. Bourdieu carefully recounted his initiation into the rites of philosophy and the acquisition of the "prestigious identity" (2000b: 35) attached to philosophy at the time. He compared himself to a Native American initiate (citing *Hopi Sun*). Bourdieu argued, however, that the student who excels in that milieu must already have an "innate sense of the game" in order to be "chosen" by the institution, and that what happens in the institution is more a "consecration" of the identity of philosopher than a creation of one.

SCHOLARSHIP BOY/LE MIRACULÉ

When Bourdieu died, he was in the process of writing a memoir of his youth, excerpts of which were published in the French magazine *Le Nouvel Observateur* but later retracted after Bourdieu's family filed a lawsuit charging that this had been an unauthorized publication.[2] The narrative dealt with his experiences as a boarding student when he left to continue his secondary education in the city of Pau. This is a theme that he had already explored in his essay on "Auto-Analysis" in his last lectures at the Collège de France (2001a), and he expanded upon this experience in *Esquisse pour une auto-analyse*. Bourdieu described himself as a rebellious student who sometimes got in trouble for challenging the strict controls over the boarding students. He participated in what the French term "le chahut" to identify a form of resistance (primarily through pranks) unique to high school students. Bourdieu was a "scholarship boy" (cf. Hoggart 1992 [1957] and Rodriguez 1983), who succeeded in education and won state-funded grants to attend elite educational institutions. As a scholar, he was interested in the consequences of becoming educated for children from rural and/or working-class backgrounds, and his own experiences of estrangement from his origins motivated his interest in education. In a published dialogue with Loïc Wacquant, Bourdieu referred to himself as "class defector," unveiling the shame of his origins and guilt at being upwardly mobile. He also noted that his having undertaken research in his native region of Béarn was part of a personal quest:

> I spent most of my youth in a tiny and remote village of Southwestern France, a very "backward" place as city people like to say. And I could meet the demands of school-

ing only by renouncing many of my primary experiences and acquisitions, not only a certain accent. . . . Anthropology and sociology have allowed me to reconcile myself with my primary experiences and to take them upon myself, to assume them without losing anything I subsequently acquired. . . . The research I did, around 1960, in this village helped me to discover a lot of things about myself and about my object of study. (Bourdieu and Wacquant 1992: 205)

Those experiences of being the "other" at school, and thereby being made to be self-conscious of one's difference and of one's own ways of thinking, dressing, and speaking, are central to some of Bourdieu's eventual theoretical positions about reflexivity. He explicitly acknowledged that the experience of boarding school and upward class mobility afforded him a unique perspective on social life, the ability to "cross" different social milieu (Bourdieu and Wacquant 1992: 205). Here, Bourdieu was articulating his role as autoethnographer and boundary-crosser. His concept of *habitus clivé* (split habitus) also articulates this position.

Toward the end of the chapter called "Disintegration and Distress" in Bourdieu's early book *The Algerians* (1962a), there is a moving passage about the "man between two worlds" that I cannot also help but read as part-autobiography for Bourdieu. Although the explicit referent is the young Algerian intellectual in a rapidly changing Algeria, I think Bourdieu himself was also this "man between two worlds": for him, the two worlds were the traditional world of rural France in which he grew up and the world of the urban intellectual, the social scientist, he was becoming. I read this passage as one speaking to his identification with young Algerian men, due to his own background. He wrote:

Constantly being faced with alternative ways of behavior by reason of the intrusion of new values, and therefore compelled to make a conscious examination of the implicit premises or the unconscious patterns of his own tradition, this man, cast between two worlds and rejected by both, lives a sort of double inner life, is a prey to frustration and inner conflict, with the result that he is constantly being tempted to adopt either an attitude of uneasy over identification or one of rebellious negativism. (1962a: 144)

This figure is compelled, Bourdieu suggested, to make "a conscious examination of the implicit premises or the unconscious patterns of his own tradition" and this was later to be part of the methods involving reflexivity in Bourdieu's work. In his more recent writings (2003c: 292), Bourdieu admitted to having "two parts of myself" that he tried to reconcile in part by continuing to do research in Béarn, which was a way of doing "self-analysis" (*auto-analyse*).

It is interesting to compare Bourdieu with three other men from modest backgrounds who excelled in school and later wrote about their experiences: Richard Rodriguez, a Mexican American writer and author most notably of the book *Hunger of Memory: The Education of Richard Rodriguez;* Richard Hoggart,[3] a British sociologist from a working-class background and author of numerous books, including *The Uses of Literacy* (1991[1957]) and a three-part autobiography (1994); and Pierre-Jakèz Hélias, author of *The Horse of Pride* (1978 [1975]) and son of peasants in Brittany who became a professor of folklore. Rodriguez and Hoggart both wrote of the relationship of the working-class academic to schooling experiences and to intellectual life. All of these authors speak of their ambivalence associated with becoming educated and of their ambivalence toward "home" now that they had done so. They were, in Hoggart's terms, "scholarship boys" (1992 [1957]: 224) who were "at the friction-point between two cultures" (225). Hoggart described the characteristics of this type of student thus:

> In part they have a sense of loss which affects some in all groups. With them the sense of loss is increased precisely because they are emotionally uprooted from their class, often under the stimulus of a stronger critical intelligence or imagination, qualities which can lead them into an unusual self-consciousness before their own situation (and which makes it easy for the sympathizer to dramatise their 'angst'). Involved with this may be a physical uprooting from their class through the medium of the scholarship system. (1992: 225)

Bourdieu and Passeron took note of this category of student in *Reproduction* (1990: 175, fn. 34), referring to the "wonderboy" or *le miraculé,* the working-class child who "succeeds 'against all the odds'," and who is the opposite of the "inheritor" (the bourgeois child who already has by nature of class position the qualities valued by the school). Bourdieu returned at more length to the topic of the working class or provincial student who succeeds in higher education in his book *The State Nobility.* In this context, he criticized what he called the Republican myth of the "liberating school" for viewing such students as evidence of a democratic institution open to all intelligent students. He wrote:

> Those whom the school distinguishes and consecrates, as far back as we can go, have already been separated or, as we say, *cut off* from their peers. Often "pushed" by a father who has frequently made a break himself, one undoubtedly all the more noticeable the weaker it was and the less it physically removed him from the group he left . . . these students have from the outset been set apart by the slight gaps that are at the source of a cumulative process of distancing: knowing how to read before going to school, skipping grades, receiving exemptions, scholarships, grants, top prizes. (1996a: 106)

He goes on to show how the successive "consecrations" by the school build up this image of the good student (*bon élève*) that continues to bind the student to the school institution. It is very clear that this passage can be read, as in the case of many such statements by Bourdieu, in terms of his own autobiography.

In the two essays, "Esquisse pour une auto-analyse" (2001a; 2004), Bourdieu wrote of some painful aspects of his own childhood experience related to his father's having left farming to become a civil servant. Bourdieu's own father had already made the rupture of which Bourdieu speaks in the passage cited above that led to his own school success and further rupture from his social background. He described, in autobiographical terms, what he described in "experience-far" terms in *The State Nobility*. Bourdieu related his feelings of estrangement more directly in his *auto-analyse*. He wrote that grew upon in a village that was only twenty kilometers from the city of Pau, but it was so remote and obscure that his classmates at high school in Pau had never heard of it. He and his father had both made a break from their backgrounds: his father, through a switch from farming to civil service as a postman; Bourdieu, through education that took him far from the village. Bourdieu's grandfather, a tenant farmer, and uncle continued to work the farm that his father had left. Bourdieu wrote that his childhood experiences as the child of a "turncoat" (*transfuge*) to his social origins had marked him and predisposed him to get involved in struggles and polemics:

> Very close to my friends at primary school, sons of small farmers, of artisans or of shopkeepers, with whom I had almost everything in common, except success [in school] which distinguished me a bit, I was also separated by an invisible barrier, which expressed itself at times in certain ritual insults against *lous emplegat,* the salaried workers "always in the shadows," a little like my father was separated (and he gave lots of signs of the fact that he suffered, like the fact that he always voted to the extreme left) from these peasants (and from his father and his brother who had stayed on the farm and who he went to help each year during his vacation). (2001a: 213)

The "invisible barrier" is one not only of his school success but of the estrangement from social origins that his father had already experienced and which in some sense paved the way for Bourdieu's school success, made it easier for him to take the second step in leaving the peasant habitus. Bourdieu wrote of the "social estrangement" (2004: 121) that occurred during his junior and senior high school years as a boarder, and of his need to rehabituate himself each time he returned home for weekend visits. He also confessed that he did not mind that he returned home less and less

often because his misbehavior at school and challenges to its authority resulted in his being kept at school as a punishment. What is striking here is
not only Bourdieu's experiences but that he was writing so much about
himself in his sociological work, and increasingly conscious of the ways in
which he was doing that.

In his autobiography, Richard Rodriguez wrote: "It is education that
has altered my life. Carried me far" (1983: 5). For both Bourdieu and
Rodriguez, there is a private set of behaviors, language use and values (what
Bourdieu would call the class habitus) that is different from the public
world of the school. Whereas Rodriguez captures the distinction between
the family and school through the lens of ethnicity, a very American way of
looking at things, Bourdieu, who was from a nation in which cultural differences are ideologically minimized,[4] focused on social class issues. Although Bourdieu did make reference to the provincial student with different accent, way of dressing, and so on, his primary focus was on social
class. Whereas Rodriguez views the rupture between family and school as
ultimately a liberating and inevitable experience, despite some guilt and
feelings of loss in distancing himself from parental culture (1983: 28–29;
46), Bourdieu saw this rupture only in terms of a symbolic violence exerted upon the provincial and/or working-class student, for whom the primary habitus is devalued as the student acquires the secondary habitus
associated with education. Both, however, distanced themselves from academics from more privileged backgrounds. Rodriguez writes of "those
middle-class ethnics who scorn assimilation . . . and trivialize the dilemma
of the socially disadvantaged" (27). Bourdieu, as I already noted above,
wrote of his bourgeois peers in academia who were less "objective" because
they have "accounts to settle with the bourgeois family" (1990b: 4).

Both Rodriguez and Bourdieu acquired the ability to see their familial
cultures with fresh eyes because of their educational experiences and what
Bourdieu would call the "rupture" that this entailed. For Bourdieu, this is
the "scholastic point of view." Rodriguez wrote that, going home after college, he was "a kind of anthropologist in the family kitchen" (1983: 160).
Bourdieu, of course, made this his profession to be a sociocultural observer, and undertook ethnographic research in his own natal region, among
people he knew, even having his own mother serve as an informant
(Bourdieu 2003c: 289). Both authors viewed education as giving one the
ability to think abstractly, and thus setting one apart from those who have
not been schooled in this way. Rodriguez wrote: "My mother and father
did not pass their time thinking about the cultural meanings of their experience" (1983: 72). For Bourdieu, this is part of his theory of the relationship between commonsense and sociological understandings of the world
articulated in *The Logic of Practice*. He more recently elucidated this by

writing that most people do not have "in their heads the scientific truth of their practice which I am trying to extract from observation of their practices" (2003c: 288).

I have already written (Reed-Danahay 1997b) of the ambivalence about becoming educated for French peasants in an essay called "Leaving Home" that compared the autoethnographies of Pierre-Jakèz Hélias and Emilie Carles, a schoolteacher. When I wrote that essay, it had not yet occurred to me that Bourdieu's own life story would be relevant, and I had only made use of some of his theoretical ideas in my analysis. But not only are there interesting comparisons to be made between Bourdieu and Hélias, particularly in the ways they narrate their experiences, but also Bourdieu's auto-analysis is helpful to me in further explorations of the work of Hélias and other former peasant autobiographers. I also instinctively feel that Bourdieu would be appalled by this comparison, because he would have viewed Hélias as someone who, as Claude Grignon (1991: 14) noted, indulged in the "fetischizing" of "one's roots," but I shall plough on nonetheless. Of an earlier generation than Bourdieu, Hélias, born in 1914, was from a peasant background but his father was an artisan, a clog-maker, who had some schooling himself—in Bourdieu's terms, therefore, someone who had already made the break himself from the peasant background, like his own father. Much of the educational narrative contained in Hélias's story centers on primary schooling in the village and then the rupture that occurred when he went on to secondary school in the city. Like Bourdieu, Hélias describes painful experiences associated with education, for him a very harsh schoolmaster and later, his marked status at boarding school because of his rural background, his different clothing, his different accent—again, a collective experience, at least in France, also shared by Bourdieu and others. Hélias, like Bourdieu, also recounts his estrangement from his social origins as he became more educated and spent more time in the city, and he expressed a mixture of nostalgia and regret toward his trajectory. He wrote of leading a "double life" (1978: 309) and later of the guilt and ambivalence about having left home:

> There was one sure thing: the whole region was in flux. And we were responsible for all the agitation, we who were studying elsewhere and would come home for our vacations behaving like strangers, bareheaded, wearing knickers, and making the kind of revolutionary remarks that bewildered our childhood friends, who were still making every effort to stick to the rules. (1978: 313–14)

Hélias and Bourdieu both described their having become educated as a somewhat inevitable process, not an active choice, although in different terms. Neither positions himself as having actually desired to leave, or to have actively rejected rural life. Each described having been "chosen" by the educational system and somewhat swept up by it. Hélias described in vivid detail the process of the teacher encouraging his family to let him continue his studies at secondary school in the city. This dilemma of leaving home is a particularly French story, because of the centralization of the educational system. During both Bourdieu's and Hélias's childhoods, most rural children completed all of their education at the village school, which was obligatory to age fourteen. Any student who continued on in secondary education had to "leave home" at that age. The geographical break with the family, associated with education, for working-class children occurs later in the United States, not until university studies or even graduate school. Hélias continued his links to rural Brittany by training as a folklorist and carving out a career in which he worked toward a form of salvage ethnography, as what he called a "memory collector," who worked to protect and record traditional peasant culture. He worked out some of his own ambivalence about his marginal status as both native and outsider through the writing of his autoethnographic memoir, which is part-memoir and part-ethnography, and by his career in folklore studies. For Bourdieu, ethnographic research in his natal region and on educational institutions, as well as the ethnographic work in Algeria helped, as he has written, for him to come to terms with his life trajectory. He wrote: "I learned a lot from two research projects, carried out in very different social milieux—the village of my childhood and the Paris universities—which enable me to explore some of the most obscure areas of my subjectivity as an objectivist observer" (2000b: 4).

THE BIOGRAPHICAL ILLUSION

Those fragments of his own experience that Bourdieu shared in interviews and other writings provide some insights into his trajectory and his attitudes about it. They help us to understand his "point of view." Bourdieu's long-term translator Richard Nice remarked about him that:

> I think there are two versions of Bourdieu's past. One is the mythical one in which he is the peasant boy confronting urban civilization, and the other one, which he actually thought more seriously, is what it's like to be a petit bourgeois and a success story. And all this obsession with other people's language, and with the use of language to dominate and put down in non-rational ways is perhaps also the rethinking of his own experience. (Nice 1985, from an interview quoted in Mahar 1990)

How would Bourdieu have explained his own trajectory, his own "success story," in light of his theory of social class reproduction? In none of his writings did he explicitly set out a coherent life history narrative, and his self consciousness about the "biographical illusion" would, undoubtedly, have inhibited him from doing so. In *Esquisse pour une auto-analyse* (2004), Bourdieu wrote against the conventions of a linear life narrative even as he revealed many aspects of his life experiences. He began that intellectual memoir with his experiences at ENS, and did not deal with his childhood until the latter portion of the book. He also revealed details about his relationships with mentors and colleagues that he had not hitherto addressed— explaining, for instance, how he had come to be incorporated into Raymond Aron's group at the École des Hautes Études en Sciences Sociales (related to a contact made in Algeria and their common ties to ENS). Bourdieu described most of the "choices" in his career in terms of a mixture of chance and habitus. He rarely spoke of himself in terms of an active social agent who doggedly pursued his aims or got involved in political maneuverings in order to achieve them. For example, he portrayed himself as a reluctant candidate for the Chair in Sociology at the Collège de France (2004: 137-9), who had to be prodded by colleagues to take the position. He does admit, however, that this reluctance was based on an ambivalent mixture of insecurity and repugnance for intellectual "games." There is a clue to Bourdieu's self-presentation about his social agency in his response to a question about his intellectual autobiography:

> I don't have to tell you that many things that have played a determining part in my "intellectual path" happened by chance. My own contribution, doubtless linked to my habitus, consisted essentially in making the most of them, to the best of my abilities (I think, for example, that I seized on a great number of opportunities that many people would have let go by). (1990b: 26)

Bourdieu's notion of strategy involved the social agent's ability to "play the game" or "play the hand" he was dealt (the social capital of his habitus and the social or symbolic capital he acquired through education) in the "space of possibilities" available to him. In this passage, we see the ways in which Bourdieu applied this to his own life. He was a product of his habitus, took advantage of certain opportunities that crossed his path, and thus made the most of his inherited dispositions in order to succeed in academic life (and to become a well-known public figure in France and an internationally known social theorist). Bourdieu did not, however, offer much in his autobiographical writings about how he seized opportunities. There is only one hint of this in his interview with Franz Schultheis, which was published in *Images d'Algérie* (2003a: 37–38). Bourdieu said that when he was starting his career and had been given the chance by Raymond Aron to establish his own research center (at the École des Hautes Études en Sciences Sociales), he needed some funding and wanted very much to establish his research credentials. He had to find a way to do that (*il fallait que je me débrouille*). Because he was interested in photography and had taken many photos in Algeria, he somehow obtained some contract money from Kodak that funded his study of the uses of photography in Béarn (eventually published as Bourdieu and Bourdieu 1965).[5] This is how Bourdieu would explain the exceptions to the rule of social reproduction. They are individuals who, like him, seize opportunities presented to them. This certainly affords some social agency to the individual, and Bourdieu strikes a delicate balance between attributing his success to his own abilities and attributing it solely to the social conditions or origins of his existence.

TWO

Education

Educated people owe their culture—i.e., a programme of
perception, thought and action—to the school.
—*Systems of Education and Systems
of Thought* (1967)

In the early 1960s, Bourdieu was writing on topics seeming, at first glance,
to be disparate and unrelated. He undertook his earliest educational
studies, done in collaboration with Jean-Claude Passeron and others, within
the same period during which he also continued to publish from his ethnographic work in Algeria, as well as from his ethnographic studies on
marriage strategies and on the uses of photography among peasants in southwestern France. Bourdieu's study on linguistic misunderstandings in education appeared in mimeograph version as early as 1961, and was later
published in 1965. His educational work is mostly identified outside of
France with the book (coauthored by Passeron) *Reproduction in Education,
Culture and Society,* published in France in 1970 and appearing in English
translation in 1977. Bourdieu's first two major studies on the culture of
university students, *Les héritiers* and *Les étudiants et leurs études,* were, however, published in 1964. This was also the year that one of his major works
on displaced Algerians, *Le déracinement,* was published. His ideas and
theories were developed through a juxtaposition of work in France and
Algeria, and in urban and rural contexts, using both statistical and ethnographic methods. There is not a linear progression to this work, as some
have claimed and as Bourdieu himself sometimes suggested in interviews
but, rather, an interrelationship among the various topics pursued more or
less simultaneously.

Bourdieu remarked on the continuities between his studies in Algeria
and France during the time (1965–75) that he worked on both *Distinction*
and *The Logic of Practice:* "I was able to pass imperceptibly and quite naturally from the analysis of Berber culture to the analysis of school culture"
(1990b: 23). This is a curious statement, especially given the fact that
Bourdieu made few explicit comparisons between his work in the two contexts. Why this "natural" quality to being able to work in these seemingly

disparate contexts? The answer lies partly in Bourdieu's own background, I believe, in that he was someone who had made a transition from spending his childhood in a rural, traditional society (like that of Kabylia) to that of inhabiting the most sacrosanct of positions within the French university system. Moreover, the experience of having made this transition was one that prompted much of his own research, provoking questions about French education that, he believed, were those of an "outsider" to the system. In his own mind, Kabylia and the French educational system were less separate universes than they would be for others.

ROOTS/ROUTES OF BOURDIEU'S EDUCATIONAL THEORY

Education played a significant role in Bourdieu's theoretical system and not in ways that are only relevant to scholars of schooling per se. Bourdieu felt that if you want to understand systems of power in modern societies, you must look to the educational system. In his work on the social transformations of so-called traditional societies, Bourdieu distinguished between literate, schooled societies with formal systems of education, and nonliterate societies that transmit culture through informal means. Within "modern" societies, Bourdieu distinguished between those categories of persons with greater or fewer educational qualifications, and he studied the implications of this for social class. Education, in the broadly anthropological sense having to do with knowledge construction and cultural transmission (Pelissier 1991; Levinson, Foley, and Holland 1996), is very much at the heart of all of this work. Bourdieu studied power primarily through the lens of education in its widest sense—including both formal and informal modes of cultural transmission, as well as studies of knowledge more broadly—its circulation, valuation, and transmission. He wrote in *The State Nobility* that "the sociology of education lies at the foundation of a general anthropology of power and legitimacy" (1996a: 5).

The roots of Bourdieu's interest in education can be traced, in part, to his own biography. He was an educationally and geographically mobile individual throughout his life, a boy of modest background from a remote region of France who nevertheless succeeded in schooling and rose through the most prestigious institutions of higher education in France during his career. This is indeed an exceptional accomplishment. We can see that, in terms of Bourdieu's life history, he was able to dodge many of the obstacles to higher education and became labeled as "gifted" through good performance in the exam system required to entrance to elite institutions, despite the potential handicaps of his rural, provincial background.

Bourdieu's preoccupation with education also can be understood in the wider context of French culture and its educational system. The school system in France is central to national identity—both in that it was largely through primary schooling that notions of citizenship and national belonging were constructed, and in that the rigor and reputation of their educational system has long been part of national pride for the French. I can think of few other nations in which national identity is as closely associated with being a cultivated, educated, schooled person (even though, as Bourdieu himself demonstrated, many are excluded in reality from this category in France due to social class background). France is probably unique in having a popular television show that centers on "*La Dictée,*" a common pedagogical method in French classrooms for teaching spelling and grammar. Hosted by Bernard Pivot,[1] this contest is watched by a wide spectrum of viewers who want to test their own skills.

Education is one of the major values, sources of identity, and points of pride for the French. That Bourdieu should turn to education in order to examine systems of power in French society, and by extension, in all stratified societies, is directly connected to this national context within which his thought was shaped. That he should largely ignore education in Algeria, is also connected to specifically French notions of center and margin (with Algeria positioned as more "traditional" and pristine).

HISTORICAL PERSPECTIVES ON FRENCH EDUCATION

Despite Bourdieu's claims that the implications of his research are not specific to France, as he argued in the introduction to the English version of *Distinction* and as Loïc Wacquant argued on Bourdieu's behalf in his forward to *The State Nobility,* a full understanding of his work depends on the historical context of French education, a topic that he did not himself specifically address, taking it as a "given." The modern French Republic was founded upon the promise of mass education, and the nation was in large part constructed, or "imagined" (Anderson 1991; Hobsbawm 1992), through the primary education system and its introduction of notions of citizenship and French language to the remote provinces (Weber 1976; Mendras and Cole 1991). France also extended its colonial power through education, planting schools in its colonies and teaching the French language to its subjects.[2]

French education has been influenced by a debate over Republican ideals of equality and secularism, including free education for all citizens, as the champions of the French Revolution first proposed this.[3] The history of the idea of equality in French schooling is one with many twists and turns, however. Mass education is also associated with wider global movements toward nationalism, and was an idea attractive to other nations besides France, beginning in the eighteenth century.[4] French education had been under the direct control of the Catholic Church prior to the Revolution, and the struggle between religious education and state-controlled secular education is a constant theme in the history of education. The Third Republic (1870–1940), and its first Minister of Education, Jules Ferry, worked to restore the ideals of the Revolution after the setbacks that followed it, in large part through the establishment of universal mass education that was free and secular. Ferry was a proponent of the "civilizing mission" of French education, and his other role as Minister of Foreign Affairs and colonizer complemented his aims to take French culture to the provincial masses via village schools within the hexagon (French territory)[5] with the move to export this to the subjects of French colonial regimes (Furet 1985; Colonna 1973). At the start of the twentieth century, primary education became universally available and mandatory for all French students through the Ferry Laws of 1881 and 1882, and each *commune* (village or township) in France was to have its own primary school. The state tried to disentangle religious teachings from state-sponsored schools, promoting the idea of "l'école laïque," and all religious personnel were prohibited from teaching in state schools.

Mass primary education at the beginning of the twentieth century did not end debates on educational equality or on the question of church versus state control over education, however. The French educational system remained highly stratified and centralized. Although French primary schools spread a common language and culture through a centralized bureaucracy, this worked largely to legitimize bourgeois values and to reinforce, rather than eliminate, regional and class-based boundaries. Andy Green (1990) has suggested that even though there was a common culture disseminated in the schools, children were inserted into that culture differently according to their social class background. There has long been an ideological clash in France between those supporting the ideals of equal opportunity and those supporting a more elitist form of education that bases its arguments on the idea of merit or giftedness. Education continued to reinforce class-based differences, so that up until mid-century there were primary schools for working-class and rural children in which all schooling would be completed, and primary schools for the elite that led to possibilities of secondary and higher education. A two-tiered system of middle-school education (with schools oriented toward *lycée* and schools oriented toward technical training) continued up until the 1980s. Most children who got a primary school certificate ended their schooling at age fourteen well into the twentieth century, whereas only a select few had the opportunity to continue their studies. Although there has been some change at the level of primary- and middle-school education in terms of equality of opportunity—including the abolishment of the two-tier system mentioned above—

there continues to be stratification at higher levels. There are intricate differentiations between *lycées* or high schools in terms of the types of higher educational opportunities open to its graduates. At higher levels, there is a distinction between trade schools leading to specific professions, universities, and the elite institutions of higher education, the Grandes Écoles, populated by the children of the bourgeoisie and taught by professors from the same social class.

Mid-twentieth-century debates on French education concerned the establishment of an *école unique* (literally, a single school), a system of education that would no longer involve a two-tiered approach that excluded students from the start.[6] Struggles between church and state also continued throughout the century, with variations in intensity in different regions of the nation, and were a backdrop to other debates. The Vichy Regime (1940–44), which championed both traditional rural life and moral values, restored some of the role of the clergy in public education, but those reforms were rescinded after liberation. At mid-century, Catholic schools were permitted to enter into contracts with the state and receive funding if they followed the national curriculum, and this remains the case today. Many Catholic schools are part of the elite high school or *lycée* system that funnels students toward the elite universities and Grandes Écoles. Because of the centralized and stratified educational system and its many forms of tracking, during the period of Bourdieu's childhood (1930s to mid-1940s), it was difficult for rural children to have access to higher education, unless they were part of the provincial bourgeoisie.

In post–World War II France, as in other Western nations, a baby boom led to a huge influx of students reaching universities during the 1960s. Continued complaints about the inequality of the educational system, as well as other problems associated with jobs and social services, prompted a crisis in France, popularly known now as simply "May '68."[7] Various reforms followed this "crisis," but there continue to be dissatisfactions in French higher education as well as in the primary and secondary levels. A second large strike that involved not only education but also threats to social security in France occurred in 1995, and Bourdieu took an active and controversial role in these events. Huge student strikes in France again took place in 1999 and 2000, aimed at the policies of Minister Claude Allègre, which led to his downfall and replacement by the socialist Jack Lang, who had been Minister of Culture under Mitterrand. The contentiousness of issues of education in French society continues, most recently prompting the government to launch a "Great Debate" on the future of French education (Comité Interministériel sur l'Education Nationale 2003). The debate has its own website (http://www.debatnational.education.fr). University students participated in major protests in fall 2003 in order to challenge new reforms related to European Union (EU) standards for higher education. The issue of religious expression in French classrooms, especially the wearing of the scarf by Muslim girls, continues to be a divisive issue and resulted in legislation passed in early 2004 to ban this practice.

DURKHEIM, BOURDIEU, EDUCATION, AND RELIGION

The theoretical and institutional antecedents of Bourdieu's work on education can be traced primarily to the writings of Emile Durkheim. Pompougnac (1984: 38) has pronounced Durkheim the "grandfather" of Bourdieu and Passeron's book *Reproduction*. Durkheim established a sociology of education that drew on French and European history. His ideas about moral and secular education were also influential in the reforms of education in the late nineteenth century. Durkheim's writings on education[8] are less well known than those on religion (1961), the division of labor (1984), or suicide (1951), and few of these were published in book form during his lifetime. However, he lectured extensively on education and pedagogy to primary school teachers during his career and had a major influence on education in France at the turn of the century (Ottaway 1955; Halbwachs 1969; Pompougnac 1984). He held a university position in education at the Sorbonne toward the end of his life. A supporter of the goals of the Third Republic, he was a strong advocate of secular morality and reason, as opposed to religious teachings, in French schools. Durkheim traced the history of education, focusing on the influence of Jesuits, in a study first published posthumously in 1938 (Durkheim 1969 [1938]).

Bourdieu was influenced in many ways by Durkheim, but Bourdieu's work on education is, in some ways, only indirectly influenced by Durkheim's educational thought. Durkheim was influential in the study of schooling primarily in having established the sociology of education and inculcation as a legitimate area of study and one that helped explain the reproduction of society and its social groupings. Bourdieu shared Durkheim's focus on reason as the basis for education and the scientific study of society. He also shared Durkheim's interest in the ways that individuals internalize and express socially constituted values and behaviors—which Bourdieu explored through the concept of habitus, and which Durkheim explored with the concept of the collective consciousness and also in his study of suicide trends. Durkheim's thought on religion reflected the legacy of nineteenth-century concepts of social evolution, and he felt that reason and science would eventually replace religion and prevail in "modern" society.

Bourdieu's position on religion and education was complex. At the same time that he drew heavily from Durkheimian and Maussian concepts of religion in so-called primitive societies, and applied these to educational institutions, showing how these institutions are not wholly "rational" but depend on similar phenomenon such as magic, symbols, and charisma as do "primitive religions," Bourdieu almost entirely ignored the presence of contemporary organized religion in French education or society. He used metaphors of religion but did not directly address religion as an institution itself in the context of education. The Bourdieuian theory of education focuses exclusively on the influences of the family, on one hand, and the secular state school system, on the other. Neither in his work on rural France nor on his work in urban settings, did Bourdieu explicitly take into account the existence of the church, despite the enormous influence that the Catholic Church has had on French society.[9] I am not suggesting here that he was not aware of that influence but, rather, that he chose (or his habitus predisposed him) to marginalize that influence in his own work. Although many of his ironic references to teachers acting like clergy and other uses of religion as a metaphor to discuss educational processes were veiled criticisms of the church, he seemed unwilling or unable to address religion per se in his empirical work. This lack of attention to institutional religion as a subject of sociological research also has been noted by the French sociologist of religion Erwan Dianteill, who ascribes Bourdieu's dismissal of religion to the *culture laïque* (secular culture) prominent among intellectuals and teachers. In an address to the French Association of Sociologists of Religion in 1982 (partially reprinted in Bourdieu 1987), Bourdieu remarked that a sociology of religion was almost impossible, because if one was religious the research would be tainted by lack of objectivity, and, if one was not (as in the case of Bourdieu himself), one would be excluded from relating the experience of belief in one's analyses. Although France is increasingly a secular society with low church attendance among its predominantly Catholic population, the influence of religion is not absent in the society and, with the growing Muslim population, religion has again been at the center of debates in the late twentieth century and into the present.[10] Dianteill notes that whereas Bourdieu used a notion of religion as a symbolic system in his studies of education, he marginalized religion itself in his studies of Algeria as well as in France. Dianteill writes, "As with Catholicism, the secular ideology thus perceives the Muslim religion as an anachronism condemned by modernity over the long run" (2002: 18; my translation). Bourdieu's silence on religious institutions, particularly in the context of French education, is difficult to explain except to say that it indicates a lack of reflexivity on his part in that, like many left-wing French intellectuals, he was a strong supporter of the secular state and separation of church and state. And, like Durkheim, he was influenced by a Republican ideology that expected reason to triumph over religion.

INSTITUTIONAL POWER: BOURDIEU AS "*HOMO ACADEMICUS*"

Situating Bourdieu within the context of the highly centralized French educational system is key to a holistic perspective on his theories.[11] The centralized state controls all higher education in France, even though at lower levels of primary and secondary schooling there is some local and regional control and influence. Each scholar employed by an educational institution is technically a civil servant, whether working for a university, a research arm (like the Centre National de la Recherche Scientifique) or an elite school (Grandes Écoles).[12] Bourdieu's own relationship to the French educational and university system is vital to an understanding of his work, and I will have more to say about Bourdieu's relationship to French anthropology in the next chapter. He worked within this system, being a product of it as well, while criticizing it to the core. He has been both social actor and observer in French academia. Bourdieu operated within a system that is organized through research laboratories and centers or teams (*équipes*). He was the head of a tightly knit group of researchers at the École des Hautes Études en Sciences Sociales, through which he published the journal *Actes de la Recherche en Sciences Sociales.* There is a lot of collaboration among researchers in this system, and Bourdieu coauthored several publications. The work he published in the 1960s with Jean-Claude Passeron criticizing higher education helped fuel student dissatisfaction expressed during the May '68 crisis in French society. Bourdieu also worked with the government, preparing two reports, including a report on the future of education in France prepared for then-President Mitterrand (1985) and a report on secondary education for Minister of Education Michel Rocard (1990).

All important elite institutions of secondary and higher education are in Paris, which is still, despite efforts at decentralization during the 1980s in France, considered the intellectual and cultural center of France. Ambitious teachers at all levels who are trained in Paris but begin their careers in the provinces or abroad, as Bourdieu did in his early years, try hard to eventually find a position in Paris. Bourdieu taught in Algeria and then at the University of Lille before returning to Paris. The process of becoming educated in institutionalized systems of schooling was of central interest to Bourdieu, and part of his self-reflexive project, as he was himself deeply imbedded in educational institutions. He pointed to this several times in interviews, as in this statement from the interview "Fieldwork in Philosophy":

> It is clear that my vision of culture and the education system owes a great deal to the position I occupy in the university, and especially to the path that led me there (which doesn't mean that it is relativized by this fact) and to the relationship with the school institution—I've described it several times—that was favoured by this path. (1990b: 23)

Bourdieu has described the position of his own field of sociology in *Homo Academicus* as that "relegated to the bottom division of the major new intellectual powers" (1988b: xxi). The social sciences are a relatively new field in France, suffer a "doubly subordinate position" (121), and struggle in the field of academia with the older dominant disciplines of philosophy, French, and history, and the more recent high status of the natural sciences in this hierarchy.[13] Although sociology is not itself one of the most prestigious disciplines in France (cf. also Lemert 1981 and 1986), Bourdieu's place within the academic field was an elevated one, to say the least.[14] Charles Lemert has vividly described the scene of a Bourdieu lecture in terms that lend some of the flavor of the cultural milieu within which he worked and his place in it:

> The College de France, one of France's most venerable cultural institutions, stands fortress-like above the cafes, Tunisian restaurants, and street vendors that have changed Paris' Latin Quarter. Here France's most brilliant scholars offer public lectures as modest recompense for election to this living pantheon. Today the lecture hall is already filled with an assortment of eager auditors. . . . Suddenly the form of tradition is evoked by the appearance of a portly but serious man adorned in the uniform of France's civil servants of culture, the bluish grey of a museum guard. In a firm voice reaching octaves above his working-class station, he serves the singular purpose, announcing "Monsieur, le professeur . . ." Pierre Bourdieu enters briskly. (Lemert 1986: 689)

Lemert goes on to say that Bourdieu, in sport jacket and open shirt, provided a contrast to this imposing setting. Cheleen Mahar (1990: 28–29) describes an almost identical setting during a visit to a Bourdieu lecture at the Collège de France in 1985, and also remarks on the discrepancy between what was projected as the "prestige, status and formality of the French system" (28) and Bourdieu's own informality. But it is instructive to keep that ideology of formality in mind when considering Bourdieu's work; he sometimes, as Michael Herzfeld pointed out, "confused the ideology of his own milieu with its practices" (1987: 83).

In an essay on Bourdieu as an "Insider/Outsider" Frenchmen (2000), Derek Robbins divides Bourdieu's career into three phases. The first, lasting from the 1950s to late 1960s, was that in which he gained his training in philosophy and undertook ethnographic fieldwork. The second period, during the 1970s, was one in which he established his credentials in a "scientific" sociology and built a research team. The third period began, according to Robbins, when Bourdieu took the Chair in Sociology (1981) and "became interested in the relationship between his personal status and power and those of the institution in which he is [*sic*] employed and which, in some sense, he represents" (Robbins 2000: 2). I am leery of portraying Bourdieu's career in such handy categories, because I see continuities and interests that transcend his entire career. His interest in reflexivity and in observing his own academic milieu did increase over time, as Robbins suggests, but it was always present. For example, although *Homo Academicus* was first published in 1984, while Bourdieu was "safely" ensconced in his lofty position at the Collège de France, this scathing critique of French academia was based on research carried out in the 1970s, before he achieved his highest status. I would characterize his work more in terms of a growing interest in a critique of the state as an institution and its role in domination, which followed his work on education and on issues of social class.

EDUCATION AND REPRODUCTION

First, a brief summary of Bourdieu's educational theory, which depends on his major concepts of habitus, cultural capital, and symbolic violence. According to Bourdieu, habitus is an internalized, embodied disposition toward the world. It comes into being through inculcation in early childhood, which is not a process of deliberate, formal teaching and learning but, rather, one associated with immersion in a particular sociocultural milieu—the family and household. Through observation and listening, the child internalizes "proper" ways of looking at the world, ways of moving (bodily habits), and ways of acting. Children, thus, acquire the "cultural capital" associated with their habitus. All human children, one assumes from Bourdieu's writings, undergo this process of inculcation in order to acquire the habitus that later guides their adult life and its outcome. It is through such inculcation that traditional societies reproduce themselves in subsequent generations. In *Outline,* Bourdieu used the Kabyles as an example of traditional society, where the values of honor and of loyalty to the family were inculcated as part of the habitus, with differences in socialization for boys and girls (1977a: 88–89).

Bourdieu viewed learning as an "irreversible process" (1990f: 43–44), in which the child plays a mostly passive role. Inculcation leads to the internalization of what he called the "cultural arbitrary." In *Reproduction,* Bourdieu and Passeron distinguished between cultural reproduction (reproduction of cultural arbitrary) and social reproduction (reproduction of relationships between groups or classes). They defined the former as "transmission from one generation to the other of the culture inherited from the past" (1990f: 10); and the latter as "reproduction of the structure of the relations of force between classes" (11). Bourdieu and Passeron argued that part of cultural reproduction (in any society) is the misrecognition of the "objective truth of that culture as a cultural arbitrary (ethnocentrism)" (31). They used the concept of *doxa* to characterize this. Moreover, in societies in which there exist dominant and dominated classes, there is misrecognition of the fact that the culture considered "legitimate" is the culture of the dominant sector (31). This misrecognition contributes to the reproduction of the position of dominance of the dominant class. A common term in Bourdieu's scholarly vocabulary is "rupture"—as he viewed his own sociological method as a tool to break through the commonsense understandings of the cultural arbitrary.

In societies with formal education and class stratification, such as France, the primary habitus inculcated through the family (which will differ according to the social position of the family) then comes into contact with a system which is outside of the family and part of the state apparatus—the school. This institution inculcates a secondary habitus, the "cultivated habitus," which privileges the cultural capital (which includes world views, linguistic codes, certain types of knowledge, and material objects—such as books) of a particular social class, the dominant social class. The school does not act primarily, however, to teach children anything they don't already know, but to certify the knowledge of the children of the dominant class by giving them high marks, certificates, and diplomas. It is for this reason that Bourdieu and Passeron labeled their two major works on education (and here I give the English translations that correspond well to the original French) *The Inheritors* and *Reproduction in Education, Society and Culture*. Similarly, Bourdieu called his third major work on education *The State Nobility* in order to draw an analogy between education and the inheritance of noble titles in *Ancien Régime* France. Many of Bourdieu's other publications have dealt with formal education,[15] but I will focus on these three books here.

THE INHERITORS AND REPRODUCTION

The Inheritors takes as its premise that the function of education is to produce a social hierarchy (1979: 68), and that this conflicts with the value of a "truly democratic" system that would enable all students to have access to skills leading to school success. In *The Inheritors,* Bourdieu and Passeron provided an ethnographic and statistical study of university students, primarily those studying art, which argued that social origins are the major determinant of eventual school success or failure (what they refer to at one point as "educational death rates," p. 8). They stressed that this must not be viewed in terms of "mechanical determinism," because individual students will not all be affected the same way by their social background. It is up to a student to make the best of the chances given them. Bourdieu was aware of this factor in his own life, since his educational trajectory was an exception to the rule of social origins.

Bourdieu and Passeron argued that the unequal rate of school success occurs through a process of elimination, whereby the students from the lowest social classes are eliminated at greater rates than those of the higher social classes. Students either feel "at home" or "out of place" at school (1979: 13), and this is in large part because of the family environment that either did or did not prepare them for school through the "cultural habits and dispositions inherited from the original milieu" (14). They wrote:

> Not only do the most privileged students derive from their background of origin habits, skills, and attitudes which serve them directly in their scholastic tasks, but they also inherit from it knowledge and know-how, tastes, and a "good taste" whose scholastic profitability is no less certain for being indirect. (17)

Factors of religion, peer influence, and the media were almost casually discounted by Bourdieu and Passeron, with little attention given to them. The authors wanted to show that this system, while touted as "natural" and "rational," depends on symbolic constructions, the masking of ideology, and superstitions. Bourdieu used two metaphors that come from earlier ethnographic and sociological influences (esp. Durkheim, Weber, and Mauss) in order to describe the workings of this system of elimination: the metaphor of religion and that of "the gift."[16] Bourdieu took Mauss's critique of the concept of gift and applied it to the educational context—revealing the "ideology of gift" and its role in masking the factors of social origin and home environment that are at the heart of the success or failure of a child at school. Bourdieu and Passeron wrote that "all value is incarnated in the child prodigy, the brevity of whose path through school testifies to the extent of his gift" (71). They also explained that teachers collaborated in the perpetuation of this ideology of the gift:

> As for the teachers who incarnate scholastic success and are required constantly to pass judgment on the abilities of others, their professional ethic and morale depend on their regarding the abilities they have more or less laboriously acquired as personal gifts and on their imputing other people's acquired abilities and ability to acquire abilities to their essential nature—the more so because the educational system provides them with all the means of avoiding the self-conscious reflection that would lead them to question themselves both as persons and as members of the cultivated classes. Often originating from the lower middle class or from teachers' families, they are all the more attached to the charisma ideology which justifies arbitrary culture privilege, because it is only qua members of the intellectual class that they have some share in the privileges of the bourgeoisie. (70)

In an epilogue to *The Inheritors*, the authors took up the issue of how the dominant class works to maintain its position in times of the inflation of academic qualifications, and of the ways in which economic capital continues to be converted through educational credentials into academic capital. Although the concept of cultural capital had not been used in the first edition of *The Inheritors,* it was added in the epilogue. This book dealt with university education and the ways in which it excludes children from modest social origin while promoting the advancement of the children of the elite—who thereby "inherit" the social positions of their parents. It argued against the meritocratic view that educational achievement was either the result of native intelligence or was earned through diligence. Children succeed in education primarily, Bourdieu and Passeron argued, because of their social origins and the type of cultural capital that they bring to school as a consequence.

In *Reproduction* (1990), a more explicitly theoretical text, the authors took their analysis further and put forward a theory of education and power as a symbolic process. Bourdieu and Passeron further theorized the role of pedagogic action (PA) in sorting children according to social origin, showing how it works to disguise its methods and intent. Children fail in school and internalize those failures as having been caused by their own shortcomings—lack of intelligence and lack of hard work. A child sees that he or she is doomed to fail in school and thereby "chooses" to do poorly or drop out. This is evidence, according to the theory, of the symbolic violence exerted by the educational system. Inculcation at school through the PAu (Pedagogic Authority), which is invested in the teacher but also permeates the entire educational environment, works to exclude the children of the working classes. What is inculcated at school is not so much knowledge that can be useful to the child but the value of the legitimacy of the dominant culture. This process is strongest when it "assumes the guise of self-exclusion" (42) so that children accept that they are destined (either through their own choice or through their own failures) to be unsuccessful at school.

In *Reproduction,* Bourdieu and Passeron argued that schools are essentially conservative, traditional institutions, aimed at self-preservation and replication. As in *The Inheritors,* they used non-Western ethnographic examples to jolt the reader with parallels between schools and traditional societies. Evoking Malinowski to critique teacher attitudes, and with not a small touch of irony, they wrote that "as in the Kula cycle, where the armshells always go round in one direction and the necklaces in the other, all the wit and wisdom go from teachers to students and all the dullness and crudity from students to teachers" (112). Although Bourdieu and Passeron posited resemblances between social conservatism and systems of authority in schools and traditional societies, they viewed the school's mode of pedagogy, or inculcation, as very modern because it depends on impersonal social relationships. They distinguished between "implicit" pedagogy, which produces a habitus with unconscious forms of inculcation, and "explicit" pedagogy, characteristic of schools, where a secondary habitus is inculcated through articulated and formalized principles (47). Whereas the primary habitus of all children is inculcated in the family through implicit forms, bourgeois children are more exposed, the authors claimed, to explicit forms of verbalization and classification at home. This thereby makes their primary habitus closer to that inculcated in the school and gives them an advantage over other children.[17] The main argument in both *The Inheritors* and *Reproduction* was that the French educational system has assumed part of the bourgeois family's role in cultural and social transmission to its heirs, serving to reproduce the class interests of the dominant class.

The State Nobility

In *The State Nobility*, Bourdieu focused on the elite system of higher education at the French Grandes Écoles, demonstrating, in his most forceful and nuanced arguments about this topic, the ways in which social position is "reproduced" through education—but not in any mechanical or straightforward way. Bourdieu departed from his earlier studies in two important ways, while retaining a focus on the reproduction of domination. First, he sought to dissolve the emphasis on a distinction between "modern" and "traditional" forms of education that had been central to the earlier books, showing that the elite schools were "traditional" in their methods of inculcation. Connected to this, he no longer described the school institution as operating primarily through explicit forms of inculcation. Instead, he emphasized the implicit forms of inculcation and pedagogy operating in that sphere to create a cohort of students who would assume dominant positions in society.

Bourdieu presented a more sophisticated version of his educational theories in this book, drawing greater attention to the ways in which his work on education is about power. The Grandes Écoles, the most prestigious institutions of higher education, are different from the universities who serve the broader population. In the various sections of this analysis, Bourdieu showed how the teachers and students work together to produce this institution, of which the teachers are themselves the product and whose students are chosen due to their own inherited dispositions which make them ideally suited to it. The analysis draws primarily from survey and interview data, and several chapters were co-written with either Yvette Delsaut or Monique St. Martin. This type of educational institution, in which Bourdieu was educated (having been a student at ENS), recruits its students from various levels of the bourgeoisie (with the occasional exception from the lower classes). *The State Nobility* constitutes a sort of autoethnography (as in study of one's own group) for Bourdieu, as it is set in a context with which he was familiar from both his own student days and his career as an academic. As in *Homo Academicus,* he obviously drew on his own experiences and intimate knowledge of this milieu in the descriptions he presents.

In his inaugural lecture to the Collège de France, Bourdieu advocated the study of elite forms of education as a way to help change the fabric of social and political life in France:

> If the sociology of the system of education and the intellectual world seems to me to be fundamental, this is because it also contributes to our knowledge of the subject of cognition by introducing us, more directly than all reflexive analysis, to the unthought categories of thought which limit the thinkable and predetermine what is actually thought: I need merely refer to the universe of prejudice, repression, and omission that everyday successful education makes you accept, and makes you remain unaware of, tracing out that magic circle of powerless complacency in which the elite schools imprison their elect. (1990b: 178)

In *The State Nobility,* Bourdieu returned to the some of the themes developed in the earlier books *The Inheritors, Reproduction,* and *Homo Academicus,* but with a more nuanced and fleshed-out description of the types of everyday behaviors on the part of students and teachers that result in the reproduction of the domination of the dominant classes. He was critical of what he called the "myth" of the school as a liberating force, arguing that the educational institution functions to legitimate domination (1996a: 5). For Bourdieu, it was sociology that is the liberating force, at least his brand of sociology, which exposes the "objective" truth of the social relations and dispositions of the habitus that lead to the reproduction of domination.

Bourdieu expanded his theory of habitus through the analysis of the social practices of teachers and students in the Grandes Écoles, and he used the metaphor of religion to describe these practices. In a chapter on "Misrecognition and Symbolic Violence," Bourdieu compared what he called "academic forms of classification" to the "primitive forms of classification" studied by Durkheim and Mauss, arguing that the words and labels applied by teachers to students operated as a kind of "social alchemy." The preparatory classes, which are mandatory for entry into the Grandes Écoles, serve as "a genuine common culture, in the anthropological sense" (81). Here Bourdieu echoed the Durkheimian sense of "mechanical solidarity" in traditional society, in that a shared body of knowledge, including ways of moving, slang, and jokes, was transmitted as a secondary habitus. He termed this community a "magical prison" of which the teachers were "ostensibly the guards" (91), even though they were themselves prisoners/products of this same system. The teachers exert their influence through the "charisma of office" and "consecrate" the students by awarding prizes, titles, and certificates. They are not aware of this, however, and "think they are making strict academic judgments" (39). Bourdieu likened the relationship between the elite preparatory schools and universities to that between the sacred and the profane (102). Like religious authority, he argued, the Grandes Écoles separate the chosen—using the justification of giftedness and ability to explain their privileging. Bourdieu also showed how alumni work to constitute and replicate these relations through an analysis of obituaries written by classmates and published in the yearbook. In these forms of biography, the shared hierarchical system of value or symbolic capital is displayed and this, Bourdieu argued, demonstrated a "successful socialization" process that will "get agents to act as accomplices in their own destiny" (45).

In *The State Nobility*, Bourdieu wanted to strike a balance between what he positioned as a "centralist perspective" on social agency associated with Althusser, whereby Ideological State Apparatuses work through symbolic coercion, and a "spontaneist perspective," that posits a voluntary servitude of the dominated. He wrote in his introduction to the book that "If it is fitting to recall that the dominated always contribute to their own domination, it is at once necessary to recall that the dispositions that incline them toward this complicity are themselves the effect, embodied, of domination" (4). He explained this in terms of the field of power relations in which social agents operate, arguing that there is a structural homology between education and power. The field of power is one of struggles, he admitted, so that social reproduction strategies of the dominant class must legitimize their domination. Bourdieu criticized the dominant ideology thesis for implying a "unique, fully unified discourse," whereas, for him, dominance involves various points of view, depending upon the form of capital needed for dominance in a particular field.[18] He continued to maintain that these strategies of domination lay in the habitus, and were not based on "rational calculation or strategic intent" (272). Bourdieu concluded his book with strong language for those who hold on to the view that education is a "liberating force" in society, calling this ideology "the new opiate for the people" (412). A "mask of modernity" associated with schooling, he argued, conceals the "magical-archaic nature of the educational institution" (376).

REPRODUCTION THEORY AND
RESISTANCE REVISITED

In English-language discussions of educational sociology, Bourdieu's studies of education are generally placed alongside work published during the 1970s such as that of Baudelot and Establet (1971) and Althusser (1971 [1970]) in France, Bowles and Gintis (1976) in the United States, and

Willis (1981 [1977]) in England. In France, Bourdieu first established his reputation as a sociologist through his work on education coauthored with Jean-Claude Passeron and published starting in the 1960s. He is still associated with theories of social and cultural reproduction in French sociology of education, where his work has been poised as opposite to that of Raymond Boudon (1973), one of his fiercest critics, who advocates a theory of individual strategy and rational choice in education. Bourdieu accused Boudon of "methodological individualism," whereas those on the side of Boudon see Bourdieu as overly deterministic. Berthelot (1982), another sociologist advocating individual strategy approaches, has accused Bourdieu of circular reasoning and functionalism. In these debates, as Marie Duru-Bellat and Agnès Henriot-van Zanten (1992) point out, extreme positions were staked out and the possibilities for seeing evidence of strategy in Bourdieu's work were thereby overlooked. They suggest that with his later work, especially in the *Logic of Practice,* Bourdieu contributed to theories of practice that are not mechanistically determinist. Duru-Bellat (2000) suggests that during the years since these two competing paradigms were established, with Boudon on one side and Bourdieu and Passeron on the other, sociological research in France continues to be influence by them and neither has been falsified through empirical work.[19] The debates within the "field" of the sociology of education in France, which positioned Bourdieu in a certain way due to the earlier work and in which he staked out his own position against rational actor theories, play a role in his subsequent writings, especially *The State Nobility,* in which he continued to answer his critics and show more evidence of how individuals as social agents participate in social reproduction through behaviors that appear as freely made "choices."

In the field of Anglo-American "critical studies of education," within which Bourdieu is generally situated, there has been controversy over issues of reproduction and social agency, particularly since the publication of Paul Willis's book *Learning to Labor,* which focused attention on modes of resistance in theories of social reproduction.[20] The customary nod to Willis's work in discussions of resistance, where it is usually contrasted with what is considered a reproduction model of education associated with Bourdieu, misrepresents the complexity of both their contributions.[21] Willis's *Learning to Labor* was originally published in 1977, seven years after Bourdieu and Passeron published *La reproduction* in French, but in the same year that it first appeared in English translation. Willis was aware of the original French version, and does briefly cite it in his book, using the notion of cultural capital to address differences between working-class and middle-class students. In no way, however, was this book an attack on Bourdieu's theories, since Willis was only vaguely familiar with his work at the time. As was an earlier study of capitalist schooling in France by Baudelot and Establet (1971), of which Willis seems unaware in his book and which has never been translated into English, Willis's approach was influenced by the Marxist approach of Althusser (1971) and his notion of "Ideological State Apparatuses." Willis primarily was working with the ideas of Althusser (1971) and Gramsci (1973)—whom he favored, trying to find a way to reconcile Marxist theories of ideology with lived practice. Willis provided an ethnographic sociological study of working-class boys in an industrial urban setting in order to challenge Marxist theories of reproduction that he felt relied too heavily on dominant ideology and ignored social agency and struggle. Willis tried to demonstrate that the "lads" had some partial understanding of their class position and also that they undertook some forms of resistance to the dominant cultural forces operating on them. Ultimately, the "lads" got working-class jobs and the social class reproduction continued.

In the context of some references to Bourdieu's work that he made after the publication of *Learning to Labor,* Willis states that what he calls the "counter-school culture" (represented by the working-class "lads" who were the focus of his ethnography) "refuses to collude in its own educational suppression" (1981: 128). This perspective is directly at odds with Bourdieu's own claim for the dominated class in various domains (peasants in terms of the marriage market as well as working-class kids at school), whereby he argued that the reproduction of socioeconomic hierarchy is indeed founded on the fact that the dominated participate in their own domination. This is because, through the habitus, they have internalized their own position in the field of power. Willis adopts the concept of "partial penetration" to explain the mechanism through which the lads come to see what is in store for them and therefore resist the forces of class domination. Bourdieu did not himself posit a total misrecognition of class position among the dominated either. He interpreted this differently: "Even the negative dispositions and predispositions leading to self-elimination, such as, for example, self-depreciation, devalorization of the School and its sanctions or resigned expectation of failure or exclusion may be understood as unconscious anticipation of the sanctions the School objectively has in store for the dominated classes" (Bourdieu and Passeron 1990: 204–5). The level of awareness of their domination among the working-class is, therefore, interpreted differently among Willis and Bourdieu. For Willis this is partly conscious, but for Bourdieu, the habitus operates primarily at the level of the preconscious, in a taken-for-granted disposition toward the world of which the social agent is not explicitly aware. Bourdieu returned briefly to the debate with Willis in *Pascalian Meditations,* reiterating that "the dominated are always more resigned than the populist mystique believes and even than might be suggested by simple observation" (2000b: 231). He noted that many adolescent males will express resistance, as Willis had shown in his study. Bourdieu also, however, pointed to the rigidity of both the lads' world and the language they used to describe it, suggesting that the cult of masculinity and social hierarchy of the lads' world was actually very conformist and rooted in a collectively guaranteed and stable world (of the urban working-class, one assumes Bourdieu meant). He seems to have been suggesting, therefore, that the resistance of the lads was (just?) part of their commonsense culture, and not a true challenge to the structures that dominated them—of which they could not be aware. Bourdieu may have been drawing on his own experiences with schooling and masculinity in his response to Willis's work here. In *Esquisse pour une auto-analyse* (2004), Bourdieu wrote of his own mixture of docility in the face of the educational system (which led him to be accepted into ENS) and challenges to authority in terms of such practices as the "*chahut*," which did not really challenge the system. He also wrote of his participation in rugby as a way to assert his masculinity among his peers who were themselves of rural social origin, even as he was growing away from them through success in his studies.

The debate over reproduction and resistance in education also must be placed in the context of radical theories of education (Giroux 2001 [1983]; Apple 1982) that posit its potential for liberation—a position about which Bourdieu gave contradictory messages in his own work. In this context, Bowles and Gintis's 1976 study *Schooling in Capitalist America* became the archetype of a mechanistic reproduction model of class relations that took into account neither social agency nor possibilities of liberating change. When Bourdieu and Passeron's book *Reproduction* was translated into English in 1977, it seemed to have the same message, especially if one relied too heavily on its title. Although Willis made scant reference to Bourdieu in *Learning to Labor*, he criticized Bourdieu on many fronts in a 1981 article through which he sought to answer many critics of his first book. He made the damning statement that "For all the richness of the Bourdieun system, once again, agency, struggle, and variety have been banished from history" (55). Willis claimed that Bourdieu's work was only helpful in understanding how the bourgeoisie pass along their cultural capital to their children and did not illuminate this process among the dominated sectors. He also argued that with Bourdieu's theory "we are left finally with a traditional socialization model—the bourgeoisie transmit, quite unproblematically, their culture to their offspring" (1981: 55). For Willis at that moment, Bourdieu's theory offered "no theoretical basis for a politics of change, for the production of alternative or radical consciousness" (1981: 56).

Although it was not evident in his earlier books on education, Bourdieu did address change and did allow for a lack of fit between habitus and individual trajectory. In an early article coauthored with Luc Boltanski and Monique St. Martin (Bourdieu, Boltanski, and St. Martin 1973), Bourdieu argued that changes in "the state of capital" (economic, cultural, or social) would lead to changes in educational strategy. These authors also argued that education had begun to limit the power of the family in cultural transmission (1973: 83), so that the bourgeoisie came to depend increasingly on the school as a mode of reproduction and to develop strategies to ensure the legitimacy of their position. The same article argued that in light of socioeconomic changes affecting agriculture, peasants in France had begun to adopt educational strategies that were "autodestructive," by encouraging girls in particular to become more educated, which was leading to their marrying outside of the villages. In *The State Nobility,* Bourdieu addressed cases in which there were individual "misfirings" of the system of social reproduction—which he also called "deviant trajectories" (1996a: 183–4). This is where there would be deviation between position and disposition, where a bourgeois child may fall in social status, or a working-class child may rise in social status. These were, however, exceptions, and as one can see from the language Bourdieu employs to describe this, exceptions to what he believed was most often a smooth process in which social agents were inculcated with the right dispositions to fit their positions in society.

Bourdieu's analyses of the events of May 1968 (1988b) illustrate his approach to resistance and to change. It is primarily one that explains these in terms of lack of fit (*décalage*) between the habituses and dispositions of social agents (especially their aspirations for the future) and the structures and fields in which they find themselves. There is no conflict in society when there is "harmony" (Bourdieu's term) between the habitus and the structure, but it can exist when this harmony is lacking due to historical circumstances. The student demonstrations were, he believed, the result of a combination of many students entering universities because of the postwar "baby boom" and the decreased value of qualifications that followed as the universities let many pass quickly through the system in order to create a teaching corps to handle the growing student population. A sense of frustration arose among lecturers whose advancement in the university system was slower than they had hoped, and among students who eventually came to see that their qualifications were not as valuable in terms of employment as they had expected. It was the "heirs" of the bourgeoisie who became most vocal (Bourdieu called it an "aristocratic revolt") as their formerly "automatic" ascension to good positions was stymied by the lowering of the value of qualifications. Bourdieu concluded that May 1968 was not truly aimed at democratization of the educational system but, rather, worked to restore the dominance of the bourgeoisie in a changing field of the value of their symbolic capital.

Whether or not Bourdieu's body of work entails what Willis referred to as a "politics of change" through education requires close scrutiny of his work to determine. Bourdieu challenged the view that schools work democratically to minimize social stratification, and tried to show that they did, in fact, contribute to social stratification despite their apparent neutrality from economic spheres. As I showed through his denunciation of the liberating myth of education in *The State Nobility*, in particular, Bourdieu appears to have been pessimistic about the possibilities of social change through schools, seeing educational institutions as linked to the reproduction strategies of the bourgeoisie. In his Prologue to *The State Nobility*, Bourdieu reiterated his position that it is the "awakening of consciousness" through a scientific sociology that will lead to liberation, not schooling per se, as even those who wish to reform schools are themselves subject to a symbolic violence of which they are not aware. Here he offered the possibility that those who read his writings could alter their habitus sufficiently to change the system.

Bourdieu's famous essay on giving a lecture, his inaugural address as Chair of Sociology at the Collège de France (1982c; reprinted and translated in *In Other Words* 1990b), is a metadiscourse on the social field in which such a lecture occurs. It also presents a strong argument for the liberating potential of sociology, and in his remarks Bourdieu argued that "through the sociologist, all social agents are able to know a little more clearly what they are and what they are doing" (1990b: 186). This will only be true, however, if sociology is a science, and "especially when it takes the form of a science of the symbolic powers capable of restoring to social subjects the mastery of the false transcendence that miscognition ceaselessly creates and recreates" (198).

The differences in interpretation between French and Anglo-American readers of Bourdieu's writings may be attributed to two factors. First, in French sociology, there is little dispute about the reproduction of the educational system, as the state routinely collects data on parental background and it is clear that, by and large, the success of children in the educational system depends on their social class. The issue then becomes that of how this occurs—either through individual choices based on a rational understanding of possibilities and constraints (Boudon) or through an internalized set of dispositions and symbolic violence (Bourdieu). Another factor is one pointed out by Richard Harker (1990: 98), who rightly explains that education has different meanings in French- and English-speaking contexts. In France, education is understood in terms of training and selection, and this is related to a system that explicitly "selects" children and orients them to different educational tracks through a system of exams and certificates, and in which "paper qualifications are a necessary acquisition" for employment, mobility, status, and so on. Notions of personal development for the individual, associated with education in the English-speaking world, Harker suggests, are less prevalent in France. Teachers and parents speak quite openly about children and their abilities, and see the school as helping the child to be placed in the right track for their abilities, rather than helping to develop what is considered an innate "gift" or lack thereof.[22] This is, of course, an idea that Bourdieu sees as leading to the misrecognition of the ways in which the school legitimates bourgeois culture and dominance. Following Harker's observation, I suggest that it follows from this that it is not as transgressive in France to suggest that children wind up in different occupations depending upon their social class origins as it would be elsewhere—for example, in the United States. In cultural contexts in which education is supposed to further individual development, even if that means resistance to hegemony, the notion of reproduction through education is more difficult to accept. It also makes sense, following this argument even further, that the concept of "practice" associated with Bourdieu's work in Algeria and some of the work on "taste" in France, was much more easily accepted and even embraced by many Anglo-American scholars because it seemed to infer a notion of individual agency and freedom (even if a close reading of Bourdieu shows that this is not exactly what he had in mind).

Several recent critical ethnographies of education have engaged with the theories of Bourdieu via the debate over agency and structure prompted by Willis's book. A major hallmark of critical ethnographers of education is their attempt to synthesize micro-level research with macro-level social processes and to be explicitly theoretical in their analyses—oftentimes using a cultural studies approach inspired by (if not accepting wholesale) Marxist and post-Marxist theory. In general, such studies have an element missing from Bourdieu's own writings, however empirical his research may be: ethnographic descriptions of social practice, of social actors in concrete situations interacting with other social actors. Bourdieu's work on education relies primarily upon interviews or questionnaire data, self-reports of behavior and attitudes that are certainly important as narratives, but fail to show us individuals "in motion."

There have been several ethnographic studies that respond to these debates on agency, structure, and practice in education. Two early books, both appearing in 1990, were based on ethnography that engaged with resistance theory, reacting to both Willis and Bourdieu: *Educated in Romance* by Holland and Eisenhart (1990) and *Learning Capitalist Culture* by Foley (1990). The first had a forward written by R. W. Connell, an Australian sociologist of education who had engaged with the debate earlier by criticizing "reproduction theory" (cf. Connell 1983). The forward to Foley's book was by Paul Willis. Both books take as their starting points critiques of Willis, and attempts through further ethnographic examples among different ethnic populations and further theorizing on issues of class and resistance, to understand the role of peers and of gender in processes of social hierarchy. Both studies attempt to bring anthropological perspectives on the study of culture to a more central place in critical theories of education. Neither book is an explicit attempt to refute the reproduction approach of Bourdieu's early educational writings; rather, one draws on concepts of practice (Holland and Eisenhart) and the other of taste (Foley) from his other writings. In a more recent ethnography of a diverse urban Mexican high school, Bradley Levinson (2001), engages with Bourdieu's concepts of habitus and his use of a game metaphor to articulate the lived practice of students who negotiate and respond to various influences. Levinson is particularly interested in the ways in which student aspirations are affected not only by their primary habitus but also subsequent influences coming from national discourses, school culture, peers, and the mass media.[23]

In my own ethnographic and historical research on education in rural France (Reed-Danahay 1986; 1987; 1996; 1999; 2000; 2003), I work on Bourdieu's own terrain in France, but my focus has been on primary education at the village level and youth culture, rather than secondary and higher education. I adopt the view of Bourdieu and others (Apple 1982) that schooling plays a role in the reproduction of social stratification, but take a perspective on this which shows how this gets worked out at the local level and is nuanced by factors such as regional identity, religion, gender, and peer culture. Bourdieu's research generally took as its starting point either secondary or higher education, and his work did not explain how the children were socialized prior to arriving at these levels. He assumed that the family is the main factor in inculcation yet did not focus on family socialization in France in any of his work.[24] My research has taken place in a region where many children stay in farming (primarily dairy) and I have been interested in explaining why this is so during a time of overall national trends away from this type of agriculture. I argue that the reproduction of the family farm today, in an era of the European Union's Common Agricultural Policy, which increasingly applies bureaucratic demands and restrictions on farming, and in an era of growing mechanization and capitalization of farming, is itself a form of resistance to bourgeois hegemony. Schooling in Lavialle is a site of conflict, and it is a site that provides ambiguous messages to children about their futures. My approach is not an outright rejection of Bourdieu, because I see evidence of social reproduction strategies among families and the role of schooling in the reproduction of bourgeois hegemony. I do, however, reject his notion that the dominated accept their domination and internalize their failures. In

Lavialle, people are aware of some of the factors working against them, and employ what can be considered, after Scott (1985), as "everyday forms of resistance." With their own French concept of *se debrouiller,* the Laviallois express this form of "making do," or "making out" in the situations presented to them (Reed-Danahay 1993). It is, in many ways, odd that Bourdieu should downplay those forms of everyday resistance that would have been so evident to him, being raised in a peasant milieu. Although he did acknowledge forms of "getting around" marriage strategies in Béarn (1972b), and certainly contributed much to our understandings of Kabyle men's everyday social manipulations, Bourdieu seems to have adopted the ideology of French education as central to the society and thereby ignored ways in which people may subvert this in everyday life. He never wrote ethnographically about education in the village settings in which he worked.

"CONTROLLING PROCESSES" IN EDUCATION: BOURDIEU, ELIAS, AND FOUCAULT

The idea of an internalization of social control is present in the work of Bourdieu, Norbert Elias, and Michel Foucault. Elias and Foucault shared with Bourdieu an interest in the workings of power in European societies, and all three rejected of the notion of the autonomous individual ("methodological individualism") in their theorizing of power.[25] Those who draw on their theories are interested in answering questions about the ways in which social actors are, at once, producers of culture and constrained by habitus (in the case of Bourdieu and Elias) or discourses (in the case of Foucault). In an article on what she labeled "controlling processes," Laura Nader (1997) proposed a useful analytical distinction in studies of power between social control and cultural control, relating to internal versus external forms of control. She uses the term "cultural control" for forms that are internalized and implicit. Nader writes: "The distinction between social and cultural control allows for the distinction between control over groups or relationships and control of the mind, both part of any controlling process" (1997: 719). Nader suggests that the use of social (external and explicit) control has become less acceptable in contemporary times, so cultural control "becomes more central to the whole mechanics of power" (1997: 720).

Whereas Bourdieu focused more attention on education as a "controlling process," Elias and Foucault also touched on education in their work, with implications for understandings of social and cultural forms of control. In many ways, an attempt to synthesize these three approaches illuminates these issues more than can each theorist on his own. The historical approach of Elias complements Bourdieu's focus on empirical studies that lack historical depth, while Foucault's focus on discourse and surveillance balances the emphasis on habitus or internalized control in the work of both Elias and Bourdieu. Foucault's theory of power developed primarily in the context of the institutions of the prison and the asylum, but it has much to say about schools (Ball 1990; Rousmaniere et al. 1990). Foucault viewed power as diffuse, permeating all aspects of social and cultural life, and operating through discourse and technologies or regimes that serve to "normalize" forms of governance. The child in school is both "compiled and constructed . . . in the passive processes of objectification, and in an active, self-forming subjectification" (Ball 1990: 4). Knowledge about individual children is acquired by schools, through techniques of surveillance and record keeping, that are then used to shape their behavior and attitudes, and even their own self-knowledge. As Stephen Ball describes Foucault's thought on this, "These discourses and practices have not only been used to change us in various ways but are also used to legitimate such changes, as the knowledge gained is deemed to be true" (1990: 15). Internalized self-regulation is a result of these disciplinary regimes in modern life. Foucault (1977) described the Panoptican, Bentham's architectural feature of prisons that would permit easy surveillance of all prisoners in their cells, as a metaphor for all forms of institutional surveillance that shape the self-disciplining of inmates.[26]

James Marshall suggests that an important contribution of Foucault to studies of education is in the area of his questioning of "normative notions of legitimacy and illegitimacy." Foucault demonstrated that power is implicated in a "host of shaping processes—learning to speak, read, and write, for example—which the liberal framework would not normally identify as acting contrary to the interests of the child" (Marshall 1990: 25). Whereas what Marshall terms the "liberal" approach in education sees power operating only when it conflicts with what pedagogical experts see as what is in the best interest of the child, Foucault alerted us to the permeation of power throughout the educational process. This is similar to Bourdieu's critique of French Republican ideologies of education in *The State Nobility*. Like Foucault, despite his distancing from him, Bourdieu was interested in questioning forms and processes of the legitimization of power and knowledge in society.

Norbert Elias viewed all socialization as contrary to the "animalistic" nature of the child (although he did not question *this* discourse on the construction of the relationship between humans and animals, as would a Foucauldian), and thus also called into question the legitimacy of educational processes. Elias identified problems of parent-child relations (and, by extension, one could add, teacher-child relations) as problems of civilization—through which the child's "animalistic spontaneity" must be converted into adult self-regulation, and the "domestication of the natural needs" (Elias, 1980: 200). Elias wrote: "Just the learning of reading, writing and arithmetic requires a considerably high degree of civilizing drive and af-fect-regulation; it takes, even in its most elementary form, at least two or three years of childhood and mostly demands some activity in the context of a special institution outside of the family—in a school, a symptom of the partial defunctionalization of parents" (203). Elias's theory of the "civi-lizing process" used a concept of habitus (although one that is not entirely congruent with that used by Bourdieu) in order to explain changing cul-tural constraints on individual comportment.

For Elias, the civilizing process is a process of socialization at the indi-vidual level, as well as a macrohistorical trend that began in Europe in the court society of the Middle Ages. Even though Elias did not focus on school-ing per se in his writings, this concept has relevance for an understanding of schools as places of both social action and constraint. The origins of modern schools can be traced to medieval institutions, so that formal edu-cation and "civilization" (in Elias's sense of the term) arose in tandem. In the context of French education, the phrase "the civilizing process" has particular resonance, given the important rhetoric of schooling as part of the *mission civilisatrice* during the Third Republic. In the history of France, the notion of civilization has been paramount in concepts of nationalism. The "civilizing mission" of both primary schooling in rural France and colonialism abroad was a key ideology of the nineteenth century, advo-cated prominently by both François Guizot and Jules Ferry. Theodore Zeldin notes that the French word *"civilisation"* did not enter the vocabulary until the late 1700s and was not admitted into the dictionary of the French Academy until 1798 (1980: 6). "Civility," the word that *"civilisation"* came to replace in nationalist rhetoric, is a much older term and it this term that Elias draws on in his historical studies of court society. Huppert defines the sixteenth-century usage of "civility" to mean: "politeness, urbanity, a rejec-tion of savagery and rurality, aspiration towards justice, order, education" (1971; quoted in Zeldin 1980: 6). Zeldin points out that as the term *"civi-lisation"* came to be used in the nineteenth century by figures such as Guizot, it took on a connection with the state. As people became more "civilized" (meaning educated and polite), the country would prosper and improve overall. Civilization was thus a moral, economic, and political issue.

In *The Civilizing Process,* Elias linked the bourgeoisie in France to the emerging concept and value of *"civilisation."* As the bourgeoisie rose in power in relation to the nobility, they adopted the values of court society, and, Elias wrote, "the bourgeois revolution in France, though it destroyed the old political structure, did not disrupt the unity of traditional man-ners" (1978: 49). The bourgeoisie came to "express the national self-im-age" so that *"civilisation"* (like Kulture in Germany) became a tool in which to justify their superiority and therefore that of the nation. French primary schools have long been a key vehicle for the spread of this *"civilisation"* to the masses, both as a Republican ideal of egalitarianism, linked to nationalism, and as a program that reinforced class stratification. There has, however, been relatively little use made of Elias's ideas in studies of the schooling process as a civilizing process, and while Bourdieu drew on Elias in his studies of taste and distinction, he did not make much use of them in his own educational studies.

In a 1980 paper on "The Civilizing of Parents," Elias wrote that both parents and children in contemporary society have developed increasing forms of self-regulation and control. Parents have done so because physical violence against children is no longer acceptable, and they must control their own emotions in dealing with children and socializing them in "civilized" norms of behavior. Children must, for their part, develop increased self-regulation, at earlier ages, in keeping with societal values for autonomy. External forms of "social control" develop, therefore, into increased "cultural control" in the form of ideologies and internalized self-regulation of behavior. This cultural control comes from a variety of avenues—messages from advertisements, mass media, peers, and authority figures such as teachers and parents. Although Elias did not carry this idea into the realm of the classroom, it is equally relevant there. Physical punishments for children at school are giving way to forms of self-regulation among children, who must monitor their own behavior and internalize school norms of "civility."

One of the major differences between Bourdieu's approach and that of Foucault and Elias is his focus on social class and stratification, showing that socialization processes and educational institutions work in different ways for different segments of the population. Whereas Elias saw the civilizing process as originating in the bourgeoisie, he also saw it as then spreading to the general population and did not focus attention on the ways in which the bourgeoisie continues to assert its domination. According to Bourdieu, schools serve primarily to legitimize the dominance of the dominant bourgeoisie, and his theory calls this legitimacy into question. Although the system works to present class stratification and school failure among certain sectors of society as a "natural" state of affairs, Bourdieu argued that the symbolic capital associated with the habitus of some children is more highly valued and rewarded by the school than others, simply because the school embodies this habitus itself. Notions of civility and manners come into play in Bourdieu's thought, but as he demonstrated in *Distinction* (1984), the social class structure works to separate and distinguish between the "tastes" of various segments of the population, rather than to spread the norms of "civilization" throughout.

The relationship between Elias and Bourdieu has been thoughtfully analyzed by Jean-Hughes Décheaux (1993), who points out that both employ the concept of habitus and field (*champ*). Décheaux suggests that Bourdieu was more concerned with illuminating the process of social re-production than social transformation, which was of major concern for Elias. Bourdieu operationalized the workings of power through economic, social and cultural capital, however, while Elias used a concept of "power chance" without specifying the dynamics of how this works. Their views of habitus were similar but not entirely congruent. For both, the habitus was a site for the articulation of social and mental structures (or, in Nader's terms, social and cultural control) and work toward self-regulation. The internalized cultural control of the habitus in Elias's work reflects the civi-lizing process. For Bourdieu, the habitus was a generator of behavior; it is a locus of both cultural control and social practice or agency. The trajectory of the child at school, therefore, depends on not only the social constraints of the habitus or the internalized self-regulation it entails but also on the ability of the child to make use of the forms of symbolic and economic capital in his or her repertoire.

Foucault claimed that resistance and power are inseparable processes, although critics point out that he never specified how resistance operated. Bourdieu did not reject a concept of resistance, but this was never a major focus of his work—aimed more at social and cultural reproduction. For Elias, children's resistance to the civilizing process comes primarily from biological or "natural" resistance to cultural constraints. He wrote that our modern understanding of childhood rests on the discovery that they are not "little adults," and have more difficulty controlling their impulses and emotions. In his discussion of contemporary parent-child relationships, Elias suggested that the power chances of parents used to be much greater than those of children, but that the balance has shifted. He wrote, "It is not only that parents have power over children—normally children, and even new-born children, also have power over parents" (1980: 195). His expla-nation for this lies in the role that children play in the fulfillment of desires for their parents, a role that rarely existed in previous eras, according to Elias. "Earlier societies were generally more set up than industrial ones so that the people composing them would try to exploit their power chances to the last, relatively unconcerned about the destiny of subordinate people" (Elias 1980: 195). Although this last statement must be viewed with some skepticism in a cross-cultural perspective, and is too broad a generaliza-tion, Elias was pointing to an important development associated with modern schooling. As historians such as Minge-Kalman (1978) have sug-gested, the modern family is primarily oriented toward the production of children (rather than material commodities). The ways in which children become both object and subject of modern advertising and mass media in a child-centered era reflect this desire-fulfillment aspect of children for adults.

Schools, as the places that segregate children from adults and produce the "educated," "civilized" person, have become the symbolic focus of much national attention and concern. Elias work suggests that we should examine more closely the ways in which this might be lending children more power chances vis-à-vis parents and teachers than they had previously. Elias was interested in balances or ratios of power. Although his work placed greatest emphasis on socialization within the family, where the "civilizing process" occurs, he did suggest that the establishment of separate institutions for children as a trend in modern society worked to alter the role of parents. He usefully called into question the "natural" function of the family and showed that the family is a process, and ever changing as society changes. This perspective also was shared by Bourdieu, who argued, using a different vocabulary, that the family strategies of different class strata will change as their interests and the value of their cultural capital changes (Bourdieu, Boltanski, and St. Martin 1973).

The three theorists discussed here were all concerned with state power as it operates through schooling. Foucault's interest lay in governmentality in a broad sense, and in the production of docile bodies and regulated minds. For Bourdieu and Elias, the bourgeoisie represented a dominant force in state power, and the state worked to legitimize their dominant position. As the concept of civilization became associated with nationalism, and the bourgeoisie representing the epitome of the good citizen, the role of schooling in the reinforcement of state power has been important since nation-states mandated school attendance.

Some of the perspectives of Elias and Foucault can complement those of Bourdieu, despite some important differences among the three. Foucault's perspectives on surveillance and discipline in controlling processes provide a way of looking at the continued monitoring and control over behavior that becomes internalized throughout one's life, whereas Bourdieu's focus was primarily on the habitus as something acquired during early childhood and then set into motion in various social fields. Bourdieu undertheorized inculcation over the life course, even though he did articulate a theory of a secondary habitus acquired through education, and placed an almost exclusive emphasis on schools as sites for inculcation and class domination, rather than looking at other forms of control. Although educational institutions are crucial places to look for forms of domination and control, with Bourdieu's theoretical approach, one is encouraged to assume their primacy rather than to interrogate elsewhere. All roads lead back to the school in Bourdieu's work.

Elias's approach, particularly his suggestion (unfortunately not given full attention in his work) that there are differential power-chances among parents and children, could usefully complement Bourdieu's arguments about the differential influences of families and the school over social reproduction. Bourdieu afforded children little social agency and portrayed them as primarily passive in the face of the inculcation they receive. This is why he did not devote much attention to peer relations, dismissing them as irrelevant (as in *The Inheritors*) or showing how peers simply work to reinforce the messages of the educational institution (as in *The State Nobility*). Although Willis's work (1977) emphasized peer relations among the lads, the lads similarly reinforce the norms of masculinity and manual labor shared by their parents. By examining the possibilities for power among parents and children and schools, and "chances" to exert power, Elias opened up space for looking at the agency of children and youth. This might be further theorized to explain what Bourdieu called the "misfirings" of the reproduction system as being not due to malfunctions, but changing relations of power.

BOURDIEU AND THE LEGACY OF FRENCH REPUBLICANISM

Two critics of Bourdieu (Lane 1999 and 2001; Kauppi 2000) have suggested that he had a vision of education rooted in notions of the French Republic, despite his critical stance toward education, and that the two are contradictory. Niilo Kauppi sees Bourdieu as following in the tradition of French sociology in its "public defense of Republican ideals such as equality and liberty" (2000: 15). He argues that Bourdieu combined this with the other tradition of French intellectual as hero and liberator of "society's underdogs" (15). Rather cuttingly, Kauppi also argues that Bourdieu could not position himself as intellectual hero if he did not also construct a sense of urgency about a dangerous world of domination that reigns over common sense (14). Jeremy Lane also sees a Republican vision in Bourdieu's criticisms of French education, related to the influence of Durkheim, and coexisting "with a residual belief that, suitably reformed, French universities might indeed realize the duties with which the Republican tradition had charged them, namely to ensure democratic and universal access to knowledge and culture" (2000: 57). Lane (1999) argues that Bourdieu's stance toward Republicanism was ambivalent, but that appeals to universal reason and values of truth and knowledge associated with Republicanism can be traced in his work from the early studies of art appreciation and museum attendance (Bourdieu and Darbel 1966) to the later criticisms of television and the mass media (Bourdieu 1996b). In his essay *Sur la télévision,* Bourdieu argued that education should teach not only reading and writing but also the rights and duties of citizenship, ensuring universal access to the ideals of the French Republic. As Lane points out, this is contradictory to some of Bourdieu's other more pessimistic appraisals of the possibilities of liberation through education. His increasing emphasis on this later in his career was accompanied by a plea for the autonomy of the intellectual field and ideal of the intellectual as free from the market and the media (see Bourdieu 2002b).

Bourdieu championed the possibilities of liberation through the insights of a critical sociology, and he felt that he had to stay autonomous in order to objectify the objective conditions of existence that were commonsensical to most people. Lane (1999: 468–9) sees some danger in Bourdieu's celebration of Republican ideals as separate from the neoliberalism that he felt was invading them from the outside, and suggests a lacuna for Bourdieu in not understanding the relationship between the two. There is evidence of these Republican ideals in Bourdieu's early work in Algeria as well, which would support Lane's thesis. Although Bourdieu neglected to mention the existence of formal schooling in Kabylia in *Outline* (Reed-Danahay 1995), he collaborated with an Algerian sociologist, Abdelmalek Sayad, who was himself a former schoolteacher in Algeria, and the two made mention of schools in their coauthored publications. In their references to schooling, Bourdieu and Sayad used an almost utopian-sounding tone in order to stress the important role of education in the future of Algeria, in which the concerns Bourdieu voiced about the state and social reproduction in his work on France were absent. In a very early book, *Le déracinement* (1964), published the same year in which *The Inheritors* appeared, Bourdieu and Sayad dealt with the displacement of Algerians in resettlement camps during the Algerian war. At the end of the chapter in *Le déracinement* called "Le sabir cultural" ("Cultural Pidgin"), there is a section on "the educator and the bureaucrat." Here Bourdieu and Sayad addressed the dilemmas facing displaced Algerian peasants, who were stuck between a traditional world they can't return to and a modern economic system for which they were not equipped to cope. They suggested that "the intervention of centralized authority seems indispensable and, in any case, inevitable" (175), and that "only educational action, entirely and total, can overcome the contradictions" (177). Because the Kabyle peasant was "enclosed in the contradiction" (between tradition and modernity) and could not have an "adequate representation" of his situation, according to the authors, it was necessary to develop a pedagogy sensitive to his needs. Bourdieu and Sayad argued that:

> The literal meaning of educative action, in its ideal form, is precisely to adapt itself to the aptitudes and the desires of those it seeks to nurture and transform, therefore to know them and to respect them, to define, in each case, a system of demands calibrated to these aptitudes and desires, so as to transform them through the influence of education action, briefly to prohibit itself from arbitrarily proposing demands defined abstractly for abstract subjects. (Bourdieu and Sayad 1964: 177)

It seems clear from this that Bourdieu was proposing a system of education in Algeria that, if developed from the start in order to avoid the ways it operated in France, could be a liberating and empowering institution rather than a hegemonic force working to reproduce the power of the dominant.

Because Bourdieu did not attribute his own ability to objectify the *doxa* to anything else in his background other than his educational experiences, which created the rupture between village and school that permitted his sociological vision, we must assume that he did view education as potentially liberating—for him, at least. That education was for Bourdieu both a source of uncomfortable detachment from his origins and, paradoxically, afforded him a way to understand and theorize his own position, helps us understand the ambivalence in his views toward education. That he should seek a possible alternative in Algeria fits closely with his other uses of Kabylia as a foil to France.

THREE

Insider/Outsider Ethnography in Algeria and France

> Having worked in Kabylia, a foreign universe, I thought it
> would be interesting to do a kind of *Tristes tropiques* . . . but
> in reverse . . . : to observe the effects that objectification of
> my native world would produce in me.
>
> —*An Invitation to Reflexive Sociology* (1992)

In 1959, Bourdieu went to his native region of Béarn, in southwestern France, to do fieldwork, after having conducted his initial research among the Kabyles in Algeria.[1] In speaking of his turn back toward his own region as fieldsite, Bourdieu employed terms such as "foreign," "native," and "objectification" that articulate a long-standing (some would say, defining) opposition in ethnographic fieldwork between near and far (cf. Zonabend 1979; Fabian 1983; Gupta and Ferguson 1997; Segalen 1989). In his introduction to a recent volume that collects key writings on Béarn, Bourdieu returned to the theme of why he chose to work in France, writing of "throwing himself" into this very familiar world of his own region that he "knew without knowing" (2002a: 10) and which he could now "objectify" because he had distanced himself by immersion in another way of life (and here one assumes he means Algeria, although he does not explicitly say so).[2]

By doing fieldwork in France, Bourdieu was working against a stance commonly taken by Claude Lévi-Strauss, who was the dominant voice in French anthropology at mid-century, that the only way to be truly objective and to question one's own cultural assumptions as an ethnographer was to go to an unfamiliar environment. Bourdieu did not question Lévi-Strauss's conviction that objectivity was the goal (and in some ways, privilege) of social science, also the legacy of Durkheimian sociology, but sought to unpack the dichotomy between subjectivity and objectivity in much of his work. Going to Béarn was a way to seek objectivity in the familiar. Working on the French educational system afforded him a similar opportunity to do so, although he was less a "native" to this system and fell more into the category of convert or oblate, not having been an "heir" of the educated bourgeoisie.

What does it mean for Bourdieu to have constructed his research in Béarn as the "inverse" of Lévi-Strauss's part-ethnography, part-travelogue, and part-autobiography *Tristes Tropiques*? Lévi-Strauss wrote that:

> While remaining human himself, the anthropologist tries to study and judge mankind from a point of view sufficiently lofty and remote to allow him to disregard the particular circumstances of a given society or civilization. (1992: 55)

It was this perspective that Bourdieu intended to invert by going to his own environment in rural France in order to conduct ethnographic fieldwork. It was what Bourdieu called the "objectification" associated with structuralism that he later came to reject as he developed his "theory of practice." Moreover, in neither the case of his ethnographic research in late colonial Algeria, nor that of rural France, did Bourdieu seek what Lévi-Strauss described as the "no more thrilling prospect for the anthropologist than that of being the first white man to visit a particular native community" (Lévi-Strauss 1992: 326). In both cases, Bourdieu immersed himself in fieldwork situations that were impossible to close off from "the West" or its influences.

Bourdieu's writings nevertheless betray a nostalgic view of peasant society—a melancholy, or "*triste,*" portrait of the disruption and rupture with the past that produced dislocated, marginal, people. Bourdieu substituted Lévi-Strauss's *tristes tropiques,* and its critique of modern civilization, with an image of *tristes paysans,* and an attendant critique of the influences of modern capitalism on traditional socioeconomic peasant societies. Bourdieu adopted a linear historical approach that could position peasants as examples of the past societies in the present. Bourdieu's work was marked by a dichotomy of traditional and modern society that overshadowed at times even his own experience, so that he made little explicit connection in his writings between his ethnographies of Algeria and rural France, while at the same time using these cases at various times as a foil to "modern" France. Although Bourdieu wrote reflexively about the relationship of the two research experiences to his work later in his career, explicit ethnographic comparisons between the peasant societies of Kabylia and Béarn are rare in Bourdieu's writings. In a footnote to his article on honor among the Kabyles, he addressed the "Western reader," stating that he deliberately avoided comparisons with Western society in order to avoid "ethnocentric identifications" (1966a: 241, fn. 36). He claimed that in the West ("in our society") there is more of an individual orientation in behavior concerning honor, whereas among the Kabyles, behavior is connected to relationships among groups. What is left unclear, however, is how Bourdieu would have incorporated rural French society within the same category as Western in this opposition.[3] In a sense, the two sites of Kabylia and Béarn were "worlds apart," kept separate in his writings on each; but, at the same time, as we can learn from Bourdieu's own later reflections, these served as parallel worlds in which he worked on similar themes and developed his theoretical perspectives on habitus, field, and symbolic violence.

BOURDIEU AS "NATIVE" AND "OUTSIDER"

Bourdieu's earliest ethnographic studies in rural France and in Algeria were carried out during the late 1950s and early 1960s. The work was published at around the same time in France and operated within, to use of one of Bourdieu's own terms, the same intellectual field. It is significant to point out, however, that the Algerian work reached English-speaking audiences over a decade earlier than the rural French research, and most of the latter has never been translated into English. For example, *The Algerians* (orig. French version, 1958) appeared in 1962, and other articles on the Algerian work appeared in English translation during the 1960s. The earliest French article dealing with his rural French ethnography also appeared in 1962 (Bourdieu 1962c). It has never been translated into English. It was not until 1976 that the first English-language publication of the Béarn research appeared, in an article on "marriage strategies," included in a compilation of *Annales* articles translated into English. Although *Outline* is devoted to the Algerian material, with occasional examples drawn from France, the reworking of the Algerian ethnography in the *Logic of Practice* was accompanied by a chapter on marriage strategies in Béarn. This work, originally published in the early 1970s, is from the same *Annales* article already translated in 1976, cited above. To the best of my knowledge, the only other translation into English of Bourdieu's Béarn ethnography appears in fragments throughout the book *Photography: A Middle-Brow Art,* where he draws on his early studies of the cultural meanings and uses of photography among Béarnaise villagers that he carried out with his wife (Bourdieu and Bourdieu 1965).

Bourdieu's roots in rural France informed both the Algerian and French work. He made use of his origins to establish his ethnographic authority in Algeria. Bourdieu's position in Algeria was, as a Frenchmen and former soldier, that of member of the dominant society and colonizer—and he was keenly aware of this. In his preface to the sociological study he conducted among Algerian workers (Bourdieu et al. 1963a), Bourdieu cited Michel Leiris's 1950 article on ethnography and colonialism, in which Leiris wrote of the complicity of the ethnologist working in colonial contexts and of the impossibility of any "pure" science. Leiris stated that, whether or not they wish to be complicit, ethnographers are funded by their governments to do research in areas colonized by these governments. Anticipating discussions in Anglophone anthropology two and three decades later about the position of the native anthropologist, Bourdieu asked "Must we think like those who often say that there is no 'pure' ethnology other than that done by the natives? But why this ethical and epistemological privileging?" (1963a: 258).

An alternative perspective was voiced two decades later by the Algerian anthropologist Mafhoud Bennoune (1985), who was raised in what he called a "peasant mountain community." Bennoune wrote about his situation as a native anthropologist, by definition cast as an "other" in a discipline that romanticized pristine traditional cultures, whose frame of reference was not the West (as was the case with his professors in the United States) but the possibilities for change in his own society. He suffered a "double alienation: from the majority of scholars who constitute the international anthropological community and from an authoritarian bureaucratic environment within which he exercised his profession in his own Third World country" (363). He asks about the role of the anthropologist who is cast as "other" in a discipline devoted to the study of "the other." By paying attention to the voices of anthropologists who are come from outside of Euroamerican contexts, such as Bennoune, we are made more aware of the assumptions, frames of reference, and asymmetrical power relationships that dominate the discipline of anthropology. Although Bourdieu may have been justified in questioning a view that ethnographers from Europe were necessarily too implicated in the colonial relationship to Algeria, Bennoune reminds us to question the assumptions of an anthropology and a sociology that prompted Bourdieu to go abroad to undertake research.

When conducting ethnographic research in rural France, Bourdieu positioned himself as the native anthropologist. As a child, Bourdieu was surrounded by those who spoke the local dialect and he was raised in an agricultural milieu—if not strictly on a farm, as his father was a postman. As Jenkins (1992: 13) points out, his immediate origins were more petit bourgeois than peasant, because civil servants (such as a postal worker), along with small shopkeepers and artisans in rural France, are considered to be in that class. Although I have not found this phrase in Bourdieu's own work, one can speak of the "internal colonialism" (Hechter 1975; Lafont 1967 and 1971; Hind 1984) that occurred in France as regional populations with their own languages and local particularisms were brought into the control and under the hegemony of the dominant French society and culture.[4] Bourdieu's 1977 article on the class position of the peasantry, as well as his 1980 article on the social construction of the idea of region, both focus on the peasantry in France and highlight the symbolic domination to which they have been subject. In these articles, he discussed the ways in which local culture and local language are devalued by dominant

French culture. Whereas primary schools in France were instrumental in the project of constructing understandings of the nation and its regions, it is significant to note that Bourdieu rarely explicitly addressed the content or historical significance of French schooling in national, ethnic, or regional terms in his scholarly writings and sociological studies of education, choosing to focus on the social class reproduction of the school. An exception to this is in his brief discussion in *Language and Symbolic Power* (1982a) of regional languages in France, and the role of schooling in legitimizing the authority of the dominant language.

Bourdieu remarked several times on the reciprocal relationship between his fieldwork among the Kabyles and Béarnaise and the ways in which this influenced his own theoretical development. Part of Bourdieu's self-reflexive project was to remain critically aware of one's position vis-à-vis one's informants, and to seek an understanding not of their "native point of view" but of the logic of their practices. In his preface to the *Logic of Practice*, Bourdieu made reference to his social origins and the advantage this gave him as a rural ethnographer in Algeria, making him aware of the dangers of assuming a naïve empathy with his informants. He wrote: "Perhaps because I had a less abstract idea than some people of what it is to be a mountain peasant, I was also, and precisely to that extent, more aware that the distance is insurmountable, irremovable, except through self-deception" (1990b: 15). Here Bourdieu legitimized his claims to study the Kabyles, despite his association with the colonial power of France, through reference to both his rural origins and his theoretical stance. He was, like the Kabyles, familiar with peasant life (having come from a rural background), but he also was a self-reflexive researcher who was aware of the construction of this relationship. Distance and closeness were thus associated not only with geography and culture, but with one's theoretical stance. Despite Bourdieu's own "proximity" to the Kabyles because of his rural origins, he maintained a stance of self-reflexive distance in his observations of them. He continued in this passage: "The distance lies perhaps not so much where it is usually looked for, in the gap between cultural traditions, as in the gulf between two relations to the world, one theoretical, the other practical" (15).

This theme of these differences between practical logic and theoretical logic, and between objective and subjective approaches, was central to Bourdieu's work in both the Algerian and rural French contexts. He wanted to overcome the dichotomy between objective and subjective, while also maintaining a distinction between the practical (experience-near) logics of both researcher and informants and the theoretical (experience-far) logic of the sociologist. Bourdieu articulated the relationship between Algerian and French peasants largely through an inversion of the opposition between insider and outsider research. He positioned himself as insider in

Algeria and outsider in Béarn. One place contained "exotic" others with whom he claimed some affinity because of his own rural origins, while the other place was inhabited by people he knew, including his own relatives—yet he adopted a stance of "distant intimate" in that research as he tried to be objective in a milieu that was familiar. Bourdieu adopted a position as outsider to the French educational and academic systems, because of his social origins.

PAYSANS EMPAYSANNÉS
[ENTRENCHED PEASANTS]

Despite the rarity of Bourdieu's explicit comparisons between the two rural regions of his research, parallels between his thinking about peasants in Algeria and Béarn are striking. In two articles published in *Etudes Rurales* within two years of each other—an article on French bachelors (Bourdieu 1962c) and an article on uprooted and resettled Algerians (Bourdieu and Sayad 1964a)—Bourdieu dealt with the social change and disruption associated with urbanizing influences on traditional peasants. The theme of rupture and a break with tradition is prevalent in both articles, despite important differences in the ethnographic context. In the article entitled "Paysans déracinés: Bouleversements morphologiques et changements culturels en Algérie" (trans. Uprooted Peasants: Structural Disruptions and Cultural Changes in Algeria), which draws from material also appearing in *Le déracinement* (Bourdieu and Sayad 1964b), Bourdieu and Sayad described what they called the "cultural contagion" occurring as a result of peasant groups from the mountains being resettled with other groups with whom they would not normally have had contact. Bourdieu drew an analogy between these resettlement camps and cities—both of which were contrasted with traditional clan social organization. Algerian peasants mixed with those having had more contact with the city in these camps, and Bourdieu noted the "devaluation of peasant virtues, the breakdown of 'collective controls'" (79) on behavior, generational conflicts, and changes in women's roles. Changes in greetings, café behavior, food, and eating habits also were noted. It was the traditional peasant (*paysan empaysanné*) who was left most emotionally displaced in this setting, according to the analysis, no longer feeling comfortable in his bodily habitus (87). The language of the peasant body was out of place in the resettlement camp. The concept of *"empaysanné"* refers to the peasant being trapped in his condition of peasanthood, and Bourdieu attributed this to a disjuncture between the traditional habitus of the peasant and the socioeconomic conditions (what he would later come to call the economic field) in which he found himself.

In his earlier article on Béarn (1962c), "Célibat et condition paysanne" (Bachelorhood and the Peasant Condition), similar themes of a rupture with the past and dislocation for the traditional male peasant are present. Here, Bourdieu also made reference to "*paysans empaysannés,*" with the connotation of being locked or enclosed within the condition of peasanthood. These peasants became "out of place" within their own village, however, rather than being geographically dislocated. This article on bachelors was produced during the postwar period in France, a time of alarm about "rural exodus" and the high rate of bachelorhood in many regions. Bourdieu argued that the traditional social system, in which marriage was primarily a concern of the peasant family and its worries about inheritance, had been disrupted by socioeconomic changes affecting the meaning of the dowry itself but also attitudes toward the individual. Marriage had become, by the 1960s, more a matter of individual choice than of the authority of the patriarchal family system. As girls became more educated, Bourdieu argued, and had more access to urban ways of life, they increasingly ignored male peasants from isolated hamlets as potential husbands, preferring urban men, despite concerns of inheritance. In the article, Bourdieu addressed the ways in which unmarried men were produced within a marriage system that favored male primogeniture, and in which women tended to "marry up" the economic and social scale. Men from isolated hamlets were the most likely candidates for remaining in an unmarried state. They were also, he maintained, most aware of their condition and the limitations of "peasanthood." In both the Béarn and Kabyle cases, the traditional peasant habitus was not in harmony with the social and economic conditions. Bourdieu described this in terms of the emotional turmoil it created for the peasant and his writing is sympathetic for these *tristes* members of the dominated class.

Bourdieu exhibited ambivalent feelings, however, about the settings of rural life that he analyzed in Béarn and Kabylia—both a romanticizing nostalgia and a critique of the sentiment of honor that structured systems of domination within traditional society. Bourdieu's understandings of peasant life, and its emotional implications for the individual, are evident in two early passages with similar messages that twin the two sites of his research—Kabylia and Béarn. When referring to Kabyle society as a "primary society" in which the group is central to the individual, Bourdieu described the feelings engendered by this: "Penned inside this enclosed microcosm in which everybody knows everybody, condemned without the possibility of escape or relief to live with others, beneath the gaze of others every individual experiences deep anxiety about 'people's words'" (1966a: 212). This also would describe life within a mountain village in southwestern France, and in finding this passage while preparing this book, I could not help but wonder if Bourdieu wasn't aware of this parallel to a life he had himself escaped. I soon found that, in fact, Bourdieu made an almost identical statement to that on Kabyle villages in describing life in his village in Béarn. In his early article on uses of photography in his natal village, Bourdieu described an "enclosed world where one senses at each moment without escape that one is under the gaze of others" (Bourdieu and Bourdieu 1965: 172; my translation). Despite his lack of explicit comparisons between the two settings, it is obvious from these examples that Bourdieu saw parallels and that his own emotions were stirred by (memories of?) these settings. Bourdieu's ambivalence about these *tristes paysans* comes through in these two examples. He was both critical of the effects of change for the displaced male but at the same time critical of the traditional society that had existed before the effects of modernization. Having left the gaze of village society himself, Bourdieu lets slip both his nostalgia for that society and also his acquired sensibilities (dispositions) that caused him to be critical of the lack of privacy that "enclosed world" entailed.

The notion of the entrenched peasant that Bourdieu used in both Algeria and France is sympathetic to the plight of the traditional peasant whose habitus is not in harmony with the structure. A decade later, the French sociologist Henri Mendras (1970) would declare "*la fin des paysans*" (the end of the peasantry) in France, based on his distinction between farmers and peasants. In contrast to industrial England, whose agrarian population was depleted in the nineteenth century, France, Mendras wrote, "stopped in her tracks; she passed for a century and a half while her peasants, though slowly accepting technological innovations, remained peasants" (1970: 5). In the postwar period, Mendras argued, the engine of urbanization and industrialization accelerated, transforming those remaining peasants into farmers. Mendras would later write a book on the French Fifth Republic (1988) that championed its economic and social progress and Republican ideals. In stark contrast to Bourdieu, who focused on the casualties of French postwar society and continued class struggles, Mendras has an optimistic vision of a cohesive middle-class society from which both peasants and the bourgeoisie have been banished. By comparing the perspectives of Bourdieu and Mendras, we can see the different visions of peasant life operating at this period of French history. Although Mendras declared the demise of the peasantry as a class, the term *paysan* continues to provoke emotional, political, and economic consequences in France, and has recently been rejuvenated as a term of self-reference for farmers in the context of new peasant uprisings associated with the popular figure José Bové.[5]

Bourdieu was working out his theories of habitus and symbolic violence in a climate in France of social upheaval and what was called "rural exodus." His approach to peasants in both Algeria and France is informed by French ideologies of attachment to place or to the soil that became increasingly salient as the rural population declined following World War II. As I have argued in my analysis of rural French women's autoethnographies (Reed-Danahay 2002), the land (*la terre*) has a particularly important place in French national memory in comparison with other European nations, such as England and Germany, to which urbanization and industrialization came much sooner. Fremont (1997) argues that "*la terre*" is a site of memory in France, a country where many people have genealogical ties back to a great-grandparent, if not a grandparent, who was a peasant. Postwar rural depopulation in France created a powerful nostalgia for the peasant past of family farms. Rural romanticization has often been linked to conservative political regimes in France, such as the Vichy ideology, but as Susan Carol Rogers (1987) has pointed out, the relationship between images of peasants and political values can shift. In the contemporary period, the "green movement" and leftist critiques of neoliberalism and the World Trade Organization (WTO) have become associated with nostalgia for rural France.

The normative idea of the farm family and attachment to the soil as part of French identity was established in earlier centuries, and can be seen in the nineteenth century thought of the historian Frederic Le Play and the geographer Vidal de la Blache. This ideology also can be traced in French novels, as Rose-Marie La Grave (1980) found in her studies that point to the gendered nature of a proposed "man-land dyad," in which women were seen as less naturally attached to the land than were men. In his study of French immigration, Philippe Noiriel criticized Braudel's *The Identity of France* (1988–90) for being "profoundly marked by this philosophy of rootedness" (1996 [1988]: 40). Noiriel is critical of the approach to the history of France in this and other works that take the French family to be the link between past and present, and he feels that an idea of the "deep-rootedness" of the French people cannot be sustained in the face of the evidence that one-third of today's French population have foreign roots, so that "the all-encompassing role of the family as an explanation for continuities and discontinuities falls apart" (1996: 41). Bourdieu's *paysans empaysannés* in France are, thus, best viewed as key symbols of tradition in French society.

Drawing on her anthropological studies of the history of the French family, Martine Segalen affirms Noiriel's critique. She writes:

> Up to now studies have tended to concentrate on the stable family. . . . Even though our information regarding family migrations is still very thin, the image of the rural family as being static and rooted to the soil is one which must be corrected. Families were more or less stable according to the times. The nineteenth century appears to have been an age of resumed mobility, often over great distances, for economic ends, as seen in the emigration of younger sons debarred from inheritance, and seasonal migration which became permanent, etc. (1983: 41)

Other studies of French internal migration,[6] as well as Noiriel's work on immigration, point to the ideological nature of the emphasis on the family, on rootedness, and on historical continuity in understandings of contemporary French peasants.

Paul Silverstein (2002 and 2003) has pointed to Bourdieu's (with his collaborator Abdelmalek Sayad) reliance on a metaphor of "uprootedness" in his work on social transformation among the Kabyles, comparing it to other uses of this term in earlier literature on migration in France and the United States. Although not tying this specifically to French ideologies of the land and the peasant family, Silverstein does suggest that this metaphor (like that of attachment to soil) can be used both by conservative ideologies and for the anticolonialist intentions of Bourdieu and Sayad. His useful foregrounding of this metaphor in Bourdieu's work and its relationship to Berber cultural movements and their nostalgia for a "rooted cultural past" complements the analysis of French ideologies of attachment to land that inform discourse both at home and in the colonial context. It is vital, in understanding Bourdieu's constructions of his own position as outsider or insider in research, to take into account the broader historical and ideological connections between rural France and Kabylia in which his thought has been shaped. His theory of habitus and dispositions would not, moreover, dispute an effort to see that what he felt as affinity (between himself and the Kabyles) on a very personal level was the product of larger social and historical processes.

BOURDIEU AND FRENCH ANTHROPOLOGY

Bourdieu's relationship to French anthropology (apart from his rejection of structuralism) has rarely been addressed in discussions of his work, and he is generally placed within the context of French sociology. Key discussions of Bourdieu and the sociological milieu include Lemert (1981), Swartz (1997), and Berthelot (2000). Bourdieu and Passeron (1967c) wrote a lengthy article describing the postwar sociological field in France, and Bourdieu also wrote about his early educational experiences in philosophy in *Pascalian Meditations* and *Esquisse pour une auto-analyse*. This neglect of anthropology is, in part, understandable in that Bourdieu's institutional affiliations were in sociology and most of his research network was composed of sociologists. But it misses an important element in understandings of the context in which Bourdieu worked in France.

Several recent publications have contributed to our understandings of these links. In his intellectual autobiography, *Esquisse pour une auto-analyse*, Bourdieu wrote more explicitly than previously about his relationship to ethnology in France in the 1950s. He revealed why he was attracted to ethnology and the journal *L'Homme* founded by Lévi-Strauss—because it offered a different view of the scientific study of society than that of philosophy—and he discussed the influences of his work in Algeria for his identity as an ethnologist early in his career. Bourdieu's early fieldwork in Béarn and Kabylia was shaped by anthropology in important ways and he remained engaged with the field of ethnology (if often adopting a critical stance toward it) throughout his life. Anthropology, in turn, paid attention to his research and theories. Durkheim and Lévi-Strauss both argued for the integration of sociology and anthropology. Bourdieu himself advocated the merging of the two in his Huxley lecture—ending with the statement that he wished "to see the unity of the sciences of man asserted under the banner of Anthropology designating, in all the languages of the world, what we understand today by ethnology and sociology" (2003c: 292). He also wrote that his own attempts to reconcile anthropology and sociology are attempts to "exorcise the painful schism, never entirely overcome, between two parts of myself" (292), referring to his work in both disciplines. Bourdieu's call for a reunification of the social science disciplines under the rubric of anthropology formed the basis for a posthumous homage to him in a special issue of the journal he founded and headed until his death, *Actes de la Recherche en Sciences Sociales* (Bourdieu, Champagne, Poupeau 2003). In an introductory essay to that issue, entitled "Pierre Bourdieu and Anthropology," the editors comment that Bourdieu's early work in Algeria (which constitutes the major theme of the issue) used both qualitative methods of ethnology and quantitative methods of sociology, demonstrating that his work, from the outset, synthesized the two disciplines.

Recent considerations of its history place the roots of French anthropology in two projects of the French government: colonial expansion during the eighteenth and nineteenth centuries; and studies of the various regional populations within France during the same period. Bourdieu participated in both of these, as a colonial anthropologist in Algeria and as an ethnographer of rural France. Anthropological research at home and abroad initially had two strands—that of folklore, and that of anthropology or ethnology. Folklore, which was a discipline never completely accepted by the university system in France, focused on the traditional cultures of French regions and was primarily a field of collection of artifacts and description of customs, traditions, and beliefs. Ethnology developed as a field dedicated to study abroad, and was associated from the start with a strong theoretical emphasis (cf. Weber 1989; Chiva 1992; Rogers 2001). It was first institutionalized with the opening of the Ethnology Institute in Paris in 1925, founded by Marcel Mauss, Paul Rivet, and Lucien Lévy-Bruhl, and had deep connections to colonialism in France. The Musée de l'Homme was created later, in 1937. The field of rural sociology, which similarly developed through uneasy relationships between folklore and sociological theory, has overlapped with that of anthropological studies in France as well, although sociology was more receptive to taking French society as an object than was an anthropology that had carved out the study of "exotic" societies as its area of focus. As Florence Weber (1979) has pointed out, however, the major historical figure in French sociology, Durkheim, devoted little attention to European peasant societies in comparison with the German theorists Marx and Tönnies, whose work came to be more influential in the field of rural sociology. This was not true to the same extent for Durkheim's nephew Marcel Mauss, who continued to influence anthropology and sociology in France after Durkheim's death.

Folklore studies were always less important to the French state than they were in Germany, with the exception of the Vichy regime during the German occupation of France, when Marshall Pétain sought to romanticize rural, traditional life as part of his conservative program (Weber 1979). The taint of collaboration that touched folklore studies during this period led to its decline in the postwar period, despite some important work that had been carried out in the 1930s and prior to that. Arnold Van Gennep, the major figure in French folklore studies, had only briefly held a university position, and remained largely outside of the academic establishment (Belmont 1974). Although largely known outside of France as the author of *Rites de passage* (1909), a comparative study of rituals of status change, Van Gennep undertook massive local studies of folklore in France that resulted in multiple volumes of work (1937–58). Folklore studies were connected with a journal in France, *Revue de Folklore Français,* and Georges Henri Rivière was a figure bridging ethnography and folklore who helped create the current Museum of Popular Arts and Traditions (Musée des Arts et Traditions Populaires) in Paris, where collections of rural French artifacts as well as recordings and fieldnotes are housed.

As I trace this brief history, it also must be acknowledged that one cannot study French anthropology in isolation from British and American anthropology and sociology. Even a cursory reading of Lévi-Strauss's work shows how he was influenced by American anthropologists, such as Lowie, as well as by the German linguistic traditions, and he was in close contact with American institutions—living in the United States for long periods and lecturing often at U.S. universities. Rural sociology in France, whose major figure in the second half of the twentieth century was Henri Mendras at Nanterre, was heavily influenced by Redfieldian community studies and the Chicago school (in turn, influenced by a British social anthropology that was influenced by Durkheim). Bourdieu and Passeron (1967c: 183) themselves noted with some irony the necessity for the postwar generation of taking a tour in the United States in order to gain legitimacy in French academic circles. Bourdieu spent time in the early 1960s at the Institute for Advanced Study at Princeton and at the University of Pennsylvania, where he encountered Erving Goffman's work, and he later facilitated the translation of Goffman's work in France (Swartz 1997: 26). Later in his career, he would spend time at the University of Chicago (among other institutions), working with students in both anthropology and sociology (Bourdieu and Wacquant 1992). French anthropology also was influenced by philosophy in France. Before anthropology or sociology were institutionalized as legitimate subjects for study in higher education, most intellectuals were trained first in philosophy, as was the case for Bourdieu at ENS. Early anthropologists, such as Lévi-Strauss, attempted to establish it as a science and to differentiate it from philosophy through empirical studies of the human condition. Whereas the work of phenomenologists, such as Merleau-Ponty, was influential on both Lévi-Strauss and Bourdieu, there is a long history of animosity between the existentialist positions of Sartre and those of the anthropological perspective (Lévi-Strauss 1991 [1988]: 116–19; Bourdieu 1990b: 3–33).

In an interesting article written from the (somewhat condescending) perspective of British social anthropology, Michael Mendelson (1958) described the state of anthropology in France at the time of Bourdieu's earliest experiences in it. The prestige of philosophy, noted time and again by Bourdieu himself, dominated the academic field, but there were important influences on anthropology from geography and history. Research interests were centered around "area studies"—so that there were Africanists, Asianists, North Americanists, South Americanists, and so on (in contrast to what Mendelson saw as a focus on problem-oriented work for the British). There was some urban research at the time both within and outside of France (i.e., Chombart de Lauwe 1956). Lévi-Strauss had already emerged as the leading figure, praised by Mendelson for his efforts to create a comparative approach. Georges Balandier, working in Africa, was also a major figure at the time. The study of kinship and religion dominated the work conducted in various regions of the world. Two key observations by Mendelson were, first, that a humanist approach rooted in Durkheim's emphasis on morality and ethics had led many French sociologists and anthropologists to have a "strong social consciousness and interest in contemporary problems" (which recalls Lévi-Strauss's musings on modernity in *Tristes Tropiques,* as well as Bourdieu's commitment to social issues throughout his career). Mendelson also observed that there were several studies conducted on French soil—based first on Arnold Van Gennep's studies of French folklore and M. Maget's sponsorship, from his Laboratory of French Ethnography, of pilot research projects in Corsica, the Hautes-Alpes, and Touraine. Bourdieu himself mentioned the influence on his early ethnographic work of Maget's guide to field studies in the introduction to his collected works on rural France (2002a).

In his history of anthropology education in France, Gérald Gaillard, who draws on Bourdieu's concept of fields, traces the very recent growth of this field. In 1950, there were only forty-eight anthropologists (including ethnologists, folklorists, physical anthropologists, and prehistorians) in France, and the first B.A. and M.A. degrees were not established until 1966 (at Paris X-Nanterre). Gaillard identifies five generational "cohorts" of anthropologists, starting with the first generation who were taught by Marcel Mauss and Paul Rivet at the Ethnology Institute. Bourdieu would fall within the cohort of the third generation, those who began their teaching careers in the 1960s and were either trained directly or influenced by Lévi-Strauss. Although Bourdieu was never employed as an anthropologist, and worked in the field of academic sociology, he had connections to this generation of anthropologists. Gaillard notes that the history of French ethnology was merged with that of sociology in the early years, as Marcel Mauss, who was elected to the Chair in Sociology at the Collège de France in 1931, was instrumental in forming ethnology. Mauss suffered as a result of anti-Semitic laws during the 1940s that prohibited him from teaching, and lost much of his direct influence over anthropology. The first Chair in Anthropology was created at the Sorbonne in 1942 for Griaule, who had completed the first dissertation in ethnology 4 years before that. Lévi-Strauss was working at UNESCO at this time, a victim of anti-Semitism as was Mauss, and Leenhardt and Griaule dominated the discipline during the 1940s. In the early 1950s, by the time Bourdieu was doing his studies in Paris, Lévi-Strauss had returned to France and started training students through his Chair in Religious Studies at the EPHE (École Pratique des Hautes Études), and a cohort of student were trained by him during 1955 and 1964 (including Dumont, Blanchard, Balandier, Condomenias). Lévi-Strauss was elected to the Chair in Anthropology at the Collège de France in 1959, and founded the journal *L'Homme* soon after that.

During the 1950s, when Bourdieu would have studied ethnology at the Sorbonne[7] (the only place it was taught in Paris at the time), under Aron and Lévi-Strauss, it was the anthropological (rather than folklorist) perspective that most prevailed, especially what has come to be called French structuralism. One can see some influences of folklore studies in Bourdieu's work, particularly in his use of proverbs,[8] but the primary influences on his ethnographic work were more anthropological. At the time that Bourdieu worked in Béarn, the attraction and prestige of the "exotic" was paramount in French anthropology (Chiva 1992 [1987]: 9; Abèles 1999: 404). Nevertheless, three major figures in French ethnology had conducted rural studies prior to Bourdieu's work in Béarn, as Mendelson also noted. Much earlier, Robert Hertz, an associate of Marcel Mauss, and a folklorist, undertook a study of religious ritual in the Alps that was ethnographic in methods (Hertz 1913). During the 1950s, the anthropologist Louis Dumont (1951) undertook research in rural France and was attached to the Museum of Popular Arts and Traditions before turning his attention to full-time work in India. Bernot and Blanchard (1953) had conducted a fairly conventional "community study" in Normandy, called *Nouville*, under the auspices of UNESCO, and with the blessings and encouragement of Lévi-Strauss. When the American Laurence Wylie went to southern France to do a community study in the 1950s, resulting in the classic *Village in the Vaucluse* (1957), he had in mind a comparison with Bernot and Blanchard's study in northern France (Wylie 1979). There also was a study in the Rhone valley by Clement and Xidas (1956). The establishment of a field of anthropological studies in France was relatively slow to develop, however, and it was not until the late 1970s and early 1980s that this occurred, through the encouragement of Lévi-Strauss and with the establishment of the state-funded Mission du Patrimoine (Commission on the Patrimony), which now funds research in France and publishes its own journal, *Terrain* (Langlois 1999: 415). There is also an association of French anthropologists that publishes work on France in its journal, *L'Ethnologie Française.*[9] As Susan Carol Rogers (2001) points out, however, the interest in rural France has since evolved into research on "the present" and on what are considered modern rather than traditional aspects of French society.

Bourdieu's relationship to this new "ethnography of France" was not straightforward. As Joëlle Bahloul (1991) has pointed out, Bourdieu was viewed fairly strictly as a sociologist in France, and it was mainly in the United States that his ties to anthropology were appreciated, even if his approach was criticized by many. Bahloul also observes that by the time Bourdieu's critiques of structuralism had become welcomed by some American scholars (e.g., Ortner 1984), which she believes fits in with the more individualist approach of American social science,[10] the debate had long been over (if not fully resolved) in France. Although, during this early period of work in France, Bourdieu had connections to figures working in the Mediterranean region, such as Isac Chiva, his own interests and institutional affiliations took Bourdieu in different directions. Bourdieu came increasingly to identify himself as a sociologist and worked in institutional settings that were in that discipline. He continued to bring anthropological perspectives to his work, however, as this book demonstrates on numerous occasions. And many French anthropologists of rural France do acknowledge his connections. A 1992 edited volume on the state of the ethnography of France (in relation to German counterparts), with chapters written by French ethnologists, demonstrates Bourdieu's lasting contributions to this field. It is evident from this book that his work on kinship in southwestern France opened up new areas of investigation beyond strictly structuralist accounts and also brought Le Play's nineteenth-century work on the family back into the picture (Chiva 1992; Lamaison 1992). Bourdieu also was influential in symbolic anthropological approaches in France (Fabre-Vassas and Fabre 1992) in his work on distinction and taste. In another example, Zonabend (1984 [1980]) used Bourdieu's notion of symbolic capital in her analysis of marriage strategies in a Burgundian village.

Vera Mark (1987) has drawn attention to ways in which Bourdieu's work in southwestern France may be placed in the regional context of Occitan studies in France more specifically. Through her criticisms of Bourdieu, she engages with his work in the context of rural French scholarship. Mark considers Bourdieu, along with the anthropologist Daniel Fabre and the historian Emmanuel Le Roy Ladurie, to be scholars who have contributed to regionalist ideologies of the Occitan, which are primarily constructions by and for intellectuals. Although she does not use this terminology nor cite his work on that topic, Mark accuses Bourdieu of the very error of "scholasticism" to which he attributes many problems in contemporary anthropology. Bourdieu employed oppositions of north/south, national/regional, traditional/modern, rural/urban, male/female, and "authentic"/"inauthentic" languages that are, according to Mark, the "effects of academic discourses." Drawing from Bourdieu's (1980) work on representations of regional identity in France, Mark cites his claims that Occitan is a social artifact imposed on Béarnais speakers at the expense of their "authentic" dialect. From her own fieldwork in the region, Mark found a more dynamic linguistic process and interplay between social groups that she claims to be occluded in Bourdieu's ahistorical analysis, which relied primarily on the static oppositions she mentions. Her work points to the necessity, which is part of Bourdieu's own theoretical program, of examining the objectifications of the observers (ethnographers), and turns this back into a critique of Bourdieu.

BOURDIEU AND THE "FIELD" OF MEDITERRANEAN STUDIES

In the context of Mediterranean peasant studies, Bourdieu was known mostly for his research in Algeria. His publications on both Béarn and Kabylia, however, constituted part of the interest in "peasant studies" generally during the 1960s and 1970s and, more specifically, the Mediterranean as culture area. Three conferences held in Europe in 1959, 1961, and 1963 shaped the development of notions of the culture area of the Mediterranean (Peristiany 1966: 9). At that time, this field consisted of studies of peasant societies undertaken in the region from southern Europe to northern Africa through the lens of preoccupations with tradition and modernity, issues of kinship and family, and the value complex of "honor and shame." Bourdieu had essays published in two edited volumes in English that resulted from these conferences: *Mediterranean Countrymen* (Pitt-Rivers 1963) and *Honor and Shame: The Values of Mediterranean Society* (Peristiany 1966). These essays, drawing on his ethnographic research among the Kabyles (one on concepts of time; the other on concepts of honor), appeared alongside articles written by ethnographers of rural France, such as Laurence Wylie (working in southern France) and Isac Chiva (who worked in Corsica.) It was Chiva, then editor of the interdisciplinary journal *Etudes Rurales,* who published Bourdieu's first lengthy ethnographic article on bachelors in rural France in 1962. Bourdieu's connections to the British social anthropologists Pitt-Rivers and Peristiany continued, despite his turns toward other subjects beyond peasant studies. His inclusion in their more recent attempt to update Mediterranean studies, *Honor and Grace in Anthropology* (1992), with an article on "Rites of Institution" that deals primarily with higher education in France, demonstrates his continued relevance to discussions of the meanings of "honor." Moreover, Bourdieu mentioned the Mediterraneanists Pitt-Rivers, Caro Baroja, and Peristiany as figures "who accompanied and protected my entrance into the profession" [of anthropology] in his 2002 Huxley Lecture (2003c: 290).

In spite of his inclusion in key volumes on the region, Bourdieu's contributions to Mediterranean area studies have been largely overlooked,[11] whereas his membership in the group of scholars who has studied the Middle East more specifically has been more greatly acknowledged. This contrast is evident in two review articles published during the 1980s in the *Annual Review of Anthropology*. Lila Abu-Lughod (1989) names Bourdieu, along with Clifford Geertz, as the two most prominent anthropological theorists who can be claimed by Middle Eastern studies. Bourdieu is, however, absent from David Gilmore's (1982) review of the "Anthropology of the Mediterranean Area."[12] Two articles appearing in the journal *Current Anthropology* that dealt with Mediterranean anthropology likewise neglected to mention Bourdieu's contributions (Boissevain 1979; Pina-Cabral 1989). In part, this may be because of the absence of references to the Mediterranean as a culture area in Bourdieu's work, and the lack of explicit ties between the southwestern French and Algerian contexts in his writings. But, by putting together the French and Algerian work, the Mediterranean connection becomes more apparent.

Mediterranean studies during the early 1960s were informed by a dichotomy between urban and rural societies influenced by wider historical ideas central to European social thought (Baroja 1963; Williams 1973). This had been reinforced by scholarship such as Redfield's (1956) rural-urban continuum and suggestion that peasant societies were "part-societ-ies," and by Tönnies's Gemeinschaft-Gesellschaft dichotomy (1957), in which the "community" of the village was privileged over the anonymity and anomie of the city. This theme was also, of course, present in the work of Emile Durkheim (cf. 1951 [1897]). The concept of honor in Mediterra-nean studies was tied to this system of ideas. In his introduction to one of the volumes cited above, Peristiany revealed this position with his state-ment that "Honor and shame are the constant preoccupation of individu-als in small scale, exclusive societies where face to face personal, as opposed to anonymous, relations are of paramount importance and where the so-cial personality of the actor is as significant as his office" (Peristiany 1966: 11). Honor was a key theme in Bourdieu's own work.

Several articles in a recent edited collection (Albera, Blok, and Brom-berger 2001) about Mediterranean anthropology suggest that the field was first carved out by British and American scholars. As Bromberger (2001) notes, Laurence Wylie (an American) was the first to do a community study in southern France, and the Mediterranean focus in anthropology did not get underway seriously in France until the 1970s. Driessen (2001) notes that in the 1990s research in this region had lost its ambitions to compare the northern and southern shores, and had also been divided by not only national traditions of scholarship published in different languages, but by a division between those who worked "at home" and those "abroad" in this region. Bourdieu's work as insider in France and outsider in Algeria is rare according to this scheme, and Driessen notes that few work on both sides of the Mediterranean (he is himself an exception through his studies in Spain and Algeria). Christian Bromberger (2001) traces several historical influences upon anthropological Mediterranean studies in France, includ-ing that of human geography associated with Marc Bloch but especially Fernand Braudel and earlier geographers that influenced him. During the 1930s–1960s, the period that would have been most influential on the development of Bourdieu's thought, there was a quest for permanent fea-tures common to southern Europe and North Africa.

The Kabyles had a place in the development of notions of the Medi-terranean, in an approach built on notions of a "mother" culture, placing the pristine Berber culture at the origins of Mediterranean civilization— what is known as the "Kabyle Myth" (Lorcin 1995). As Patricia Lorcin explains,

> The Kabyle Myth was that the Kabyles were superior to the Arabs; it was not that they were different; which they were. The French used sociological differences and religious disparities between the two groups to create an image of the Kabyle which was good and one of the Arab which was bad and, from this, to extrapolate that the former was more suited to assimilation than the latter. The myth was an assimilationist

one in so far as it provided an ideological basis for absorbing the Kabyles into French colonial society to the detriment of the Arabs. It was also a racial myth, for the intellectual concepts of this ideology were essentially one of race. (1995: 2–3)

Although, as Lorcin points out, the Kabyle Myth was primarily a nineteenth-century ideology that was transformed into a construction of a Mediterranean identity and a hierarchical positioning of the European above the Kabyles, who were in turn above the Arabs, the Kabyles had a privileged place in the mythologizing of the origins of this Mediterranean culture. As Bromberger notes, some looked for archaeological evidence in France that would show the survival of similar traits in contemporary cultures in North Africa—viewed as archaic survivals.

Fanny Colonna found that in earlier contexts of colonial education in Algeria, liberal reformers, such as the Minister of Education Emile Combes, highlighted the similarities between French peasants and the Kabyles. Colonna quotes Combes as writing that "The [Kabyles'] . . . character, physiological constitution, love of the soil, sobriety, resistance to fatigue . . . are comparable to our highlanders of Auvergne" (1997: 347). Combes favorably compared Kabyles to other mountainous groups such as those in the Cevennes and Jura, and he also drew comparisons with Brittany. One can see influences of this in Bourdieu's approach to Béarn and Kabylia, in which he viewed them as sharing similar traits (Certeau [1984: 51] asked: "which is the doublet of the other?"). I do not mean to suggest that Bourdieu was directly appealing to an archaic Kabyle Myth but, rather, that the romanticization of the Kabyles in wider French popular culture (Lorcin notes the role of Kabyles in Algerian novels, for instance), would not have escaped an influence on him, even if he was not conscious of this. His feelings of affinity with the Kabyles, therefore, are only partially understood by taking into account Bourdieu's rural origins; his approach also was informed by a wider ideology with a long history, in which the Berbers in North Africa were believed to share similarities with the provincial French, especially those in the south or in mountainous regions, and in which such claims were contested.

The assumptions of twentieth-century forms of Mediterranean anthropology that seek common cultural traits have been challenged by several authors, most notably Michael Herzfeld (1987). In a recent essay, Herzfeld suggests that "the persistence of 'the Mediterranean' as a topos in the scholarly and political imagination of the late twentieth century is a cultural phenomenon of considerable interest in its own right" (2001: 665), suggesting that while the diversity and creolization of the region negate the search for unifying descriptors, the ways in which social actors employ the concept should not be overlooked. Herzfeld earlier pointed out that societies in this region of the world are "neither exotic nor wholly familiar" (1987:

7), a dilemma that Bourdieu scarcely overcame in his characterizations of either Béarn or Kabylia. The notion of "honor" claimed to be so central to the Mediterranean region is seized on, according to Herzfeld, as a Eurocentric move to exoticize the region and differentiate it from a more bureaucratic and rational "modern" Europe. Bourdieu used the concept of honor, interestingly, in the context of modern French education among the bourgeoisie in *The State Nobility*, illustrating his own determination to make this concept one that could be generalized beyond traditional Kabyle society. One of the few critics of his work to have placed Bourdieu within the Mediterranean areas studies context, Herzfeld (1987: 8) points out that while Bourdieu used the concept of honor in his analyses of both rural French and Algerian societies, he did not explicitly employ this concept to create any suggestion of pan-Mediterranean unity. Although this was certainly true in his earlier work and was reinforced through his antipathy to explicit comparisons between Kabyle and Béarn societies, Bourdieu did come to employ just such a notion in his later writings on masculine domination—a theme I will pursue below. At the point when many anthropologists had abandoned the search for common origins in this concept, Bourdieu (1998b) appealed to it to explain the persistence of androcentrism in contemporary France.

Bourdieu wrote extensively in several publications on the concept of honor among the Kabyles (cf. Bourdieu 1966a and 1972a). He drew an explicit (albeit brief) parallel between the Béarn and Kabyle contexts and uses of "honor" in these two societies in an early article co-written with his wife, Marie-Claire, on the uses of photography in the French village of Lesquire. In describing the rigid, full-frontal posture and solemn expression among those posing in rural photographs, especially on the occasion of marriage, Bourdieu described Lesquire as a society "that holds up the sentiment of honor, of dignity and responsibility" and in which it is important to provide the "most honorable" image of oneself to the other (Bourdieu and Bourdieu 1965: 172). He added in a footnote that "among the Kabyles, a man of honor is he who faces you, who holds his head high, who looks others straight in the face, unmasking his own face" (172, fn. 15). There is a similar description in *Outline,* where Bourdieu compared the two societies as those in which frontality and honor are connected (Bourdieu 1977a: 94). The concept of honor also came into play in Bourdieu's analyses of marriage strategies among rural French peasants (cf. 1962 and 1972b). In *The Logic of Practice,* Bourdieu, in a very Durkheimian voice, explicitly addressed the "breakdown" of honor in terms of a rural/urban dichotomy:

Urbanization, which brings together groups with different traditions and weakens the reciprocal controls (and even before urbanization, the generalization of monetary exchanges and the introduction of wage labour), results in the collapse of the collectively maintained and therefore entirely real fiction of the religion of honour. (Bourdieu 1990a: 110)

The theme of difference between urban and rural societies, peasants and city-dwellers, is a strong thread linking Bourdieu's early work in these two societies also connected through a relationship of colonialism—France and Algeria. The notion of habitus is also a concept worked out in both ethnographic contexts during the same period of time.

With his book *Masculine Domination,* appearing late in his career, Bourdieu employed his most explicit use of the concept of a Mediterranean culture area. Drawing on his earlier studies of masculine honor and relations between men and women in Kabylia, Bourdieu argued in his preface to the English edition of the book that "a well-preserved androcentric society (such as Kabyle society, as I observed it in the early 1960s) provides instruments enabling one to understand some of the best concealed aspects of [gender relations] in the economically most advanced societies" (2001b: viii). He also stated in a Prelude to the book that "This detour through an exotic tradition is indispensable in order to break the relationship of deceptive familiarity that binds us to our own tradition" (3). Bourdieu argued that the Kabyle

> represent a paradigmatic form of the "phallonarcissitic" vision and the androcentric cosmology which are common to all Mediterranean societies and which survive even today, but in a partial and, as it were, exploded state, in our own cognitive structures and social structures. (6)

Bourdieu made reference to the early edited collections (Peristiany 1966; Pitt-Rivers 1963) on Mediterranean society, with their reliance on the values of honor and shame, in order to support this claim. Bourdieu also claimed that "the whole European cultural domain undeniably shares in that tradition," this time referencing the work in folklore studies conducted by Arnold Van Gennep (1937–58) in France. His other point of reference for this claim was ancient Greece. Bourdieu's somewhat puzzling appeal to the Kabyles in his discussion of gender in France may be best understood in terms of late-twentieth-century French images of Algerians in the context of Europe (the EU). The Algerian in France today, Henry (1993) suggests, is both familiar and "foreign," a sign of alterity but also part of a shared (if painful) Franco-Algerian history.

I will not rehearse Bourdieu's entire argument in *Masculine Domination* here, but will summarize some of its main points. He drew on his earlier studies of honor among Kabyle men and the submission of Kabyle women as an example of a society in which the division of the sexes appears "normal" as a result of the *doxa* supported by an embodied habitus. The entire Kabyle social world, he suggested, supported male domination. He argued that male domination was embedded in bodily habitus and embodied dispositions, surviving in contemporary people living in modern industrialized societies. Rites of institution support this domination. Women and men are divided into two "classes" of habitus and bodily hexis, according to Bourdieu, so that women's submission to men goes unrecognized. Bourdieu employed the language of psychoanalysis in *Masculine Domination* as well, writing of the "Mediterranean mother or the mothering wife, who victimizes and induces guilt by victimizing herself" (2001b: 32). He drew on Virginia Woolf as collaborator in his theory, showing that her fiction demonstrates the same gender classifications and misrecognition among upper-class English people that he found among the Kabyles.

In *Masculine Domination*, Bourdieu used the Kabyle in order to criticize French society. I do not wish to quarrel with the existence of masculine domination in society but, rather, to argue that Bourdieu much simplified the issue by ignoring ethnographic material on gender published during the past thirty years (after the two volumes on the Mediterranean he cited). Several studies of women and men in the Mediterranean region (i.e., Brandes 1980; Driessen 1983; Herzfeld 1985; Rogers 1985; Dubisch 1986; Segalen 1987; Abu-Lughod 1993; Collier 1997) have problematized the issue of male domination, and suggested that there are local ways (depending upon the particulars of kinship organization, political and economic systems, etc.) in which gender roles are subverted, resisted, or displayed. These studies do not support the linear history running from ancient Greece to contemporary France that Bourdieu posits. His oversimplification is possible only through an essentialized portrait of the Kabyle and a lack of ethnographic evidence from France and other contemporary societies. Although I do not believe that this was his intent, Bourdieu employed dichotomies of traditional/modern and ideologies of a common Mediterranean ancestry that also have been used to support nationalism and colonialism in Europe.

James Le Sueur (2001) has suggested that decolonization in Algeria led to a crisis among French intellectuals in large part because the static concepts of modernity, the edifice of their worldview, were no longer possible in a world of transition. I find it useful to apply this perspective to Bourdieu. The concept of French universalism, in particular, was called into question so that those sympathetic to Algerian independence, like Bourdieu, were in the awkward position of defending people and a project that denied French universalism. According to Le Sueur, this crisis coincided with postmodernism as a philosophy, which Bourdieu rejected. In some ways, Bourdieu's attachment to the historical connections between the Kabyle and the French denies the ruptures of the colonial past, and seeks to affirm universalist principles.

OCCIDENTALISM

Bourdieu's understandings of the relationships between the triad of Kabylia, Béarn, and "modern" France shifted over time. He set up various dyads at different moments in order to put forth different arguments. Rarely, however, as I have mentioned above, did he explicitly twin Kabylia and Béarn. At different moments, he could view France as the epitome of "rationality" and an impersonal modernism but also could write of a France in which power relations were based on mysticism and the preconscious symbolic. In an earlier publication (Reed-Danahay 1995), I contrasted Bourdieu's two books *Outline* and *Reproduction* (published within two years of each other in the early 1970s) in order to argue that Bourdieu's views on the educational system of France reflected the ideological biases associated with occidentalism—essentialized views of the West (Carrier 1995). My argument was that Bourdieu's work on education is characterized by a complex use of the dichotomy between so-called traditional and modern societies. Even when his intent was to criticize the West through an ironic use of this dichotomy, Bourdieu inadvertently essentialized modernity in spite of himself.

Although *Outline* was billed by Bourdieu as a break with the structuralism of Lévi-Strauss, Bourdieu did retain the idea that there were two types of societies, characterized by the presence or absence of literacy, and, consequently, more or less "authenticity." In an article in which he outlined the "Place of Anthropology in the Social Sciences," Lévi-Strauss wrote:

> In the future, it may be recognized that anthropology's most important contribution to social sciences is to have introduced, if unknowingly, this fundamental distinction between two types of social existence: a way of life recognized at the outset as traditional and archaic and characteristic of "authentic" societies and a more modern form of existence, from which the first-named type is not absent but where groups that are not completely, or are imperfectly, "authentic" are organized within a much larger and specifically "unauthentic" system. (1963 [1954]: 367)

Bourdieu took France as an example of a modern, literate, class-based, differentiated society; he contrasted it with traditional Kabylia as representative of a society that was archaic, nonliterate, classless, and undifferentiated. Bourdieu studied the institutional, standardized forms of reproducing class cultures in literate societies through formal schooling in France. As a foil to France, he described traditional Kabylia as having kin-based, local-level forms of sociocultural inculcation that were informal and implicit. Bourdieu argued in his educational writings that French educational institutions, while touted as modern, actually operated as traditional societies akin to religious institutions (in a broad definition of education as dealing with symbolic processes, including magic). Literacy or its absence was a major explanatory vehicle for the theory, so that societies that were preliterate had different systems of power than did literate state societies. In his analyses, Bourdieu set up Weberian ideal types: Kabylia was essentialized as a pristine traditional society in contrast to the total bureaucracy of the French school. One system is based on interpersonal relationships and kinship connections; the other is based on impersonal social relationships. Bourdieu's other work on Algeria that shows social change and disruption (i.e., Bourdieu et al. 1963) was occluded in *Outline,* in which he attempted to reconstruct the "traditional" society. His ethnographic research on education, that showed more of the interactions between students and teachers (Bourdieu et al. 1965) was occluded in *Reproduction.* Each book references the other so as to reinforce these sharp contrasts.

When comparing *Outline* and *Reproduction,* one can see two very different forms of writing, which lend themselves to different sorts of ethnographic expression. The first half of *Reproduction* is written like a treatise of logic, with an ordered numbering of paragraphs detailing principles of the argument. There are no specific social actors in the text, and acronyms for various structural principles operating in educational processes, such as PW (pedagogic work) and PA (pedagogic authority), for the basis of the discussion. Allusion to previous empirical work using statistics and some classroom observation is made, but this work is not specifically described. Teachers become, in this language, "pedagogic agents," while the students themselves and their behaviors are largely ignored, as are everyday events in classrooms. *Outline* is much more ethnographic in approach, although it is, like the latter, highly theoretical in intent.

The tension between structure and agency that Bourdieu sought to resolve in his theory of practice is part of a wider cultural dialogue in Europe about the cultural and historical bases of such notions as social determinism and free will, as well as the very Western, capitalist origins of individualism. Bourdieu seems to have tried to invert this argument, to demonstrate the "myth" of individualism, by stressing the lack of individual agency in French schools while simultaneously stressing the possibilities for social manipulation among the Kabyles. Bourdieu used Kabyle ethnographic examples to illustrate the practical logics of behavior, inculcated through habitus so as to appear "natural" but open to some "playing the game" by social actors. One example is that of gift exchange and riposte. Another familiar section in *Outline* is Bourdieu's analysis of the Kabyle house.

Bourdieu analyzed the symbolism of the Kabyle house to show how individuals acquire the habitus as body hexis (gestures and postures) and cultural knowledge. Young children acquire an habitus in relation to the house, as they live in and through the space of the house. A Kabyle child learns how to enter the house properly and to decipher the gendered locations for activities within it, thereby acquiring the sexual identity that is "the major element in [his or her] social identity" (1977a: 93). Bourdieu drew an explicit contrast between the French school and the Kabyle house in a passage that underscores the dichotomy between literate and nonliterate societies:

> In a social formation in which the absence of the symbolic-product-conserving techniques associated with literacy retards the objectification of symbolic and particularly cultural capital, inhabited space—and above all the house—is the principal locus for the objectification of the generative schemes. (89)

Bourdieu also made a metaphorical link between the house and a book, stating that Kabyle child reads through the body (learning through space) in order to gain cultural knowledge in the same way that a French child will acquire knowledge through a book.

In his analysis of the Kabyles in *Outline*, Bourdieu downplayed the role of the state and ignored the presence of schools in the region, a device that permitted him to contrast France as a literate society and Kabylia as a nonliterate society. Algeria already had an elaborate system of Qur'anic schools in place that taught reading, writing, and the memorization of religious texts when the French colonial system arrived, so that to portray Algeria as nonliterate in contrast to France is an oversimplification. Jane Goodman (2003) has found extensive evidence of literacy among the Kabyles prior to French colonialism, but points out that there was a popular image of them in wider Algerian society as nonliterate. The French colonial system started to build schools in Algeria from the beginnings of its reign in 1830 (Hoggoy 1984; Colonna 1975). Algeria was unique among French colonies in having the status of a French province; it was an educational district (*rectorat*) of France during the colonial period (Stora 2001: 24; Colonna 1975). There was resistance by both Kabyles and white settlers to this colonial education, but by the early twentieth century there were schools established in Kabylia and teacher training schools that attracted Kabyle students (Colonna 1992). Colonna even suggests that Kabyle students at the teacher training college were preferred to their urban counterparts, because of their "traditional" background, in a system that wanted to create an indigenous elite that bridged traditional and French societies. Numerous examples could be brought to counter Bourdieu's neglect to mention schools in Kabylia in *Outline*, and even his own other writings on Algeria do deal with education there (if marginally). Bourdieu's neglect of social interaction in French schools, which would have articulated modes of practice through which social agents negotiate and resist domination, is an inversion of his focus on traditional practices in Kabyle that neglects education.

Since I wrote my original article on occidentalism in Bourdieu's work, he published *The State Nobility* and demonstrated a more nuanced version of the reproduction theory of education that lessened the split between "Western" and "non-Western" systems. As Bourdieu further developed his theory of symbolic violence and education in France, he turned to a study of the elite schools that seemed to call into question my charges of his occidentalism regarding France in relationship to Algeria. In *The State Nobility*, Bourdieu expanded his theory of explicit and implicit forms of inculcation, by which he had at first only seen the first in France and the second in traditional societies, to argue that social reproduction works most effectively through the implicit modes of inculcation in the Grandes Écoles. He wrote of the "mask of modernity," which conceals the magical and archaic nature of educational institutions (1996: 376). With this study, Bourdieu appeared to have abandoned the dichotomy between traditional and modern "ideal" types that he set up in *Outline*. This also may be the case with *Masculine Domination*, a book that also argues for the presence of the past in contemporary societies—in the guise of androcentrism. Rather than contrasting a modern France to a traditional Kabylia, Bourdieu here posed a linear connection between the androcentric societies of the Mediterranean in the past (represented by the Kabyles) and male domination in contemporary French society. Bourdieu's arguments in both books undermine a view of French society as being as rational as it believes itself to be.

PARALLEL WORLDS/WORLDS APART

Beginning in the late 1990s, Bourdieu returned to his interest in the earlier Algerian and Béarn research and began to cite it increasingly in his writings. In myriad ways, the meanings the two sites of research has shifted over the past forty years and we must reinterpret the "uses" of rural France and late colonial Algeria in the present. Two publications that appeared posthumously—one on his Algerian photos (Bourdieu 2003b) and the other a collection of his previously published essays on rural France (Bourdieu 2002a), both attest to Bourdieu's abiding interest in his original field sites and the theoretical issues they raised. These two books represent returns to sites of memory for Bourdieu, and evoke his nostalgia for the early fieldwork experiences he undertook. They also took him back to anthropology and ethnology, after his long and often controversial career as a sociologist. At the same time, these books continue the division between the Béarn and Algerian research, and there are scant references to his work in the other site in each. That Bourdieu would ever seriously synthesize these two sites in one text is doubtful given the lack of cross-referencing in these books: they remained parallel and yet apart.

Le bal des célibataires contains three previously published essays on Béarnaise inheritance and marriage strategies, and one essay on the peasantry as a class, spanning the period from 1962 to 1989. Apart from his essay on the uses of photography among peasants in Lesquire, which is not included, it is an exhaustive collection of his writings on rural France. In his introduction to the book, Bourdieu offered it as a historical view of his intellectual development (a sort of *bildingsroman*) as he reanalyzed the material over the years, further developing his concepts of habitus and symbolic violence. He also remarked that, in retrospect, he was better able to see the links between the processes of a local Béarnaise marriage market of symbolic goods and other markets of symbolic goods in other fields as he further developed the concept of field. Bourdieu noted in this introduction that rural sociology in France held a very low place in the academic hierarchy at the time of his research. He was influenced in that rural fieldwork by Marcel Maget's guide to the study of cultural behavior (Maget 1962), which Bourdieu noted served as a corrective to the symbolic analysis of Lévi-Strauss that he had himself used in his analysis of the Kabyle house. Bourdieu wrote that the idea to do research in Lesquire was prompted by seeing a class photograph shown to him by an old friend, who also pointed out to him those boys who had remained unmarried. His introductory remarks to *Le bal* also mentioned his own reticence about publishing the essays on his natal region, and his feelings of treason for having turned his familiar region into an object of social science. Perhaps also the same feelings of treason that he evoked in other writings about having been socially and geographically mobile, and about his father's having also made a break with the farming milieu. This may partly explain why so little of that work was ever translated into English, a combination of his reticence and the low status of the subject in academia.

The circumstances that took Bourdieu to Algeria, and his experiences as a soldier there, were recounted in some detail by Bourdieu in *Esquisse pour une auto-analyse* (2004: 53–75), at about the same time that he wrote about his fieldwork in Béarn in the introduction to *Le bal des célibataires*. Bourdieu had been drafted into the French army during the Algerian war, but he refused to attend officer's school, even though this was expected of a student at ENS. He was first assigned to duty in Versailles but, as a result of difficulties he had with the commanding officers there because of his opposition to the French approach to Algeria, he was shipped to Algeria and assigned to guard duty at an ammunitions depot. Bourdieu recalled his comradeship with the other "simple soldiers" with whom he served.

His parents intervened through a Béarnais colonel to have Bourdieu reassigned to a desk job in the military cabinet for the remaining months of his service. He wrote that he became increasingly interested in Algerian society and culture; he stayed in Algeria after his service, taking a teaching job in Algiers. He continued to pursue the ethnographic and sociological studies there, which resulted in numerous publications. Bourdieu revisited his fieldwork and experiences in Algeria at greater length in another book published posthumously, *Images de l'Algérie: Une affinité élective.*

The photographs that Bourdieu took in Algeria during the period from 1958 to 1961 are the subject of that book. Bourdieu was an integral part of the project of producing it, although it was also created through the intermediaries of the sociologist Franz Schultheis, at the University of Geneva, and the Austrian journal *Camera Austria.* There are several differences between this book and the one on rural France. First, it offers new material, as it is the first publication built around the hundreds of photos that Bourdieu took, and that also were the subject of exhibitions at the Institute of the Arab World in Paris and at the Kuntshaus art museum in Graz, Austria. In addition, the subject matter has a much higher status than that of rural French peasants, with its focus on alterity and the exotic and the seriousness of war, and this work did not provoke the same feelings of having revealed "family secrets" that Bourdieu felt in Béarn. He has never mentioned any hesitation about this research in Algeria, since he saw it as contributing to the noble cause of anticolonialism.

Images d'Algérie is very much a "European" project, despite its obvious subject matter. It came about through a combination of happenstance and politics. Schultheis first took an interest in the photos when he learned about them in the context of discussions with Bourdieu concerning the German translation of *Algérie 60* in 2000 (and, of course, the timing of that translation so many years later is interesting in and of itself). Almost concurrently, Bourdieu had intervened in the messy Austrian political situation of 2000 associated with the rise of a rightwing agenda, by publishing an essay in *Camera Austria* that reflected his involvement in the European social movement and public stance against globalization and neoliberalism. Funding for the project of collecting, archiving, and exhibiting Bourdieu's photos came largely from the EU, because it had selected Graz at a "European Center of Culture" for 2003, and this project was placed under that umbrella. There is no metacommentary in the essays of the text about this fact, but Schultheis draws explicit connections in his introductory essay between the displaced Algerian workers and displaced salaried workers in contemporary Europe, who are victims of neoliberal economic policies. He suggests that the economic crisis in Algeria provoked by the war for independence, and Bourdieu's photos that convey the suffering of the people at the time, can be held up as a mirror to contemporary Europe.

Bourdieu himself did not make these connections in his own comments, and was more self-reflective about his own past and intellectual history, tinged with some nostalgia for those early days of fieldwork. In his interview with Schultheis, he offered a similar statement about the work in Algeria being part of a "conversion" from philosophy to ethnology and sociology to that he made in his introduction to *Le bal des célibataires*. In response to Schultheis's question about the socioanalysis that Bourdieu spoke about in his last lecture at the Collège de France, Bourdieu made an explicit link between the work in Algeria and his rural French research:

> The holistic ethnological gaze that I took toward Algeria, I was able to take upon myself, on the people of my region, on my parents, on the accent of my father, of my mother, and gather all of that without drama, which is one of the great problems of all uprooted intellectuals, enclosed within the alternative of populism or, on the contrary, the self-shame associated with class racism. I took on people very similar to the Kabyles, people with whom I had spent my childhood, the gaze of necessary holism that defines the discipline of ethnology. The practice of photography, first in Algeria and then in Béarn, without a doubt contributed a great deal to, and accompanied this conversion of the gaze it implied—I believe that the word is not too strong—a real conversion. Photography is in effect a manifestation of the distance of the observer who records and who does not forget that he is recording (something which is not always easy in familiar situations, such as the dance), but it implies also all the proximity of the familiar, attentive and sensitive to the imperceptible details that familiarity allows him and enjoins him to understand and to interpret in the field. (2003a: 42–43)

In this quote, Bourdieu is drawing an analogy between the photographer and the ethnologist (who both combine a gaze at once distant and close), and this is reflected in the subtitle of the book—"an elective affinity" (between photography and sociology). He seems to be saying that his work in Algeria permitted him to accept his own social origins in France, and that both sites enabled him to become conscious of the tension between distance and familiarity during research. He also made a very explicit statement about his conviction that the Kabyles were similar to the Béarnaise.

It is worth thinking more about the ways Bourdieu asserted his ethnographic authority in both settings. In his work on Béarn, he stressed his method of objectification and scientific approach, so as to avoid any claim that he was too close to the material; at the same time, Bourdieu also used his "insider" perspective as "native" to validate his work there through his closeness to the people. He also sought to legitimize his work in Algeria by using his own rural roots in France to claim a sort of "insider" status among Kabyle peasants, and to distance himself from others associated with the colonial power of France. By positioning the two sites as both "worlds apart" and "parallel worlds," he was able to move back and forth between France the metropole, Béarn the traditional French society, and both a traditional Kabylia and an Algeria full of disruption and crisis. In a similar way, Bourdieu moved back and forth between sociology and anthropology, thereby maintaining some distance from each.

This chapter began with Bourdieu's evocation of Lévi-Strauss and *Tristes Tropiques,* and with his desire to invert that approach by going to his familiar region of Béarn and making it "exotic." Quite another type of inversion of *Tristes Tropiques* was attempted by Jean-Paul Dumont, in his book *The Headman and I* (1992 [1978]), which recounts his experiences during fieldwork in the 1960s among the Panare in Venezuela. Rather than returning to his native France to undertake research and thereby invert the site of fieldwork, Dumont sought to invert the "objective" approach of Lévi-Strauss. Although an admirer of *Tristes Tropiques,* which inspired his interest in anthropology, Dumont writes "I find there an interobjectivity where I had hoped for intersubjectivity" (1992: 11). Dumont and Bourdieu adopted different solutions to their readings of Lévi-Strauss. Both wanted to balance objectivity and subjectivity, to avoid the "lofty gaze" and to avoid what Dumont calls the "self-indulgent emotions of a fieldworker vainly attempting, by confessional narratives, to create an introspective travelogue" (3). Whereas Dumont wrote one of the landmark "reflexive" ethnographies that seeks to examine the mutual gaze of ethnographer and informants, Bourdieu worked to objectify the familiar at home and to objectify the entire construction of objective versus subjective. But Bourdieu did not completely reject affect and emotion in his work, or escape "intersubjectivity," a point to which I will now turn.

FOUR

Habitus and Emotion

Body hexis is a political mythology realized, em-bodied, turned
into a permanent disposition, a durable manner of standing,
speaking and thereby of *feeling* and *thinking*.
—*Outline* (1977) and *The Logic of Practice* (1990)

In anthropology, the past twenty years has seen a growing interest in
research that focuses on the cultural construction of emotions, and on
discursive practices associated with emotion. The implications of Bourdieu's
concept of habitus for the study of emotion have been overshadowed by
the debates concerning agency and structure with which this concept is
most commonly associated.[1] An understanding of Bourdieu's approach to
emotion is, however, an important piece in understanding his overall approach to the articulation of agency and structure. Bourdieu's notion of
"dispositions" is directly connected to emotion and affect, and this is particularly evident in his work on honor, marriage strategies, and taste. In
spite of this, Bourdieu's work has thus far remained largely marginal to the
study of emotions, neglected by many scholars working on this topic.[2]

Bourdieu's interest in emotion and affect can be traced to his earliest
work. There is a reference to his unfinished doctoral thesis (*Thèse d'état*),
on "The Temporal Structures of Emotional Life" under the direction of
Georges Canguilhem at the Sorbonne, in the "gray literature" section of
the online bibliography HyperBourdieu.[3] Bourdieu made reference to this
early work in describing his turn to ethnography from philosophy in the
interview "Fieldwork in Philosophy," when he stated that "I had undertaken research into the 'phenomenology of emotional life,' or more exactly
into the temporal structures of emotional experience" (1990b: 6–7).[4] He
went on to say that he sought a more rigorous approach that might have
drawn him to biology had not Lévi-Strauss been raising the reputation of
ethnology at this time, making it suddenly a more attractive option for
study.

Bourdieu's work is further connected to the anthropology of emotions
through his stance on reflexivity, and his continued efforts to synthesize
objective and subjective approaches to research. Although he more often

than not advocated and adopted an "objective" and scientific tone in his writings that never made his own emotional responses explicit, except during the last decade of his life, these were not, however, absent in his writings. At times, as I will argue in this chapter, emotion erupts in Bourdieu's writings in a way that seems contradictory to his more rational, scientific sociological approach but that confirms his place in the Enlightenment tradition of ambivalence about the opposition between reason and emotion. Bourdieu's work has a place not only within the context of an anthropology of emotion that looks toward the cultures we study but also an anthropology of emotion that is connected to reflections on the proper role in ethnographic writing of the ethnographer's own emotions and feelings during fieldwork.

ANTHROPOLOGY, EMOTION, AND THE BODY

In her oft-quoted statement that emotions are "embodied thoughts" (1984: 143), Michelle Rosaldo was drawing on similar concepts of emotion and the body to those articulated by Bourdieu in his concepts of habitus and dispositions.[5] Drawing on her fieldwork among the Ilongot of the Philippines and its implications for understandings of the cultural construction of the self and the emotions, Rosaldo wrote that "cultural idioms provide the images in terms of which our subjectivities are formed and, furthermore, these idioms themselves are socially ordered and constrained" (1984: 150). With these comments, and in her ethnography on the Ilongot (1980), Rosaldo articulated a growing interest in the emotions among sociocultural anthropologists. Similar trends were taking place in sociology,[6] where Hochschild's (1983) research on the "management" of emotions in the workplace among airline employees similarly pointed to the cultural construction of emotion. This was not an entirely new development, as there are examples of anthropological interest in emotions from the 1930s, such as Gregory Bateson's work on ethos (1958 [1936]), Jules Henry's (1936) early analysis of linguistic expressions of emotion (particularly anger) among the Kaingang in Brazil, and Ruth Benedict's (1989 [1934]) work on configurations and affect.

Vincent Crapanzano (1994) has traced some French roots in the current American interest in the topic, especially in the work of Lévy-Bruhl and Durkheim, and also has suggested that confrontations with alterity, during fieldwork among "others," are at the base of an anthropology of emotions. Much of the literature on the anthropology of emotions has been developed outside of European or North American settings,[7] attesting to Crapanzano's observation. It is worth noting here that the only research of Bourdieu's that is cited in the context of emotion is that on honor among the Kabyles in Algeria—a setting of "otherness." Lutz and White have attributed the interest in emotion to the growth of "interpretive approaches to social science" (1986: 405), which would include the influence of Clifford Geertz, and which came to oppose more universalist views of emotion that tied it to biology and relegated it to a marginal position in social or cultural anthropology. They also point to the distinction between reason and emotion (seen as irrational) as one that hindered anthropological studies of emotion, and to the public/private dichotomy as one that positioned emotions as private and thereby out of bounds for the cultural anthropologist. Marcus and Fischer (1986: 45) have connected ethnographic attention to emotions to a growing interest in cultural concepts of "personhood" as a way to describe cultural distinctiveness. Scholars of culture and emotion vary in the degree of primacy that they attribute to culture—culture can be seen to shape, elicit, and give meaning to emotions or it can be seen as constructing those emotions in the first place. Embedded in these theories of emotion is a distinction between the biological (or universal) basis for emotion among humans and the cultural variations that might change its meanings or expressions.[8] Bourdieu's work sought to break down this mind-body dualism with the concept of habitus as embodiment.

In her ethnography of emotions among the Ifaluk in the South Pacific, Catherine Lutz made much of a Western versus non-Western distinction in approaches to emotion, and of the impediments to understanding emotion ethnographically arising from Western notions of individualism and of the "natural" basis of emotion. She has written that her aim was to "treat emotion as an ideological practice rather than as a thing to be discovered or an essence to be distilled" (1998: 4), so that "emotional meaning is then a social rather than an individual achievement—an emergent product of social life" (5). In her attempt to deconstruct the dichotomy between rationality or irrationality that informs much Western thought on the emotions, she suggested that "rather than modeling people as either thinking or feeling, we might view people as almost always 'emotional' in the sense of being committed to 'processing information' or understanding the world in certain culturally and personally constructed worlds" (225). Although as stated in these terms, the study of emotion risks explaining everything and so explaining nothing, Bourdieu's concept of dispositions similarly posits feeling or emotion as connected to all social action. In this, he articulated a view of culture in which there is no distinction between cognition and affect, and in which social agents operate (and compete) within fields of symbolic power in ways that are structured by the thoughts and feelings that are part of their dispositions.

Bourdieu discussed the body as a "memory pad" (2000b: 141), through which learning takes place and is inscribed. This is primarily a one-way process of inculcation that affords little social agency. Nevertheless, it draws attention to the relationship between the body and culture. The implications of Bourdieu's work for the study of embodiment (which is related to emotion) have been recognized by several scholars, including Thomas Csordas, who, in his essay "Embodiment as a Paradigm for Anthropology" (1990) analyzes his ethnographic work among American Pentacostals using Bourdieu's notion of habitus. Csordas refers to the habitus as "the socially informed body." For Csordas, the body is not "an object to be studied in relation to culture" but is "the existential ground of culture" (5). Csordas describes different versions of a religious habitus among the groups he studied, in which emotion is an inseparable part of the "spontaneous" religious behaviors enacted in a "behavioral environment much broader than any single event" (39). Religious rituals, Csordas suggests, drawing directly from Bourdieu, evoke "preorchestrated dispositions." Loïc Wacquant also has developed Bourdieu's notion of embodiment in his work on the culture of boxing, and has incorporated self-reflexivity into his analysis (cf. Wacquant 2003). In a recent study of apprenticeship in Rome, Michael Herzfeld (2003) examines the learning of skills and artisanship through a theory of embodiment that explores notions of tradition and modernity. In contrast to Bourdieu, Herzfeld connects embodiment to social agency and argues that embodied dispositions are not passive in the face of power but can mask challenges to it.

For Bourdieu, emotion and feeling are part of the habitus, which is both structured by, and helps structure, systems of power and domination. In the following passage from his book *Masculine Domination,* a version of which also appeared in *Pascalian Meditations* (2000b: 169), Bourdieu explicitly discussed emotion, and distinguished between bodily emotions and (more cognitive?) passion or sentiments:

> The practical acts of knowledge and recognition of the magical frontier between the dominant and the dominated that are triggered by the magic of symbolic power and through which the dominated, often unwittingly, sometimes unwillingly, contribute to their own domination by tacitly accepting the limits imposed, often take the form of *bodily emotions*—shame, humiliation, timidity, anxiety, guilt—or *passions and sentiments*—love, admiration, respect. These emotions are all the more powerful when they are betrayed in visible manifestations such as blushing, stuttering, clumsiness, trembling, anger or impotent rage, so many ways of submitting, even despite oneself and "against the grain" (*à son corps défendant*), to the dominant judgment, sometimes in internal conflict and division of self, of experiencing the insidious complicity that a body slipping from the control of the consciousness and will maintains with the censures inherent in the social structure. (2001b: 38–39)

Here Bourdieu addressed the preconscious nature of emotions, and the ways in which dispositions that lead to various emotional reactions are inculcated in the body in ways that are beyond the conscious control of the individual. We also see here some evidence that Bourdieu did not take a wholly social constructivist position on emotion but viewed some aspects of emotion ("bodily emotions") as less controlled by the dispositions of the habitus than were the "sentiments" such as love and respect. What he called the "bodily emotions" are elicited in various contexts of power relations (as bodily responses to symbolic violence, for example), but appear in his argument to be less cultural than natural. Sentiments, however, that include honor (which is both a value and an emotion), are culturally constructed. In her discussion of socialization among the Tonga, Morton (1996: 13–14) emphasizes the importance of not conflating values and emotions, as her informants sought to socialize children with values and ideals by eliciting various emotional responses (for example, emotions of love and respect were distinguished by them, but both were used to inculcate obedience as a value). With the concept of honor, however, the value or ideal and the emotion of pride associated with it are closely linked. While mostly discussed in terms of a societal value in much of the literature on the Mediterranean, Bourdieu is somewhat unique in pointing to the emotional component of this ideal.

HABITUS AND DISPOSITIONS

Bourdieu addressed emotions through the concepts of habitus and dispositions, which must be more fully elucidated here before I can turn to examples of his references to emotions and his approach to them. The concept of habitus was central to Bourdieu's theoretical positions elaborated in *Outline,* in which Bourdieu offered his earliest systematic discussion of this concept and the ways in which he was breaking with structuralism in his theory.[9] To depend entirely on this portrait of habitus in *Outline* affords only a partial view, however, because this concept has antecedents in his earlier work and, most important, was further developed by Bourdieu in relationship to the notion of field over the next three decades. Over the many years of his career, Bourdieu used a variety of wordings to explain what he meant by habitus, but a "classic" definition, from *Outline,* is this:

> Systems of durable, transposable dispositions, structured structures predisposed to function as structuring structures, that is, as principles of the generation and structuring of practices and representations which can be objectively "regulated" and "regular" without in any way being the product of obedience to rules, objectively adapted to their goals without presupposing a conscious aiming at ends or an express mastery of the operations necessary to attain them and, being all this, collectively orchestrated without being the product of the orchestrating action of a conductor. (1977a: 72)

Bourdieu's concept of habitus as articulated in *Outline* and the *Logic of Practice* can be viewed as a synthesis of the more psychological theory of habitus used by Norbert Elias (1982 [1939]) and that of the theory of bodily habits and habitus in the work of Marcel Mauss (1979 [1950]), via "Hegel, Husserl, Weber, Durkheim" (Bourdieu 1990b: 12) and others who also used this term.[10] For Elias, habitus was associated with drives and impulses that determine tastes and habits. It was connected to what Elias called the "civilizing process," through which he referred to a certain way of understanding the relation of the individual to the social and the manners and tastes that reflected the perceived "civilized" person, and which he understood to be an historical process. In their Preface to Elias's book *The Germans: Power Struggles and the Development of Habitus in the Nineteenth and Twentieth Centuries,* Eric Dunning and Stephen Mennell write that "by 'habitus'—a word which he used long before its popularization by Pierre Bourdieu—Elias basically means 'second nature' or 'embodied social learning'" (1996: ix). Elias, influenced by Freud, saw habitus primarily as a form of personality structure. He used the concept of figurations, much like Bourdieu used the concept of field, in order to avoid overemphasis on the individual, and to theorize a network of people with shared habitus. For Elias, the habitus was "the self-image and social make-up" of individuals (1987: ix), and he described it as "soil from which grow the personal characteristics through which an individual differs from other members of his society" (182). Elias continued to write that individual style could emerge from the shared habitus, using the metaphor of "an unmistakable individual handwriting that grows out of the social script" (182) to describe this.

In what he termed the "we-I balance," Elias focused more on the national, rather than class, habitus, and associated it with "national character"—although he did not see this as the only component of the habitus and argued that habitus was flexible and could accommodate various hybrid forms of identity. He wrote that "the individuality of the particular Englishman, Dutchman, Swede, or German represents, in a sense, the personal elaboration of a common social, and in this case national, habitus" (210). For Elias, the entire I-we construction, or split between individual and social, was a social invention and the product of particular types of social habitus. It resulted in what Elias called a "habitus problem," which inclined scholars (as Westerners) to view the world in terms of this dichotomy. Similarly, the dichotomy between rational and irrational was, for Elias, part of an historical social habitus (associated with the Enlightenment) that persisted, through what he called "the drag effect," to influence thinking about behavior. Elias described emotion in terms of "we-feelings" and suggested that these are part of the social habitus and can be provoked by the nation state to enhance its power; he also argued that some social groups, in order to survive as a group, resist this power because of their own we-feelings, and are thereby positioned as irrational or as having conflicting values to those of the dominant society. Elias countered this view with the perspective that "in relation to their own group identity, and, more widely, their own social habitus, people have no free choice. These things cannot simply be changed like clothes" (225). It was not values that were at stake but "we-feelings" that are associated with one group rather than the "higher-order" group and "the fading or disappearance of the lower-order group appears in reality as a kind of death threat, a collective destruction and certainly a loss of meaning to the highest degree" (125). Elias and Bourdieu were both concerned with power struggles between different groups in society, and there are echoes of Elias's thought in that of Bourdieu and vice versa. In Bourdieu's description of *paysans empaysannés,* there are parallels to this issue of lagging social habitus in the face of changing circumstances to which Elias refers with his discussion of we-feelings. Whereas Elias spoke mainly in terms of the nation state in relationship to other regional or ethnic populations, Bourdieu articulated a theory of habitus in terms of social class. For both, however, the state ultimately represented and protected the interests of the bourgeoisie.

Marcel Mauss also had a concept of habitus related to internalized dispositions. In his essay on "Body Techniques," Mauss used the concept of habitus to refer to customary habits of moving the body that were socially constructed and, as he wrote, "do not vary just with individuals and their imitations; they vary especially between societies, educations, proprieties and fashions, prestiges. In them we should see the techniques and work of collective and individual practical reason" (1979 [1950]: 101). Although Mauss primarily was describing the physical manifestation of this in bodily movement, rather than mental or psychological qualities, he did mention that these body techniques were connected to modes of life and manners. These techniques were the product of training, and so could be connected with what he noted was the psychological a well as sociological concept of "dexterity" or cleverness. Here we see some origins of Bourdieu's use of the term habitus as a "feel for the game" in which the individual can exercise various strategies within the generative capacities of his or her habitus. The concept of practical reason, used by Mauss, is also one taken up by Bourdieu (one of his books—Bourdieu 1994a—takes this as a title) and it is a concept that he contrasted with the scientific or objective reason of the sociologist.

It is likely that the first example of the use of "habitus" by Bourdieu was in his 1962 article on the condition of bachelorhood in his natal village. In his earliest uses of the term, Bourdieu associated habitus with the "traditional" and with the family, and it referred primarily to bodily hexis. This meaning of the term also appeared (but less prominently than in the rural French material) in some Algerian writings of the early 1960s, as in his 1964 article on uprooted peasants (Bourdieu and Sayad 1964b). And, in some of the early Algerian writings, one can see the concept being developed, but without the use of the term, as in the following statement from the essay "The Attitude of the Algerian Peasant Toward Time":

> If the future is not postulated as a field of infinite possibilities, it is because the order founded and defended by tradition is viable only when it is seen, not as the best possible, but the only possibility, that is to say, only by the elimination of the whole range of collateral possibilities which challenge the inexorability of its dictates. It is essential to the survival of traditionalism that it should not recognize its own exclusion of unknown alternatives. (1963: 70)

In his later writings, Bourdieu would label this process of misrecognition and elimination of possibilities that of the preconscious dispositions of the habitus.

Another early use of the concept of habitus was in Bourdieu's introduction to a collaborative book on the social uses of photography, *Un art moyen* (Bourdieu, Boltanski, et al. 1965), translated as *Photography: A Middle-Brow Art* (1990d). This book foreshadows *Distinction,* in its interest in class and aesthetic taste, and also shows the very early concerns with a sociology of art in his work. In *Photography,* Bourdieu introduced the concept of habitus to capture "objectified subjectivity" and "the internalization of objectivity," and also in terms of "systems of unconscious and durable dispositions that are the class habitus and ethos" (4–5). Here he tied habitus to orientations toward the future, which he would do again in later work, writing that "the class habitus is nothing but this experience (in its most usual sense) which immediately reveals a hope or an ambition as reasonable or unreasonable, a particular commodity as accessible or inaccessible, a particular action as suitable or unsuitable" (5). This is similar to his passage about Algerian peasants and time cited earlier. Bourdieu and his coauthors argued in this book that class habitus determined what an amateur photographer would consider an appropriate subject for a photograph, as well as the bodily postures the subject of a photograph would take.

In his 1992 book on the literary field, *Les règles de l'art* [*The Rules of Art,* 1996c], Bourdieu explained that he adopted the concept of habitus in order to reject "a whole series of alternatives into which social sciences (and, more generally, all anthropological theory) was locked, that of the conscious (or the subject) and the unconscious" (1996c: 179). According to Bourdieu (1990b: 12 and 1996c: 179), he first introduced this term in his comments (1967b) on two essays by Panofsky on architecture, drawing on Panofsky's notion of mental habits. In making this statement, he ignored his own earlier uses of the term associated with fieldwork in Béarn and Algeria, perhaps because he considered these to be less sophisticated. He wanted to avoid an approach, which he found in the structuralist theories of both Lévi-Strauss and Althusser, which "made the agent disappear by reducing it to the role of supporter or bearer of the structure" (1996c: 179). Bourdieu claimed that his own approach was closer to that of Noam Chomsky and his theory of generative grammar, although Bourdieu did not share Chomsky's notion of the universal nature of the structure. Bourdieu described his latching onto the concept of habitus as a way of satisfying his "desire to escape from the philosophy of consciousness without annulling the agent in its true role of practical operator of constructions of the real" (180).

Habitus was described by Bourdieu in terms of dispositions, which are feelings, thoughts, tastes, and bodily postures.[11] Although this word has connotations in both French and English of being "natural," Bourdieu wanted to show that dispositions were socially produced. Dispositions are internalized, preconscious, and largely determine the actions social agents take. He described disposition as another term for "ethos" (Bourdieu and Passeron 1990f: 156). The concept of dispositions has parallels in the much earlier work of Gregory Bateson in his study of the Naven (1958 [1936]). Bateson defined "ethos" as the "expression of a culturally standardized system of organization of the instincts and emotions of the individuals" (1958: 119). Whereas Bourdieu developed his notions of habitus and dispositions in relationship to (or against) structuralism (especially in the work of Lévi-Strauss), Bateson's concept of ethos was developed in relationship to (and against) the structural-functionalism of Malinowski and Radcliffe-Brown. Bateson wrote in his introduction to the book that artists and scientists employ different ways of writing about culture, and that a structural-functionalist approach in anthropology missed elements of culture, particularly its "emotional background," that could be grasped by a novelist, such as Jane Austen. Bateson wrote that "no functional study can ever be reasonably complete unless it links up the structure and pragmatic working of a culture with its emotional tone or ethos" (1958: 2). For both Bourdieu and Bateson, the problem with structuralism (in either the French or British form) was that culture and society were somehow outside of the individual, and they each wanted to put forth a model of how internalized affect was a factor in society. In his analysis of the Naven ceremony among the Iatmul of New Guinea, Bateson posited that there was a different ethos among men and women, with consequences for the sexual division of that society.

But he also was interested in using the concept in his own society, and included a section on ethos among the English, using examples from the academic milieu with which he was most familiar. Although he felt that more fleeting types of ethos could be created in certain interactional situations, there were more lasting dispositions among stable and formal groups, such as dons at college. His brief description foreshadows Bourdieu's descriptions of academic ("secondary") habitus inculcated in students and teachers at the Grandes Écoles in *The State Nobility*. Bateson noted that what he calls their "cultural structure" and their ethos have developed hand in hand, in circular fashion, so that attitudes, tastes in alcoholic beverage, traditions, and so on are all part of the ethos, historically formed. He wrote: "The Latin Grace, the architecture of the college, the snuff after dinner on Sundays, the loving cup, the rose water, the feasts—all these cultural details constitute an intricate set of channels which express and guide the ethos" (121). He added in a footnote that this type of description must not be taken to mean that cultural structure and ethos are different things, but, rather that they "are only different aspects of the same behavior" (121).

Bateson had another concept, eidos, which he felt was the cognitive part of culture that coexisted with the emotional tone associated with ethos. Bourdieu recalled those concepts in a discussion of "point of view" in *Pascalian Meditations,* without directly referencing Bateson. He defined the eidos as a "mode of thought" and the ethos as "prereflexive belief" (2000b: 100). There is a strong parallel between their pairings of these concepts. Bateson did not focus on a conflict model of society, as did Bourdieu, but stressed the harmonious complementarity of different ethoses, even among lords and peasants in Western Europe. Conflict would "break down," Bateson suggested, only when the lords or the serfs questioned their power or submission and if social differentiation "proceeded too far" (1958: 122). In some ways, this is not entirely different from Bourdieu, who also used the term harmony to describe the fit between habitus and structure in many cases. Bourdieu used a much more explicitly Marxist perspective, however, of the ways in which the dispositions of the dominated are a function of their domination, even if they are not questioned as such by the social agents involved. Despite any differences, the work of Bateson and Bourdieu shares emphasis on emotion as an integral part of cultural anthropology and not just a subject for psychological studies of the individual. Bateson argued for the cultural and gendered nature of ethos and affect, rather than seeing emotion as a "natural" human quality. For both, ethos was a factor in human motivations—what Bourdieu referred to as strategies.

According to Bourdieu, for whom the concept of dispositions was linked primarily to social class and social stratification, dispositions guide the actions of social agents through future-oriented perceptions of chances for success or failure. An illustration of this is lies in the emotions of negative self-image discerned in the habitus of working-class children at school, as they anticipated the failure that awaited them. Bourdieu and Passeron wrote:

> Even the negative dispositions and predispositions leading to self-elimination, such as, for example, self-depreciations, devalorization of the School and its sanctions or resigned expectation of failure or exclusion may be understood as unconscious anticipation of the sanctions the School objectively has in store for the dominated classes. (1990f: 204–5)

This passage reflects the dimension of time, also noted above in the cases of Algerians and of French peasants using photography, in the acceptance of what is to be on the part of the child—who actively makes their own destiny happen by internalizing various attitudes and negative feelings of self-worth that lead them to fail in school.

In the *Logic of Practice*, Bourdieu argued that agents "become the accomplices of the processes that tend to make the probable a reality" (1990a: 65), because they distinguish between what is accessible and what is inaccessible ("what is and is not 'for us'"). This is based on the dispositions of the habitus, which anticipate and adjust expectations as the "the universe of possibilities" changes. Although this appears as a future orientation, it is actually, Bourdieu argued, based on the past conditions that have produced the present. He tied this to emotion, writing in a footnote:

> Emotion, the extreme case of such anticipation, is a hallucinatory "presenting" of the impending future, which, as bodily reactions identical to those of the real situation bear witness, leads a person to live a still suspended future as already present, or even already past, and therefore necessary and inevitable—"I'm a dead man"; "I'm done for." (292, fn. 12)[12]

Because the "future" anticipated by social agents is rooted in the perception of past and present conditions, and harmonized with the "objective" possibilities in the structure for the agent, one cannot, as Bourdieu (1977a: 73) accused Jean-Paul Sartre and Alain Touraine[13] of doing, attribute "conscious and deliberate intention" to social agents. Agents may explicitly state plans and strategies, but these practices are the product of habitus and not rational calculation. By inverting Sartre's own vocabulary to criticize him, Bourdieu suggested that to be able to consciously choose one's "emotions, passions, and actions" (1977a: 74) would be an act of "bad faith" and mere acting.[14]

There are several references to the emotions in *Pascalian Meditations*, a book in which Bourdieu was, in part, struggling with the relationship between reason and affect—drawing on Pascal's own approach to reason. Bourdieu wrote that everyday choices were guided by "sympathies and antipathies, affections and aversions, tastes and distastes" (150). People want to feel "at home," he wrote, and desire happiness. The dispositions were acquired in concert with emotions. Bourdieu also wrote in that book that it was because the body was "exposed and endangered in the world, faced with the risk of emotion, lesion, suffering, sometimes death" that it had to be serious about the world and was able to acquire dispositions that made it open to the world (140). The childhood acquisition of habitus takes place, he argued, largely though emotion and affect. The child "incorporates the social in the form of affects" (167). Emotions become self-evident because inscribed in the body.

Bourdieu described the expression of emotions, such as love, as an example of the "ritualization of practices." He quoted a young Kabyle woman as having explained that "A girl doesn't know her husband beforehand and she looks to him for everything. She loves him even before they marry, because she must; she has to love him, there is no other 'door'" (1977a: 233, fn. 11). Agents subjectively experience feelings that are for them self-evident, and part of the world "as it ought to be." In *Outline,* he juxtaposed examples from a Kabyle woman's statements about illness and death with a passage from Marcel Proust on illness in order to show that this ritualization of practices, which connects emotions to "practical reason," is not just associated with the Kabyle peasant worldview (1977a: 166–7). Bourdieu's interest in emotion is evident in examples drawn from his ethnographic work in all three contexts of Kabylia, Béarn, and urban France.

TASTES AND EMOTION

In *Distinction,* Bourdieu focused on what he called the "cultivated" habitus of the bourgeoisie, and on the interaction of inculcation in the family and in the educational system to produce this habitus. Legitimate culture and legitimate "aesthetic" judgments of taste are associated with the bourgeoisie. By looking at "taste" among artists, the bourgeoisie and petit-bourgeoisie, and the working classes, Bourdieu sought to denaturalize judgments of taste and demonstrate their very social and cultural origins (as opposed to a Kantian view of "pure aesthetics"). Tastes, as habitus, "function below the level of consciousness and language, beyond the reach of introspective scrutiny or control by the will" (1984b: 466) Bourdieu strongly associated taste with emotions. He wrote that "tastes are perhaps first and foremost distastes, disgust provoked by horror or visceral intolerance ('sick-making') of the taste of others" (56). Because one's tastes appear to be natural, those of others can seem unnatural. Class endogamy results in large part, he argued, from aversion to and intolerance of different lifestyles. Taste operates, therefore, in the boundary maintenance between social classes, and acts as a system of classification. Transgressions of the boundary-maintenance socialized in tastes can, Bourdieu wrote, provoke "visceral, murderous horror, absolute disgust, metaphysical fury" (475), feelings associated with stigma.

The notion of taste is a bourgeois notion, Bourdieu argued, because it implies freedom of choice in one's lifestyle. Bourdieu contrasted this with what he called "the taste of necessity," which refers to the fit between dispositions of the habitus and the possibilities of existence for a person. As he wrote: "An agent has what he likes because he likes what he has, that is, the properties actually given to him in the distributions and legitimately assigned to him in the classifications" (175). Bourdieu called (the illusion of) choice *amor fati:* choice of destiny. In his explication of taste, Bourdieu used several examples from questionnaires, from descriptions of home interiors, and from popular culture and the media. Taste in food was a focal point in the analysis, because it is inculcated so early in life. He argued that food becomes a moral issue, and is intricately connected to the body—in that it is taken into the body and also "makes" particular bodily forms appropriate to different social classes. The bourgeois are, as a whole, more comfortable in their bodies, he argued, than the working classes. This discomfort is expressed through unconscious reactions and emotions of timidity, embarrassment, and so on (207).

Among his many examples of bourgeois taste, Bourdieu provided profiles of bourgeois individuals and also reprinted want ads for professional jobs in order to examine "ideal" qualities that were highly valued. Control over emotion plays a role in the bourgeois male ideal. Bourdieu concluded that there is a new version of the bourgeois man emerging, but that continuities are also present: "Bourgeois distinction is still defined, both in speech and bearing, by relaxation in tension, ease within restraint, a rare and highly improbable combination of antagonistic properties" (311).[15] Bourdieu also illustrated what he called "middle-brow" taste, which occurs among the petit-bourgeoisie who aspire to legitimate culture and a higher social position. One example is an extract from a home decorating journal, which combines emotion language and taste: "If she loves painting or reading, the walls and shelves proclaim her tastes. Through her home, a woman whose job often requires her to adapt to other people's opinions, rediscovers the very feminine pleasure of saying, "what I like is . . ." (321).

This middle-class approach is contrasted to that of the working classes. Bourdieu characterized the working classes as having a distaste for pretension, which they associate with the bourgeoisie. He wrote: "Thus nothing is more alien to working-class women than the typically bourgeois idea of making each object in the home the occasion for an aesthetic choice, of extending the intention of harmony or beauty into the bathroom or kitchen"

(379). In writing about the dominated classes, Bourdieu argued that their lifestyle reflects domination and their own recognition that they are dominated, with a consequent "sense of incompetence, failure or cultural unworthiness" (386) Their response is an "art of living" based on "wisdom taught by necessity, suffering and humiliation" (394), and that expresses a hedonism and materialism "which constitute both a form of adaptation to the conditions of existence and a defense against them" (395).

Bourdieu thus used emotion language to describe taste and its expression among the different social classes in France. He associated emotion with taste, thereby denaturalizing emotion as well as taste, showing its social and cultural construction within a stratified society. He described "ready-made feelings" and wrote of taste that:

> There is no better image of the logic of socialization, which treats the body as a "memory-jogger," than those of the complexes of gestures, postures and words— simple interjections or favourite clichés—which only have to be slipped into, like a theatrical costume, to awaken, by the evocative power of bodily mimesis, a universe of ready-made feelings and experiences (474)

He had touched upon this much earlier, in *Outline,* when he pointed out that social interactions expressing sympathy, friendship, or love are connected to class homogamy, and arise "through the harmony of habitus, that is to say, more precisely, the harmony of ethos and tastes—doubtless sensed in the imperceptible cues of body hexis" (1977a: 82).

HONOR AND EMOTION

Bourdieu's analyses of the timing of gift exchange and riposte among Kabyle men (1966a; 1977a: 4–15; and 1990a: 104–11; 189–90), demonstrate his concern with the political uses of displays of emotion. His premise was that the parties to gift exchange must "misrecognize" the material aspects of the gift by establishing an appropriate interval between gift and counter-gift, or riposte and counter-riposte. The timing of exchange is symbolically charged with meaning, differently in different cases. In the case of vengeance ("the exchange of revenge-murders"), the interval must not be too long; in the case of gift exchange, not too short. Bourdieu explained this in terms of the "sentiment" of honor and its opposite, dishonor or shame. The Kabyle man of honor is discrete and in control of his emotions; he is the opposite of a man whose behavior is uncontrolled and impulsive. This "ritualization of interactions" in the timing of exchange is not dissimilar from what F. G. Bailey (1983) labels the "tactical uses of passion" in relations of power. The difference between the two analysts, however, is that Bailey sees emotional display (or nondisplay) as more or less consciously manipulated, whereas Bourdieu located this in the "feel for the game" that resides in the preconscious dispositions of the habitus.

In his early article on "The Sentiment of Honor in Kabyle Society," Bourdieu used an explicit language of emotion to describe the behaviors and norms of Kabyle men:

> The man who, incapable of preserving his dignity, grows impatient or angry, speaks at random or laughs without reason, is precipitate or uncontrolled, acts without thinking throws his weight about, shouts, vociferates (*ah'amaq*), in short, abandons himself to his first impulse, such a man is unfaithful to himself and falls short of the ideals of dignity and distinction, of modesty and shame, which are summed up in one word, elh-achma. The man of honour, on the contrary, is essentially faithful to himself (Constantia sibi, as the Romans said), and this is revealed in the care he takes to be worthy of a certain ideal image of himself. Level-headed, prudent, restrained in his speak, he always weighs pros and cons . . . he pledges his word frankly, and does not evade his responsibilities by a . . . perhaps . . . a reply that is fitting only for a woman. (1966a: 210–11)

In this early work, Bourdieu was still in transition from the structuralist approach to what he later termed that of the "logic of practice." He focused in that article on emotions and sentiments associated with honor and dishonor, and attributed conformity to norms of behavior largely to considerations of public opinion and reputation. He was still trying to work out the relationship between the value of honor as an "ideal norm" that people consciously felt compelled to respect, and "unconscious models of behavior" that "color one's attitudes without ever being formulated" (1966: 231). The question could also be posed in emotional terms—that is, do people conform because they fear the shame of embarrassment that they will experience if they behave in a dishonorable way? Or, as Bourdieu wrote, is it the case that "the essential point is that the norms, felt and experienced so deeply that they do not need to be formulated, have their roots in the system of the most fundamental cultural categories, those which define the mythical vision of the world"? (1966: 232). Bourdieu referred to honor as "ethos" in that article, although he would later refer to honor as a form of "symbolic capital." As he wrote in the *Logic of Practice,* "The conducts of honour, seen no longer as the product of obedience to rules or submission to values (which they also are, since they are experienced as such), but as the product of a more or less conscious pursuit of the accumulation of symbolic capital" (1990a: 16). In his view of honor as articulated in *Outline* and the *Logic of Practice,* the Kabyle "sense of honor" is embedded in both bodily and mental dispositions, and orchestrates (through the "feel for the game") their responses to the emotions associated with dishonor, shame, anger, and so on.

MARRIAGE STRATEGIES, GENDER, AND EMOTION

In most of his writings dealing with kinship, the family, and marriage, Bourdieu addressed the meanings of emotion and sentiment in systems tied to social reproduction and material interests. This work can be seen in the context of a dualism in kinship studies cogently expressed in the title of Medick and Sabean's edited collection *Interest and Emotion* (1984). For Bourdieu, this supposed contradiction between interest and emotion could be dissolved with the concept of the habitus. In my discussion of Bourdieu's thought on these topics, I will start with some of the later (post-1990) writings, because they most clearly articulate his theories on this. In his article "On the Family as a Realized Category" (1996d; orig. 1993b), Bourdieu tackled the question of how it is that people come to express emotions and feelings toward their families if, as he believed was the case, the family is a socially constructed "fiction." He wrote about the power of "family discourse," language used by and about the family to describe the family, as a classificatory concept. "In the social world," he wrote, "words make things, because they make the consensus on the existence and meaning of things, the common sense, the *doxa* accepted by all as self-evident" (1996d: 21). In this article, Bourdieu gave a concrete example of what he meant when articulating his theory of habitus as the "structured structure," by describing the family both as an objective social category ("structuring structure") and mental or subjective social category ("a structured structure"). This "circle," as he put it, "is that of reproduction of the social order," and produces a "near-perfect match" between the subjective and objective categories. Social agents thereby experience the world, and the family, as "natural" and self-evident.

The family is socially constructed and not at all a natural social group, he argued, but this is not adequately understood through the perspective of ethnomethodology (which focuses on the folk categories created by the "natives") because it stops with that assertion. The key for Bourdieu was to determine the "instruments of construction" that lead to a particular normative category of family; in modern societies, this is the state. Through its demographers, sociologists, and social workers (all inculcated with similar dispositions regarding the family), the state "gives reality" to the family. This also occurs through what Bourdieu called rites of institution which

> aim to constitute the family by constituting it as a united, integrated entity which is therefore stable, constant, indifferent to the fluctuations of individual feelings. And these inaugural acts of creation (imposition of family name, marriage, etc.) have their logical extension in the countless acts of reaffirmation and reinforcement that aim to produce, in a kind of continuous creation, the obliged affections and affective obligations of family feeling (conjugal love, paternal and maternal love, filial love, brotherly and sisterly love, etc.). (22)

Bourdieu concluded that "the family is indeed a fiction, a social artifact, an illusion in the most ordinary sense of the word, but a 'well-founded illusion,' because, being produced and reproduced with the guarantee of the state, it receives from the state at every moment the means to exist and persist" (25).

Bourdieu argued that it was through continuous "practical and symbolic work" that intense affective bonds were formed among members of a family, transforming "the obligations of love into a loving disposition" (22). As examples of this work, he cited "exchanges of daily existence," often orchestrated through women in the family, including gifts, services, visits, and correspondence. Family photographs also work to sanction and memorialize the family. Being able to create the "normative" family in this way, Bourdieu cautioned, is a privilege not available to all in society. He wrote "not all families, and within a given family, not all members, have the same capacity and propensity to conform to the dominant definition" (23). The family is itself a field with struggles within it, connected to inheritance issues, male domination, and so on. Bourdieu stressed that the bourgeoisie has extensive families which are integrated not only through shared habitus but strong interests of capital, social capital, and symbolic capital. The state supports the dominance of these families by perpetuating the bourgeois family type as natural and normative.

I will now turn to some earlier work of Bourdieu's on marriage in traditional societies. In his article on matrimonial strategies in Béarn, first published in 1972 (Bourdieu 1972b) but reproduced in revised form in *The Logic of Practice* (1990a; orig. 1980a),[16] Bourdieu was interested in explaining the relationship between social reproduction and family sentiment—particularly the emotion of love as expressed by young couples. Bourdieu described the two main principles guiding matrimonial strategies in "traditional" Béarn, beyond the value of impartible inheritance, as the preference for older men to marry younger women and for women to "marry up" in social status. Families seek to make "good matches" for their children, particularly the male heir and any daughters, in order to ensure the reproduction of the family patrimony—at the least its maintenance, and at best, its expansion and increased economic and symbolic capital. Bourdieu explained that marriage strategies are like other strategies, including educational and inheritance strategies, that work to "transmit inherited powers and privileges, maintained or enhanced, to the next generation" (1990a: 161). In most cases, Bourdieu found, appropriate matches are made. This does not occur through calculating reason or mechanical determinism, however, but through a "kind of socially constituted instinct which causes the objectively calculable demands of a particular form of economy to be experienced as an unavoidable call of duty or an irresistible impulse of feeling" (161). Young people experience the emotions of love and affection toward the type of person who is the most favored type of marriage choice.[17]

In explaining how appropriate couplings happen, without forcing children into arranged marriages, Bourdieu relied on socialization and the habitus, stating that:

> The earliest learning experiences, reinforced by all subsequent social experience, tended to shape schemes of perception and appreciation, in a word, *tastes,* which were applied to potential partners as to other things: and even without any directly economic or social calculation, these tastes tended to rule our misalliances. Socially approved love, love predisposed to succeed, is nothing other than that love of one's own social destiny that brings socially predestined partners together along the apparently random paths of free choice. (160)

Bourdieu did not argue that this process occurs without struggle or conflict, and, although he did not describe the family as a "field" during this earlier work (as he did in the 1992 article cited above on the family), he suggested this context. The male heir of even a very important family ("great house") must still be constantly guided by the whole group and reminded of his responsibilities. He may experience conflict between "sentiment and duty" and there will be "contradictions between structures and dispositions" sometimes leading to "subterfuges designed to satisfy personal interests within the limits of social acceptability" (153).

Informants related stories to Bourdieu of the consequences of misalliances or of parents insisting on a certain course. One family had an eldest son and five younger daughters. The informant told Bourdieu: "The boy was in love with a girl who didn't have a penny. His father said, 'So you want to marry? I've already paid for three of your sisters, you must bring in the money to pay for the two others.' The boy married one of the E. daughters instead and received a dowry of 5,000 francs. The marriage didn't work. He took to drink and went to pieces. He died childless" (153). This is a cautionary tale about the dangers (emotional and material) of resisting family pressures. Bourdieu noted that misalliances were extremely rare, as were situations in which parents had to openly exert their authority in order to "repress individual feelings" of their children, and he wrote that "the norm could remain tacit because the agents' dispositions were objectively attuned to the objective structures, in a spontaneous compliance which removes all need to point out the proprieties" (160).

Bourdieu's work on marriage strategies drew on Le Play's nineteenth-century studies of family and household. In the traditional Béarnais system, the eldest son inherited the farm, often leaving a younger son without the possibility of marriage. Le Play had noted the consequences for the younger son in this impartible inheritance system, who could be viewed as the "structural victim" of the house. Le Play wrote that many of these bachelors accepted their lot, as a result of inculcation of the family values promoting the collective and economic unity of the house, so that they came to actually value this state which lends to those in it "the serenity of bachelorhood along with the joys of the family" (quoted in Bourdieu 1990a: 158). Bourdieu challenged this "subjective" approach of Le Play, which posits a misrecognition on the part of the younger son of the exploitation of his labor and domination he experiences within the family, by inferring that the bachelor is content with his situation. Neither, Bourdieu wrote, would a wholly "objective" approach, that sees only brute power relations at work in the relationship, be adequate. There is, rather, an ambiguous quality to the relationship, whereby both duty and feeling are recognized by the participants.

Bourdieu's research took place in a region in southwestern France with a particular form of kinship and family structure, centered around "the house" or "*mas*," and which is not present throughout all of France. Martine Segalen (1984) has suggested that family relationships are organized very differently in the region of Brittany, in northwestern France, where she has conducted most of her own ethnographic research on kinship and family, than in the region studied by Bourdieu. As she points out, Béarn is a region with a tradition of impartible inheritance, in which there is one heir and the other children are given dowries. This is also the case in the region of Auvergne where I have conducted my own fieldwork on dairy farming families (Reed-Danahay 1996), and in the region of Aveyron (Rogers 1991). This type of inheritance leads to an attachment to land and its acquisition, and produces, Segalen suggests (1984: 129), a notion of family lines, a long family memory, and attachment to the family "house." In Brittany, by contrast, the system is based primarily on tenant farming and partible inheritance. Segalen has elsewhere argued that direct farm ownership, of the type existing in Béarn, leads to various "emotional ties between household and dwelling: the aim is to keep it or extend it; its possession reinforces and justifies family strategies which, in their turn, tighten the ties between the family and the land they work: it imposes particular responsibilities in maintaining its status and honour" (1983 [1980]: 75). Segalen's historical and comparative perspectives on kinship and marriage are useful in placing the material presented by Bourdieu in its sociohistorical context. Bourdieu also did this himself, in the appendix of "bibliographic notes" that cites background historical literature on the region; he also included extensive background material in the appendix to his 1962 article on bachelors.

Bourdieu felt that Béarn might be a special case of a peasant society in which there was an explicit recognition of the economic bases of domestic power that was "more realistic than other societies," so that "its representation and strategies are closer to the objective truth" (156). This comment suggests that there is no conflict for the Béarnais between what is posed by scholars as "interest and emotion," as individuals and families could simultaneously appreciate the "openly respectable criteria" for a choice of mate, such as "virtue, the good health and beauty of a girl" or "the dignity and zest for work of a young man" *and* be aware of the "pertinent criteria beneath these appearances"—economic (patrimony and size of the adot or dowry). Bourdieu concluded that "one sees how artificial or quite simply beside the point it is to ask questions concerning the relationship between structures and sentiments" (156). He suggested that the Béarnais example shows that the sociology of the family is more like a political sociology than a study of "pure sentiment."

LOVE AND DOMINATION

In his more recent book *Masculine Domination,* Bourdieu made his clearest statement about the relationship between emotions, habitus, social reproduction, and domination. In his attempts to explain the persistence of male domination over women, despite the women's movement and legal changes in women's status, he turned to the dispositions of the habitus as deposited "at the deepest level of the body" (2001b: 38) and as difficult to overcome, even in the face of the "weapon of consciousness" (39). Bourdieu defined symbolic violence in his preface to this book as "a gentle violence, imperceptible and invisible even to its victims, exerted for the most part through the purely symbolic channels of communication and cognition (more precisely, misrecognition), recognition, or *even feeling*" (2; my italics). Bourdieu argued that women, like any dominated group, internalize their domination and participate in it. Bourdieu suggested that women are kept in a state of "bodily insecurity" and exist under the gaze of others, through an "embodiment of social judgment," and are expected to exhibit behaviors associated with "femininity"—including "smiling, friendly, attentive, submissive, demure, restrained, self-effacing" (66–67). Romantic love helps justify, through feeling, their condition, but also can offer some advantages for women. Bourdieu wrote in a footnote: "If women are particularly inclined to what is called romantic love this is no doubt partly because they have a particular self-interest in it; not only does it promise to free them from masculine domination, but, both in its most ordinary form, with marriage, in which, in male societies, women circulate upwards, and in its extra-ordinary forms, it also offers them a route, sometimes the only one, to upward social mobility" (66, fn. 13).

Like the marginalizing placement of this statement in a footnote, Bourdieu wrote a longer treatise on love in a postscript, placing it in a liminal position between the body of the text and the conclusions. In a rupture from the overall text which had argued for the ubiquity of masculine domination, Bourdieu proposed in the "Postscript on Domination and Love" that "pure love" offered the possibility of freedom from state consecrations of masculine domination. Whereas he most often characterized reflexive sociological knowledge as the path to freedom of consciousness, in this essay Bourdieu positioned pure love in that role. After having written a book that underscored the symbolic domination of women and explained this in historical and sociological terms, a domination that he believed was for the most part misrecognized in contemporary society, Bourdieu chose to break with the sociological analysis and offer an almost mystical solution. Borrowing Virginia Woolf's concept of the "pleasure of disillusioning," which he added was "no doubt one of the satisfactions surreptitiously pursued by sociology" (109), Bourdieu noted in a footnote that "violently negative reactions aroused by sociology" can be attributed to the sociologist's "lucid vision" (109)

In this postscript on love, however, Bourdieu distanced himself from sociology and science, and perhaps from his own complicity in masculine domination that was implied by his sociological analysis, by evoking the mystical union of two selves through love as a way out of domination. Although Bourdieu did not, in typical fashion, cite antecedents to his thinking about love, this discussion recalls some of Max Weber's writings on brotherly love as opposed to both erotic and marital love (see Bellah 1999 and Bologh 1990 for interpretations of Weber on these topics). Bellah quotes Weber as having written that the lover "knows himself to be freed from the cold skeleton hands of rational orders, just as completely as from the banality of everyday routine," and suggests that in his theory of religion, Weber posited love as a "sacrament" or form of salvation that could obviate the disenchantment of the modern world. For Weber, "brotherly love" was the form of social association common in traditional societies and we can see the influence of Weber on Bourdieu's analyses of Kabyle honor that draw from that idea. Bourdieu's emphasis on love here also must be viewed in the context of contemporary feminist writings on the subject that see "love" as an alternative to masculinist rational thinking, particularly in the work of the French feminist philosopher Luce Irigaray (2001). The African-American feminist bell hooks (1999) recently has written a treatise on the possibilities of love as the basis of a new societal ethics. Wendy Langford (1999) identified an emerging field of the "democratization of love" in the work of Giddens (1992), Luhman (1986), and others. This is the notion that a form of pure love in the private sphere will effect a more democratic public sphere. In the current climate of neoliberalism, many scholars—about whom Herzfeld could write in the mid-1990s "shunned the state as a hostile and invasive presence in local social life" (1997: 1)—are increasingly looking toward ways of rehabilitating the state's role in protecting its citizens from new forms of global capitalism. These recent writings on "love" appear to point toward a refashioning of what Herzfeld labeled "cultural intimacy"—an aspect of national cultural identity that draws on metaphors of family feelings of love coexisting with knowledge of the fissures among and failures of various members. It is connected to a "structural nostalgia" about a time when things were better and there was more harmony. Scholarly appeals to love as a solution to current problems represent an appeal to intimacy and a look toward the private sphere as the locus of salvation from the excesses of a public sphere that has lost its moral sense. Bourdieu's discussion of love in *Masculine Domination,* and his critique of neoliberalism that I discuss more in the next chapter, draw upon these metaphors of family feeling and love as a possible solution to problems of inequality (based on gender as well as class) in contemporary society.

Bourdieu posed the question: "Is love an exception, the only one, but of the first order of magnitude, to the law of masculine domination, a suspension of symbolic violence, or is it the supreme—because the most subtle, the most invisible—form of that violence?" (109). He noted that, in the case of traditional Kabyle or Béarn societies, love was *amor fati* (social destiny) and thus constituted a "domination accepted, unrecognized as such and practically recognized, in happy or unhappy passion" (109). He distinguished this type of love from more recent forms, in line with forebearers Weber and Simmel, who also linked romantic love with modernity. Bourdieu also suggested, however, that love can overtake men, causing them to "forget the obligations linked to their social dignity" (here, one assumes he is referring to honor), and that a "suspension of power relations" can thus be "constitutive of the experience of love or friendship" (110). He suggested that "pure love," is a more recent invention, that is rarely found but does exist. It is, he cautioned, extremely fragile, and "endlessly threatened by the crisis induced by the return of egoistic calculation" (111). Furthermore, he wrote, its existence as an ideal and its place in literary traditions can be understood because this "pure love" offers a possibility of the suspension of the struggle for symbolic power, and "can lead, in its perfect reflexivity, beyond the alternatives of egoism and altruism, and even beyond the distinction between subject and object, to the state of fusion and communion, often evoked in metaphors close to those of mysticism, in which two beings can 'lose themselves in each other' without being lost" (111). He concluded that this ideal could potentially rival the "consecrations" of the state, which have become the "secular substitute for God" (112). Here he is alluding to the "rites of institution" that create the family as a "realized category" (with all the accompanying sentiments) that I discussed earlier.

In this treatise on the possibilities of freedom through love, Bourdieu reveals a mysticism that coexisted with his "rationality" and shows him to be a complex product of his times. One is tempted to sum up this postscript with the Beatles' refrain of "All you need is love!" On first reading this essay, I was at a loss to reconcile it with his other writings on emotion and dispositions as socially constructed and intricately connected to power and domination. One explanation is that Bourdieu anticipated the criticisms that his book would arouse, and wanted to temper the bleak assessment of masculine domination and women's submission with a note of optimism. His own implication in the androcentric system he described offers another explanation, however. Whereas he used his background in peasant France to his own advantage in discussions of French education and in analyses of Kabyle society, showing that he had a somewhat privileged "inside" view, it was more difficult for him to make use of that in the case of masculine domination. He positioned both Béarn and Kabylia as andocentric societies in *Masculine Domination,* and his own primary habitus was the product of one of these (with his secondary habitus also implicated). He used an example of masculine domination from his childhood memories in Béarn, through which he also tried to distance himself by explaining that these were "buried memories," of men playing cards all afternoon while women did the labor of processing the pig after a ritual pig-killing (30–31). The limits of Bourdieu's reflexive methodology are on display here as he came up against a situation in which his sociological approach would implicate him in masculine domination; he turned to a mystical discussion of love in order to (cunningly) deflect this.

Another more sympathetic reading, however, suggests that as Bourdieu was becoming increasingly engaged as a public intellectual and proponent of new forms of collectivity to battle social ills (such as masculine domination and neoliberalism) in society, he began to reject a wholly rational approach to these problems. As evident in the recent interest in love among social theorists,[18] whose potential is not perhaps yet fully realized at the time of this writing because so recent, Bourdieu's arguments can be seen as being on the verge of new understandings of collectivity and social relationships based not solely on struggle and domination but also on a form of *communitas.* His call for a social Europe (1999a), which would foster collective struggle across national boundaries against domination, reflects that impulse. *Pascalian Meditations,* a critique of scholastic reason, also, perhaps, was pointing in that direction.

THE VILLAGE DANCE AND THE "NATIVE ANTHROPOLOGIST"

Although not explicitly dealing with emotion, Bourdieu's early article on bachelors in Lesquire (1962c), reprinted in *Le bal des célibataires,* contains his most emotionally evocative writing, embedded in an "objective" account of the social production of bachelors that drew on statistical research as well as interviews. Bourdieu took the village dance at Christmastime, which he described ethnographically, as a focal point with which to express the condition of bachelorhood. Bourdieu remarked over three decades after undertaking this research:

> I can say that I spent nearly twenty years trying to understand why I chose that village ball. . . . I even believe—this is something that I would never have dared say even ten years ago—that the feeling of sympathy (in the strongest sense of the term) that I felt then and the sense of pathos that exuded from the scene I witnessed were surely at the root of my interest in this object. (Bourdieu and Wacquant 1992: 164)

The dance was a setting in which Bourdieu was native and outsider, objective and subjective observer. The article does not, however, state that this is Bourdieu's natal region, and an uninformed reader would not know this. He wrote (2002a: 11) that this "return to origins was accompanied by a controlled return of the repressed" for him, adding that the text bears no traces of this, however. The stance of distance and seeming objectivity toward this material, with which he was so intimately familiar, was deliberate. As Bourdieu explained, "the point of departure of this research is a very personal experience that I recounted in the article, but in a veiled form, because at the time I felt compelled to "disappear"' (Bourdieu and Wacquant 1992: 162).

Bourdieu cast the analysis within the context of short narratives about marriage and bachelorhood told by married and unmarried men, mostly translated from the local dialect, that he collected in the field. His facility with the local dialect in his Béarn ethnography was obvious from the amount of material collected in the dialect during interviews. At the same time that Bourdieu provided a statistical and "objective' analysis of the marriage system in which the males of Lesquire are a part, he called on subjective material on the emotions and attitudes of both married and unmarried men to explain the high rate of bachelorhood. He also provided a 'thick description" of the ethnographic setting of various dances in Lesquire. The Christmastime dance, in particular, was emblematic of the dilemma faced by the bachelors. For Bourdieu, it was not the movements of the dance per se that were of interest but the entire social setting and cast of characters involved who attend the dance and participate in different ways depending on their gender, age, and social position. He used this setting of the dance to describe a situation arising from socioeconomic change and modernization.[19]

Bourdieu explained that men from isolated hamlets were particular candidates for remaining in an unmarried state. He evoked the habitus, the evolving concept in his theoretical corpus at that period linked to symbolic domination, in the context of the village dance to describe the bodily techniques of these confirmed bachelors. Because of gender segregation in the community, chances for young males and females to socialize together were limited, and the dances permitted a rare occasion for social mixing.[20] The structural position of these bachelors made it difficult for them to marry, but the bachelors themselves embodied ways of moving and dressing and acting that made it difficult for them to attract a wife. They were clumsy in their movements, Bourdieu wrote, and their clothing was in outdated styles. They didn't really know how to dance or to talk to girls. The bachelors had a way of dressing, a way of moving, a way of drinking, a way of singing, and so on that was part of their bodily hexis, or "habitus." These were *paysans empaysannés*. He wrote:

> This is not the place to analyze the motor habits particular to the Béarnaise peasant, this habitus, which reveals the backward peasant, the lumbering peasant. The folk observation perfectly captures this hexis which fuels the stereotypes: "The peasant of olden times," remarked an elderly villager, "always walked with his legs curved in an arc, as if he were knock-kneed, with his arms bent backwards." (2002a: 114–15)

At this period of the early 1960s, Bourdieu had not yet articulated a theory of habitus that saw it as the generating structure of the structure, or as a set of dispositions that created various limits to strategies (cf. Bourdieu 1977a and 1990a). He was focused on the bodily habitus. We can see here, however, the interest in what he labeled "bodily emotions" in relationship to domination.

Bourdieu first set the scene of the dance, which took place in the backroom of a café. There were smartly dressed couples, dancing to popular tunes. There also were some unmarried girls and boys there. Bourdieu's style of writing is distant, clinical, avoiding the "I" (as he later pointed out himself); and yet, it can't help but convey the emotional reaction he had to this scene. He later wrote that the only evidence of the "emotional atmosphere" in which he conducted that research was the "nonstop tenderness of the description of the dance" (2002a: 11). The picture he painted is bleak, conveyed through terms like "somber mass." He wrote:

> Behind, on the margins of the dance floor, gathers a somber mass, a group of men who are older, who look on, without speaking: all at least 30 years old, they wear a beret and a dark suit, of outdated style. Almost as if tempted to dance, they come forward, taking some of the space of the dancers. They are there, all the bachelors. The men of their age who are already married no longer attend the dances. (2002a: 111)

We can see in the passage the internalized body image and ways of moving associated with this habitus, in turn associated with traditional forms of behavior confronting emerging "modern" ways of operating that have been adopted by other youth in the community. Bourdieu briefly described other dances where the entire community came either to dance or to gossip about possible marriages. This dance, however, was a dance primarily for the youth, and he wrote, "At the dances like this one at Christmastime or New Year's, the bachelors have nothing to do. Those are the dances for the youth; that is to say, those who aren't yet married. They aren't yet old, but they know they are unmarriageable. These are the dances to which one goes to dance; yet they don't dance" (112). Occasionally a young girl would ask one of these bachelors to dance just to be polite, and they would reveal their heaviness and clumsiness as they danced with the girls. As the night grew later, Bourdieu wrote, "they stay there, until midnight, barely speaking, in the light and noise of the dance, gazing at the inaccessible girls. Then they will go into the bar and drink face to face. They will sing together the old béarnaise tunes . . . and, by twos or threes, they will slowly take their leave, at the end of the evening, toward their isolated farms" (112). His remark that they sit "face to face" alludes to the sentiment of honor expressed through "frontality" among traditional Béarnais men that Bourdieu felt was an important part of their habitus, as also among the Kabyle peasant men. Bourdieu described the bachelors in such a way that the reader may see them as pathetic or sad figures, yet he also expressed their sense of dignity with this description. His writing about the dance conveys a sense of intimacy, emotion, and sympathy for the participants, despite his attempts to adopt a tone of "objectivity," which was so often masked in his theoretical and sociological writings. As a result, his writing about the dance evokes emotion among the reader.

FIELDWORK AND EMOTION

Bourdieu has mentioned his own emotions in the context of his research in both Béarn and Algeria numerous times, mostly in brief comments, and mostly starting in the 1980s. In his preface to the *Logic of Practice*, where he traced some of the background to his approach, Bourdieu looked back on his early Algerian research during the war and its aftermath, and noted the "emotional context" in which he was trying to "to work towards a scientific analysis of Algerian society" (1990a: 2). Despite his criticisms of structuralism, Bourdieu also wrote of the "emotional impact" for him of Lévi-Strauss's analyses of Native American mythologies that avoided ethnocentrism and looked for the internal logic of thought. In an interview with Franz Schultheis about his photos of Algeria, Bourdieu said that he took the photos as a way to distance himself from the suffering and his own emotional reactions to that: "I was at once very upset, very sensitive to the suffering that I observed, and at the same time there was also the distance of the observer, that expressed itself through the fact of taking photos" (2003a: 29). He spoke of talking to people who had lost so much, and who told him of what they'd lost, and he felt not up to the task of being able to comprehend all that he was observing. He was "submerged," he said, and "the photo, that was it, a way of trying to deal with the shock of a crushing reality" (31)

There have been several approaches to the best way to handle the public and private aspects of ethnographic fieldwork.[21] The most common way historically was to segregate these into two genres of writing—the anthropological monograph (the public, scientific product), and the fieldwork account in the form of a diary, novel, or memoir (the more private and humanistic product). Bourdieu (2003a: 32) mentioned in the context of the publication of his photos of Algeria that he wished he had kept a journal during fieldwork in Algeria, in order to find again some of his first impressions and feelings. Starting during the 1980s, Bourdieu increasingly began to relate his personal experiences of fieldwork in the published interview (dialogue) genre, which is more common in Europe than in the United States, while maintaining a more scientific and "objective" writing style in his ethnological and sociological writings. One example of this is his interview with Honneth et al. in the essay "Fieldwork in Philosophy" appearing in the book *In Other Words* (1990b), and another his 2001 interview with Franz Schultheis mentioned earlier. This genre of the interview or dialogue also was adopted by Bourdieu and Wacquant in their text (1992) on his work. Thus, we learn about Bourdieu's emotional and personal reactions to doing fieldwork in Béarn, for example, not in his published scholarly work but through the interviews he did many years later and in his later reflexive writings. Increasingly since the 1970s, previously marginalized forms of incorporating both into the same text have become much more common in ethnographic writing. We can see this in Bourdieu's own work, as he came increasingly to incorporate personal reflections in his theoretical or sociological writings beginning in the late 1990s, especially, as we have seen, in the cases of *Pascalian Meditations, Science de la science et réflexivité,* and *Esquisse pour une auto-analyse.*

The entire discussion about public and private aspects of fieldwork depends on notions of the self and the individual, the public and the private, that are Western notions and are a product of particular histories and of particular forms of state control that Bourdieu has illuminated in several texts (1982b; 1994c), even though he has never drawn a connection between this and the debates over ethnographic writing. The sociologist Carolyn Ellis's work represents one end of a continuum of reflexive approaches that is at the opposite end from Bourdieu's place on that continuum. Ellis (1991: 126–7) has drawn attention to the posture of marginality and distance adopted by ethnographers, and to the admonition against "going native" or distorting one's research through one's own emotions, that accompanies this.[22] Her response has been to embrace emotion, and she advocates an "autoethnography" that is unapologetically about the self of the researcher (Ellis 2003), and an "emotional sociology" that entails "consciously and reflectively feeling for our selves, our subjects, and our topics of study, and evoking those feelings in our readers" (1991: 126). Ellis suggests that ethnographers need to convey the emotions of "lived experience." Her approach assumes a shared emotional language of feeling between ethnographer and informants, which Bourdieu would have rejected. He most often rejected the notion of empathy, because of its associations with the "scholastic fallacy."

Ruth Behar's (1996) evocative writing as a "vulnerable observer," and advocacy of an "anthropology that breaks your heart" also represents forms of reflexivity that make their autobiographical and emotional intentions more explicit than can be found in Bourdieu's writings. That Behar and Ellis are female ethnographers may be a factor in their approach, as Bourdieu had much company among male ethnographers, who have been uncomfortable with autobiographical writing about fieldwork that is considered "confessional." Bourdieu repeatedly criticized what he labeled narcissism in anthropology, and distanced his own form of reflexivity from that genre of writing. Dumont (1992) expressed similar efforts to distance *The Headman and I* from accusations of narcissism. Susan Carol Rogers (2001: 497) has observed that autobiographical reflection has been resisted by French anthropologists, who have associated it with "Anglo-American 'postmodern' anthropology." Exceptions to that, however, can be seen in Jeanne Favret-Saada's (1980 [1977]) reflections on fieldwork on witchcraft in western France, and Florence Weber's (1989) self-reflective discussion of fieldwork as "*être avec.*"

Judith Okely (1992) notes a strong resistance to reflexivity or autobiography, particularly in British social anthropology, and counters that reflexivity does not have to be narcissistic. She writes that "the autobiography of fieldwork is about lived interactions, participatory experience and embodied knowledge; those aspects ethnographers have not fully theorized" (3). Her insightful comment that "hesitations about incorporating and expanding the idea of autobiography into anthropology rest on very Western, ethnocentric traditions" (5), and her observation that insertions of personal narrative are often occasions for apology in ethnographic writing, are quite helpful in understanding Bourdieu's relationship to reflexivity. Okely notes that anthropological reactions to autobiography are connected to Western ideas of autobiography that prefer to keep separate a public self presented in the autobiographical narrative and a more private self that is kept hidden, as well as a view of "confession" as indiscrete and salacious. One could see *Tristes Tropiques* as an example of the classic genre of auto-biographical writing that presents a public persona for the author, espe-cially the chapter on "The Making of an Anthropologist."

Bourdieu never incorporated his own theoretical contributions with the concepts of habitus and dispositions, and embodied thoughts and feel-ings, into his reflections on ethnographic research. Two other anthropolo-gists have, however, drawn on his work in this way. Jon Mitchell (1997) employed Bourdieu's concept of habitus to suggest that an "anthropology of feeling" can incorporate cognition and emotion without a mind/body dualism. In relating a religious experience he had during fieldwork in Malta, he discusses his informants and his own reactions, and argues that, while "feelings" may be physiologically similar across cultures, the explanations given for them will differ. Using a concept of social memory, Mitchell writes that ethnographers acquire memories during fieldwork and convey these memories of their informants when they write. He suggests that emotional knowledge and memory should be recognized as part of ethnographic re-search. Mitchell's work draws on concepts of embodiment, which have increasingly captured the attention of anthropologists during the past two decades, in part influenced by the concept of habitus in Bourdieu's work. Much of that work is in the area of ritual and religion.

In an earlier study, Michael Jackson (1983) criticized the mind and body split in anthropological approaches in an article on initiation ritual among the Kuranko in Sierra Leone, arguing that a semiotics of the body had dominated research on it. By wanting to get away from linguistic em-phases that see the body as passive, as a sign or vehicle for expression, Jack-son proposes a focus on bodily movement and body praxis. Jackson drew on Bourdieu's concept of body praxis and habitus in his analysis, but in ways that take Bourdieu's initial ideas into the practices of the ethnogra-pher him or herself. Although not focusing on feeling or emotion per se, but on the commonsense movements of the body, Jackson suggests that fieldworkers best understand bodily praxis through their own adoption of routine bodily habits in the field. He writes "to participate bodily in every-day practical tasks was a creative technique which often helped me grasp the sense of an activity by using my body as others did" (1983: 340).

Bourdieu's concept of habitus, especially in the more recent versions (2000b; 2002d) that deal with ethnicity, gender, and linguistic domination as well as with social class, points toward a powerful rethinking of the cul-ture concept as either "in the mind" or exterior to the individual. It deals with embodiment, emotion, and feeling—issues that the concept of cul-ture has not always incorporated, and that have not always been recognized as an integral part of what anthropologists might study. Despite Bourdieu's concern with embodiment in his theory of habitus, he depended primarily on verbal productions and language use in his own research strategies, and did little observation of bodily practices after his early ethnographic work in rural France and Algeria. Nevertheless, his concepts of habitus and disposition challenge us to further develop the implications of emotion in social practice and cultural production.

FIVE

Situated Subjectivities

> Narratives about the most 'personal' difficulties, the apparently
> most strictly subjective tensions and contradictions, frequently
> articulate the deepest structures of the social world
> and its contradictions.
> —*The Weight of the World* (1999)

Bourdieu did not use conventional (at least in British and American circles) anthropological methods of conducting "fieldwork" that involve immersion in a particular locale (or "community") for long periods of time, methods that frequently are used to uncover cultural distinctiveness. He did some ethnographic observations in his work, but mostly used open-ended or semi-structured interviews, with a goal of uncovering universally valid principles such as the operation of the habitus, with an emphasis on social class, rather than "cultural" differences. In front of an audience in Japan, Bourdieu spoke derisively of "the lover of exoticism who gives priority to picturesque differences" (1998c: 2). He continued in that lecture to say that by seeking universal validity "it is possible to register the real differences that separate both structures and dispositions (the habitus), the principle of which must be sought not in the peculiarities of some national character—or 'soul'—but in the particularities of different *collective histories*" (3). These remarks were partly in defense of criticisms that his analysis in *Distinction* was only applicable to the French, and also in defense of misreadings of his book that characterized what he was trying to do as analyzing the ways in which people "distinguish" themselves. They also, however, reveal his emphasis on universal principles, rather than cultural difference, which he believed was an artifact of particular fields of power. These comments, furthermore, reinforce his stance toward identity and the person, his rejection of the notion of the autonomous individual and view of the individual as habitus.

Bourdieu's theoretical ideas were linked to political stances that he took, and his use of personal narrative as a research methodology was, in part, connected to politics as much as to theory—in fact, he would argue that these were inseparable. In *Homo Academicus,* he wrote that "it is not, as is usually thought, political stances that separate people's stances on things academic, but their positions in the academic field which inform the stances that they adopt on political issues in general as well as on academic problems" (1988b: xviii). Although a prominent theme in his early work on economic transitions in Algeria, Bourdieu's critique of capitalism, and its construction of rational individuals, was very much at the heart of his more recent collaborative work published in *The Weight of the World*. A critique of neoliberalism and its consequences, this book used personal narratives elicited in interview material to demonstrate the social suffering caused. Bourdieu labeled some of the interviewees as "practical analysts" who are situated at points of contradiction in structures, and who thereby, in order to "survive," develop a form of "self-analysis, which often gives them access to the objective contradictions which have them in their grasp, and to the objective structures expressed in and by these contradictions" (1999: 511).

Bourdieu's use of interviews, which included extended personal narratives and life history narratives, goes back as far as his earliest research in Béarn and Algeria during the late 1950s and early 1960s. *Travail et travailleurs en Algérie* contains extended first-person narratives of displaced workers that are included in several appendices, with extracts used in the main body of the analysis. The long article "Célibat et condition paysanne" (1962c) also contains several interviews and some longer narratives included in appendices. Bourdieu treated these texts as what I would call autoethnographies—commentaries and analysis by informants on their own sociocultural milieus. Jane Goodman (2003) has usefully drawn attention to Bourdieu's differential representations of traditional and modernizing Algeria though his uses of proverbs and interviews. He used proverbs in *Outline* to portray Kabyle "traditional" society but extended interviews in research on labor and social dislocation among Algerian workers. In his work on Béarn, it also should be noted, he integrated both types of speech in the same articles. Following Goodman's observation, I suggest that proverbs in Bourdieu's work stand for the timeless element of shared *doxa* in a traditional society, even when they sometimes offer alternative views to dominant meanings; the interviews conducted by Bourdieu reveal the subjective experiences of persons in times of change, what he called *hysteresis*, when there is no longer a harmony between habitus and structure.

The Bourdieu who used first-person narratives in his work is the same person who wrote in *Outline* that "native theories are dangerous," and it is useful to recall his original arguments in that book before proceeding. I quote him at length on this topic:

> Invited by the anthropologist's questioning to effect a reflexive and quasi-theoretical return on to his own practice, the best-informed informant produces a *discourse which compounds two opposing systems of lacunae*. Insofar as it is a *discourse of familiarity*, it leaves unsaid all that goes without saying. . . . Insofar as it is an *outsider-oriented*

discourse it tends to exclude all direct reference to particular cases. . . . Because the native is that much less inclined to slip into the language of familiarity to the extent that his questioner strikes him as unfamiliar with the universe of reference implied by his discourse (a fact apparent from the questions asked, particular or general, ignorant or informed), it is understandable that anthropologists should so often forget the distance between learned reconstruction of the native world and the native experience of the world, an experience which finds expression only in the silences, ellipses, and lacunae of the language of familiarity. . . . Finally, the informant's discourse owes its best-hidden properties to the fact that it is the product of a semitheoretical disposition, inevitably induced by any learned questioning. . . . The subtlest pitfall doubtless lies in the fact that such descriptions freely draw on the highly ambiguous vocabulary of *rules,* the language of grammar, morality, and law, to express a social practice that in fact obeys quite different principles. (1977a: 18)

Bourdieu was saying that informants produce a discourse for the anthropologist that cannot be taken at face value, and which may mislead the anthropologist into believing that the people follow rules in their behavior. His point was that native theories are not always "experience-near" concepts, to use Geertz's terms, and can reflect discourses that take a quasitheoretical perspective, but not one that accurately conveys the objective conditions—which, in Bourdieu's thinking, are often veiled from the social agent. I have always balked, however, at what I consider to be this statement's somewhat unfair criticisms of ethnography and have felt that it only represented what would be *bad* anthropology, not what "good" ethnographers do. Certainly my own assumptions are that intensive fieldwork permits a certain familiarity with the discourse and behavior of informants; questions would not be directly posed until that familiarity had been established.

I have, therefore, wondered what Bourdieu would propose as the "ideal" model, which he did not put forth in *Outline* specifically, and by interrogating his own methods of interviewing and use of interview narratives, one can do that. The ways in which Bourdieu dealt with subjective perspectives in his framework of practical logic and theoretical logic is the subject of this final chapter. Although Bourdieu often seemed to accord little validity to the subjective understandings of social agents, for whom their dispositions are in a preconscious habitus, his uses of personal narrative hint at an approach that allowed for some people who were not trained sociologists to have access to understandings that went beyond the *doxa*. This is evident in *The Weight of the World, Travail et travailleurs,* and the work on marriage and inheritance strategies in Béarn, as well as in Bourdieu's use of "schooling narratives" drawn from personal narrative and obituaries as life narratives in *Homo Academicus* and *The State Nobility.*

Bourdieu's work on personal narrative lies at the intersection of two opposing trends to which he had to respond: that of the statistical survey methods of a "scientific" sociology in France, and that of the participant-observation methods of anthropology. His approach was not that of "life history," and he was not interested in the linear life trajectory itself but, rather, a more directed method of getting his informants to tell of their experiences prompted by questions that were posed to several people. This enabled him to elicit the subjective understandings of his informants. Bourdieu's use of personal narrative in the late 1950s predated the enormous interest in "biographical methods" in France during the late 1970s, spearheaded by Daniel Bertaux and his colleagues (Bertaux 1981; Bertaux and Kohli 1984) in sociology and Philippe LeJeune (1989) in literary criticism. Bertaux (as cited in Peneff 1990: 73) has attributed his own interest in life stories to May '68, which, he claims, turned him from more statistical methods to the methods of life history in order to understand people "on the ground." In their discussion of national trends in life history research, Bertaux and Kohli stress the impact of structuralism upon this methodology in France—because of the influence of "Lévi-Strauss, Althusser, Foucault, Lacan, Poulantzis, and Bourdieu" (1984: 226). They write that "the sociologist's task is to infer from recurrent practices the pattern of sociostructural relationships that are generating or restraining them" (226). The biographical method should aim, they argue, to collect a number of stories in the same milieu and to focus on practices rather than feelings or perceptions. Bourdieu's own approach, which has attempted to depart from structuralism, is, however, closer to this than to traditions of research that emphasize either individuality or typicality in a life story. For Bourdieu, the life narrative reveals the dispositions of the habitus. However, unlike Bertaux, he took perceptions and feelings or emotions into account in his work, because these are integral to his concepts of habitus and dispositions, and he did not focus exclusively on practices or behaviors, as Bertaux advocated.

Bourdieu viewed individual lives as taking place within social and physical spaces that are connected to cultural and symbolic capital. He interpreted personal narratives within this framework. In *The Rules of Art,* Bourdieu wrote:

> The dispositions associated with a certain social origin cannot be fulfilled unless they are responsive in the shape they take to, on the one hand, the structure of possibilities opened up by the different positions and position-takings of their occupants, and, on the other hand, to the position occupied in the field, which (through the attitude to this position as a feeling of success or failure, itself linked to dispositions, and hence to trajectory) governs the way these possibilities are perceived and appreciated . . . any habitus, as a system of dispositions, is only effectively realized in relation to the determinate structure of socially marked positions. (1996c: 264–5)

In addition to his concepts of habitus and disposition, Bourdieu increasingly relied on the concept of *champ* or field (to denote particular arenas of social space) from the 1980s on, and he also introduced a focus on physical space (through the concept of *lieu* or location), during his work in the project *The Weight of the World*. These concepts provide ways of talking about "structure" in his later work and a discussion of them now is necessary before proceeding to the specifics of his uses of narrative.

CHAMP/FIELD

The French word *champ* is translated as "field," but in the context of this discussion of ethnography I also want to point out that another word is used for field in terms of ethnographic fieldwork—*terrain*. Therefore, the term "fieldwork" which, as Gupta and Ferguson (1997: 8) suggest, has agrarian and pastoral connotations in English, does not have the same meanings in French (*enquête de terrain*). The two words *champ* and *terrain* are closely linked in French, but are both used in different senses for things that are all called "field" in English. Anthropologists in France do not literally speak of going "to the field" but on the ground (*sur le terrain*). The word *champ* is one used for agricultural fields (as in *champ de blé*, or wheat field), and for battlefields. *Champ* is also the word used for the concept in physics of a field of forces. *Terrain* connotes more a sense of being "on the ground," or "on location," and is associated with an expression of "being on familiar ground." *Terrain* is also the word that is used to describe a sports field (*terrain de sport*), playground, or an airfield. Both words refer primarily to physical places, and to areas of land that are in some way cleared, cultivated, or influenced by humans through culture, and would be placed in opposition to land such as a forest. In using this metaphor of *champ* as field, Bourdieu drew on the physics concept of force field in order to characterize a realm of social interaction, which did not necessarily imply physically being in the same place. *Champ* does not have the same connotation of field as in "field of study" in English, at least not prior to Bourdieu's introduction of this notion of various fields of power that include things like academic fields. The French word *discipline* is more often used to discuss what is called a field in English in terms of vocation or career.

In *The Logic of Practice,* Bourdieu used both the concepts of "field" and "habitus" to criticize structuralism through an exploration of the differences between Kabyle society and modern French society. In that text, he can be seen to gradually substitute the term field (associated with what he called "institutions" such as the church or the economy) for structure. For example, he compared the relationship between habitus and field to that between "incorporated history and an objectified history" (1990a: 66). It was in a field, he suggested, that social agents utilize the "feel for the game" or practical sense. He contrasted the field in a game (as "the pitch or board on which [the game] is played, the rules, the outcome at stake, etc.") with the notion of social fields—"the products of a long, slow process of autonomization, and are therefore, so to speak, games 'in themselves' and not 'for themselves,' one does not embark on the game by a conscious act, one is born into the game, with the game" (67). Bourdieu further elaborated on the concept of field in his study of the university or academic field in *Homo Academicus,* and in his work on art—for instance, with the study Flaubert. Bourdieu viewed the field as a concept that was relational rather than "substantialist"—by which he meant an approach that seeks substances or essences in individuals or groups, and which foregrounds the individual. Bourdieu described the field as a:

> field of forces, whose necessity is imposed on agents who are engaged in it, and a field of struggles within which agents confront each other, with differentiated means and ends according to their position in the structure of the field of forces, thus contributing to conserving or transforming its structure. (1998c: 32)

Bourdieu identified various types of fields (literary, artistic, religious, economic, academic) and also a "field of power" that refers to situations in which people with a lot of cultural capital are able to dominate in a field. In his later writings, Bourdieu suggested that domination did not occur through direct coercion by a set of agents who could be clearly identified as a dominant class but, rather, indirectly through the actions of the dominant in fields of power.

LIEU/LOCATION OR PLACE

Bourdieu introduced the concept of *lieu* in the *The Weight of the World,* in order to describe physical location as well as location in a more abstract social field or field of power. He had already used a notion of social space (*éspace social*) to talk about social positions and position-taking, with both a geographical or physical connotation and a social connotation that did not require physical proximity (although he said they often go hand in hand) in the book *Distinction.* Whereas the translator of *The Weight of the World* has chosen the term "site" for *lieu,* I would characterize *lieu* more as a term denoting "location." The word literally means "place" in France, and is used both with the rhetorical phrase "in the place of" (*au lieu de*) having to do with ideas and in concrete physical places, such as *lieu-dit,* which is a generic term for a colloquial name for a place (like "four corners"). In Marc Augé's work on "*non-lieux,*"[1] the English translation was "nonplaces."

Bourdieu's thinking about location is similar to Geertz's famous quote that "anthropologists don't study villages . . . they study *in* villages," but he took this even further to emphasize the point that "there are compelling reasons to believe that the essential principle of what is lived and seen on the ground [*sur le terrain* in the original French version]—the most striking testimony and the most dramatic experiences—is elsewhere" (Bourdieu et al. 1999b: 123; 1993c: 249). In *The Weight of the World,* Bourdieu characterized American ghettos as an example of this, suggesting that they are defined in terms of "absences" of various basic social services like health care. Noting that humans have bodies and, like other material things, occupy space, Bourdieu defined *lieu* as "the point in physical space where an agent or a thing is situated, 'takes place,' exists; that is to say, either as a localization or, from a relational viewpoint, as a position, a rank in an order" (1999b: 123). The term location or *lieu* thus refers to both social and physical location, and Bourdieu saw both as organized through hierarchy, with any particular location being either higher or lower than another. Physical location comes to express social location because individuals with a lot of symbolic and cultural capital are able to dominate and define the most prestigious locations. He wrote that "the power over space . . . comes from possessing various kinds of capital" (124), so that where you live and where you shop become reified expressions of your cultural capital. Bourdieu also suggested that social space is inscribed in mental as well as spatial structures, and this is how physical space becomes a site for the assertion of power and of symbolic violence. Capital allows those who have it to keep their distance from undesirable people and things, and to get close to desirable people, places, and things. Bourdieu wrote that "the lack of capital intensifies the experience of finitude; it chains one to a place" (127). Struggles for power over space can take individual or collective forms. Individuals can be spatially mobile, which can either be a move up in social space or a move down. Individuals also make spatial choices in terms of avoiding feeling "out of place," as in a person in a museum who is not used to visiting museums. Collective struggles take place through housing policies or land valuations.[2]

SCHOOLING STORIES/CAREER STORIES

Bourdieu examined personal narratives of education in both *Homo Academicus* and *The State Nobility,* in order to convey subjective experiences and modes of narration of educational experiences. In *Homo Academicus,* which was a study of the social field of academic power and the positions in that field held and taken by various scholars, Bourdieu distinguished between "individuals" and "agents." He used the example of Claude Lévi-Strauss to illustrate this, seeking to distinguish between the scientific use of the name Lévi-Strauss as a signifier of a position in social and physical space, and "the proper name which we use in daily life to designate the author of *Tristes Tropiques*" (1988: 22). He also referred to this as the "epistemic" versus "doxic" Lévi-Strauss; the "social agent" versus the "individual." In the book, Bourdieu was interested primarily in the former term in each of these pairs, the epistemic position-holder and position-taker, who was "defined by the position which he occupied in the space which his properties have helped to construct (and which also partly helps to define it)" (23).[3] Much as he had analyzed the position and point of view of Flaubert in the field of nineteenth-century art, he did so for French academics.

In a section of *Homo Academicus* titled "Consecrated Heretics," Bourdieu drew from a very brief personal narrative by Lévi-Strauss about his career trajectory, which had appeared in the newspaper *Libération*. Lévi-Strauss provided an example to him of a marginal career trajectory, and his brief narrative mentioned his preference for research over teaching. At the time Bourdieu was doing this research, Lévi-Strauss was among the most prestigious and influential intellectuals in France, and his preference underscored the value system that privileged research above teaching. In his remarks, Lévi-Strauss underscored the unconventional nature of his career, much of it developed abroad, a "switchback academic career whose most striking characteristic was no doubt that it was accomplished outside the university system properly speaking" (Lévi-Strauss, quoted in 1988: 108). Bourdieu takes this narrative as evidence of the different trajectories that can be followed to academic prestige, some more conventional than others. He felt that those with a disposition that permitted them to take more risks and gamble with their careers did so from positions of "objective security." He used personal statements such as that of Lévi-Strauss not to highlight the unique qualities of an individual and his or her career but to show the social pattern it displayed.

Bourdieu also used educational narratives and drew from autobiography in his study of the rituals of apprenticeship and initiation in the preparatory classes for the Grandes Écoles, especially the ENS, in *The State Nobility*. He used Alain Peyrefitte's (1963) collection of student recollections from this institution to illustrate the subjective experience involved in the attachment to it that various "rites of institution" entailed. He also drew on Paul Nizan's autobiography *Aden arabie*, which he mentioned elsewhere (2000a: 34) was a book that personally struck a chord with him as Nizan related his own experiences as a *normalien*. Although not interjecting his own personal narratives of education in *The State Nobility*, Bourdieu turned to those of others in order to convey his own experiences. He used the collective histories of *normaliens* to make a point about shared experiences and the shared ethos of the corps.

In drawing on first-person accounts of these educational experiences, Bourdieu made use of subjective experience and seemed to feel that it was more valuable in some instances than objective accounts. He wrote that "the more or less autobiographical narratives of writers from the dominated regions of social and geographical space constitute incomparable sociological documents as first-hand accounts of the subjective experiences related to these social trajectories (and not of the corresponding "realities") that are in fact more reliable, being more naïve, than we think" (1996a: 408, fn. 14). Bourdieu was referring here to people who were transplants from rural life and had written about it, like regional novelists or ethnographers (and here he may have been referring to himself). He said that in writing about their experiences, "they pay the price of integration by giving away the game" (1996a: 108), meaning that their reflections on their experiences keep them in a marginal position. Bourdieu was articulating a view here that subordinate peoples (or those from marginal backgrounds) may be keen observers of structures of power, a view that shows his affinities with some other work on subaltern counterhegemony, such as that of James Scott (1985).

In *Homo Academicus*, Bourdieu included a postscript on "Categories of Professorial Judgment" that dealt with academic rhetoric and its classifications. He analyzed letters of reference and, of interest here, obituaries written by peers as biographical stories revealing frames of judgment and value. These can be called "career stories." He took these from the alumni yearbook of the ENS, his own alma mater and one of the Grandes Écoles that were the subject of *The State Nobility*. Some of the same material is also included, with a slightly updated analysis, in *The State Nobility*. Bourdieu's methodology here was not too different from what he used in *Distinction*, when he analyzed job advertisements in order to get at bourgeois values. The approach in the obituaries was one of biography rather than autobiography or personal narrative, but the notices were viewed by Bourdieu as reflecting the sensibilities or habitus of the writer himself—an habitus that would be shared by other former students in the same class and of the same social background. In this work, Bourdieu was closer to the sort of literary analysis he undertook with such writers as Flaubert (1996c; 1988c; 1993a), than to the sociological analysis of interview data in the previous examples. Bourdieu wrote that these obituary notices were "first-rate documents for an analysis of university values. In the last judgement made by the group on one of its deceased members, they still display the principles of classification which determined his assimilation to the group" (1988b: 218). He examined the obituaries of men in the generation born at the turn of the century and included, as was his fashion, the real names of even the most famous alumni, such as Merleau-Ponty, in his corpus. In the obituaries, Bourdieu asserted, the social value assigned to the deceased is defined in terms of the hierarchical field of academic values. Therefore, the type of praise offered and virtues extolled would depend on both the social position of the career trajectory of the person being written about and that of the writer.

The career hierarchy for *normaliens,* as the alumni are called, was based on the level of educational institution (higher was better) where they had been employed and its distance from Paris (closer was better). Within that framework, finer distinctions were made between those who had published and those who had not, what they had published, and so on. There was, thereby, a shared system of moral values among all *normaliens* based on a shared system of classification—which Bourdieu compared to an elementary form of classification (after Durkheim). In *The State Nobility,* Bourdieu called this "the space of possible virtues" (1996a: 47). For those who did not advance to prestigious career positions, the obituaries praise what Bourdieu called "the lesser virtues." He wrote, drawing from the vocabulary used in the obituaries:

> The simple, modest lives, filled with wisdom and inner sincere resignation and dignity, rectitude and devotion, of any of these ordinary teachers who cultivate their garden, go backpacking in the mountains, and care for their children cannot fail to be seen for what they are as soon as they are placed back in the field of possible trajectories. (47–48)

As with much of his work on education, Bourdieu fell back on a more schematic framework of analysis to discuss the dispositions of social agents in that system. The obituaries were not viewed as products of "practical analysts" and the teachers and students in the Grandes Écoles were not interviewed themselves in order to get their point of view on their conditions. Rather, the obituaries were used to show the practical logics of the writers, who applied the system of classification to the lives of their deceased classmates and thereby made more explicit than usual, the system of classifications. Bourdieu described the educational system as one functioning as "an immense cognitive machine," but he did not want to state this was the product of a "state ideological apparatus" or that agents were "off on vacation and hence outside the game" of social reproduction (1996a: 53). The obituaries are highly encoded and almost formulaic, not unlike the proverbs that Bourdieu used in his work on traditional societies. In this way, they exhibit the unquestioned, taken-for-granted *doxa.*

MARRIAGE STORIES

In Bourdieu's two early studies on bachelors in France and displaced workers in Algeria, he used the concept of "spontaneous sociology" in his use of personal narratives. He wanted to take into account the understandings that the social actors themselves had of their situation, and viewed those who were particularly adept as "spontaneous sociologists." For the most part, however, these were not people consciously aware of the contradictions in their lives; rather, they related their own theories to the sociologist who then interpreted this in terms of the objective structures that he could perceive. In his conclusion to the 1962 article on bachelors, Bourdieu started with the quote from an informant that "young girls no longer want to stay in the countryside" and continued:

> The judgments of spontaneous sociology are by nature partial and unilateral. . . . The first task of the sociologist is perhaps to reconstruct the totality in order to discover the unity in the subjective consciousness that the individual has of the social system and the objective structure of this system. The sociologist strives on the one hand to understand the spontaneous consciousness of the social fact, a consciousness that is, by nature not reflected upon, and on the other hand, to understand the fact in its own nature, thanks to the privilege afforded to his situation as an observer who rejects "acting the social" (*agir le social*) for thought. From then on, he must reconcile himself to the truth of the objective facts that his analysis helps him discover and the subjective certitude of those who live it. . . . Sociology is not worth one hour of trouble if its aim is only to discover the strings that move the individuals it observes, if it forgets that it is about men, even if they do, in the way of puppets, play a game in which they are not aware of the rules; in brief, if it does not take as its task to restore to men the meanings of their actions. (1962c: 108–9)

In his analysis of bachelorhood in Lesquire, Bourdieu viewed statements such as that indicating that girls don't want to marry local boys as a signal or cue, but not as the entire explanation for the problem. He also wondered why men were identifying a "problem" with bachelors at that time (late 1950s) when there had always been bachelors in the community, most often the youngest sons. He located the explanation in the traditional structure of the marriage market, something that was common sense to his informants, and the changes in the wider economy that had altered that. Bourdieu included lengthy extracts of life stories he had elicited from bachelors and married men in an earlier generation, when the youngest son frequently stayed unmarried because he could not inherit. Like the schooling and career stories cited above, these could be considered "marriage stories." Bourdieu noted that many of the interviews were originally collected in the Béarnais dialect. When he asked one of the men, who was born in the late 1800s as the youngest son in a family with a small farm, why he never married, he explained that he would have had to find a girl who was going to inherit a farm herself, as he had no hope of getting his family's farm. He had left his family as a young man to work as a farm laborer for a relative of his mother, and when the head of that household died, he stayed on to help the widow and her children. He said, "I have found myself happy like this. I am attached to this household, to the children, to the land of the elders, to the area" (128). Another man, in a similar situation and same age cohort responded "Marriage? There wasn't even a cent. How to marry?" (129), and spoke of working his little plot of land after the war and "spending great evenings with several friends from the area, bachelors like me or those unhappily married" (129). These men, as Bourdieu indicated, seemed resolved and to have accepted their own fate.

It was the younger generation of bachelors that had captured the imagination of the community, because many of them were eldest sons, not younger sons, and this was a rupture with the past. Bourdieu wrote, "The bachelor appears as the strongest sign of a crisis that is affecting the social order. Whereas in the older society, the bachelor was tightly linked to the situation of an individual in the social hierarchy, a reflection itself of the distribution of land, it appears today as linked, above all, to the distribution of geographical space" (59). The oppositions between those in different positions within the family had been replaced by an opposition between urban men and peasants living in hamlets. And the discourse on marriage had changed from that of being resolved to fate, to that of bemoaning the fact that girls won't stay and marry local boys. One man said, "Now the needs of women are larger. It is no longer a question of refusing a marriage on the basis of the dowry alone" (70). Bourdieu did not interview any younger bachelors or women, but relied on interviews with the older bachelors and a couple of younger married men (he indicated the marital statuses and ages of his informants in the text). But he did return many years later to this region to interview two farmer fathers who were of that younger generation, and those interviews were reprinted in *The Weight of the World*. Bourdieu's statistical analysis of marriage patterns provided him with the strongest basis for uncovering the "objective" structures, however, and the few interviews he did conduct provided a "commonsense" view (what he would later call "practical logic") that enabled him to argue that marriage patterns were affected by the perceptions of the social actors—rather than being the function of the rules. In this article, Bourdieu was also beginning to develop concepts of social space and geographic space in the life trajectory that were more clearly articulated in his later work. Men in the city were both spatially and socially "located" in a higher position than peasants from remote hamlets.

LABOR STORIES

Bourdieu's most extensive use of personal narrative was in the collaborative study of Algerian workers, *Travail et travailleurs en Algérie,* in which he conducted ethnographic interviews that complemented the statistical research of colleagues Darbel, Rivet, and Seibel. Here he collected what could be called "labor or work stories." There are appendices at the back of *Travail et travailleurs* that provide transcripts (some lengthy) of interviews with sixty men. The interview questions are not inserted into the narratives, but in some cases indicated generically at the beginning of the appendix. Bourdieu interspersed short excerpts from these interviews into his analyses of the ways in which men from a precapitalist economic system were being inserted into an emerging capitalist economy in Algeria. Questions were posed about employment practices and work histories, relationships with co-workers and employers, and attitudes toward the current economic crisis. Many of the men were unemployed, most were displaced workers, and some were from rural areas while others came from urban areas. Bourdieu described what he did as ethnology, and himself as an ethnologist in the text—and from remarks in the introduction, it appears that this was because he was dealing with what was considered in the terminology of the time an "ethnological" population of non-Western peoples, since the study was also labeled as "sociological" in the title. Bourdieu was sensitive to criticisms about French ethnologists working in Algeria, but defended this. To lend authority to the interviews, he described his methodology and his use of teams of interviewers—one Algerian and one French researcher, which he felt had more chance of success in getting the men interviewed to respond. In this, although he did not explicitly say so in this vocabulary, he seemed to have been controlling for the factors of insider- and outsider-oriented discourses that he warned against in the quote from *Outline* cited earlier in this chapter. With a combination of insider and outsider interviewers, he felt, the speaker's explanations would be more authentic.

Bourdieu noted that he had chosen work as a topic because it was the most visible site of structural contradictions in the colonial system—between traditional models of economy and models "imported and imposed by colonialism," or between "the imperatives of rationalization and cultural traditions" (266). In describing the overall set of interviews and responses to them, Bourdieu noted that some respondents were more "lucid" and "clever" in their responses. He wrote:

> In the course of analyzing these interviews, I had the feeling that the differences between individuals in the same category were due much more to the degree of consciousness that they had about their situation and their ability to explain it, than to the differences objectively inscribed in their comportment and attitudes. (266–7)

Bourdieu was describing a form of autoethnography here practiced by these informants who were able to provide an ethnographic perspective on their condition. The remarks of these individuals, he wrote, could offer in a single image a "more vivid and more clear" picture than "all that the others presented in paintings that were partial and hazy" (267). It is obvious from the transcripts of the interviews that some men gave cryptic and brief responses, while others launched into longer and more elaborate responses.

One informant, to which Bourdieu devoted an entire appendix entitled "The Spontaneous Sociologist," was a cook from Algiers. Bourdieu returned to the narrative of this man in a recent article in which he included excerpts from the original text, with added commentary using the concept of habitus that was absent from *Travail.* In the original text (1963), there is no commentary on this story. In his article called "Making the Economic Habitus: Algerian Workers Revisited" (2000c), Bourdieu wrote about his experiences of hearing stories and anecdotes in the field about economic behavior that made him "feel (*éprouver*) in sensible and concrete fashion the contingent and arbitrary character of these ordinary behaviors that we perform every day" and that the people he was interacting with were experiencing a conversion from the dispositions of a precapitalist economy to that of the "so-called rational" (23) economy the he took so much for granted himself. He wrote that he was able, through both statistical data and his own ethnographic inquiries, to begin to understand his own assumptions about the economy and to understand the "implicit philosophy of labour, based on the equivalency of labour and its remuneration in money" (24) as it was juxtaposed with an economy based on "the gift and counter-gift" among neighbors, which, he noted, had been the system in the late colonial period in Kabylia. Bourdieu wrote that he became aware of his own "quasi-native familiarity" with this economic system as he undertook his research, writing:

> ethnographic inquiry . . . though a kind of methodologically provoked anamnesis, had "awakened" some deeply buried memories of my own country childhood in the Pyrénées mountains—I was often sent, with the exact change counted out into my hand, to the hamlet grocer, who had to be called into his shop by shouting "hoo-hoo" on the threshold of his house. (25)

And Bourdieu continued in the passage to suggest that this memory helped him to see the oddness of monetary payments set up by boys in a private school in England as a sort of insurance policy against canings, something that must have been in the news at the time of his research in Algeria. In this way, he suggests, the rational economic system became "perfectly exotic" (25) for him. I should add here that we can also see in this passage the type of autobiographical narrative that Bourdieu had begun to include in his writings late in his career.

In the second half of the article, Bourdieu turned to the narrative of the Algerian cook who he had called a "spontaneous sociologist" in the earlier 1963 French publication, but now (in English translation) referred to as a "folk economist."[4] Bourdieu argued that this man's narrative was useful in conveying the "practical economic sense" that guided his actions and also served as a biographical document revealing details of the acquisition of an economic habitus as an experience shared collectively among members of that generation. Bourdieu's observations about this man are striking. He wrote:

> this man endowed with barely an elementary education was depicting, in his own words, alternating between French and Berber, the core of what I had been able to discover about the ongoing transformation of social and mental structures wrought by capitalist expansion and colonial war in Algeria, but only by means of a long and arduous effort of data production and deciphering. (28)

It is worth noting in passing about this statement that the mention of the cook speaking French and Berber echoes Bourdieu's work in Béarn where many of the informants spoke to him in French and Béarnais. Bourdieu further remarked that the cook articulated "a universe on which he had been able to adopt a viewpoint at once close-up and distant" (29) and that this had been influenced by his occupational mobility and various positions he had held. He suggested that this point of view was "taken from a point in objective social space at once central—unlike the vast majority of manual workers and clerks, he had seen the world of the Europeans from the inside—and yet marginal, because he had never broken his ties to his companions in misfortune" (29). Issues of distance and familiarity that were part of Bourdieu's own research trajectory and educational experiences were again raised in the context of this cook and his narrative. For Bourdieu, finding the right balance between distance and familiarity was key to sociological understanding. I will not reproduce quotes from the interview here but only note that Bourdieu included segments extracted from the longer text with what he felt were particularly insightful statements poised at the heading of each segment, a device he also used in *The Weight of the World*.

TESTIMONIES

The Weight of the World is a collection of interviews conducted by Bourdieu and colleagues with various people who were connected to forms of social suffering in France—either directly or through roles such as social worker.[5] The French title of this book, *La misère du monde* (literally, "the poverty or malaise of the world"), hints at Fanon's earlier *Les damnés de la terre* (1961; translated as *The Wretched of the Earth*), a book that Bourdieu condemned because of its utopian view of a postcolonial society in Algeria. These interviews constituted case studies for Bourdieu, and he claimed to be using scientific methods in their collection and presentation. He laboriously discussed methodology in the prefatory essay "To the Reader," in another essay on "The Space of Points of View," and again in a longer chapter called "Understanding" at the end of the book. Perhaps to balance his scientific ambitions and claims for the book, Bourdieu very early also set the emotional tone of the book and the emotional proximity of his interviewers and their interviewees, writing of the "sentiment of uneasiness at the moment of making public these private remarks" (1993: 9; my translation), "the testimonies that men and women have confided in us about their existence and their difficulty of existence" (9). He would return to this theme at the end of the book, even using the phrase "intellectual love" (1406) to describe the stance his researchers adopted toward their informants. Using the standard ethnographic practice, names and actual locations were changed to disguise identities. Bourdieu referred to the interview narratives in *The Weight of the World* as *temoignages,* or testimonies. This brings a politicized language to the work but is also a common term for life history narrative in France (rather than the more politically neutral term "narrative"). This project had a political aim of challenging neoliberalism and its effects and a sociological aim of challenging opinion polls[6] as a way to understand the responses of people to their situations. Bourdieu's theory of life trajectory, of the ways in which people make choices "without choosing" (i.e., they chose what is already their destiny) because of their inculcated dispositions, is quite clearly, however, the motor for this project.

This book represents Bourdieu's final answer to the methodological problem of incorporating both subjectivity and objectivity in social science research. Most of the book is composed of pages of first-person narratives, subjective accounts, elicited by brief interview questions that are also included in the text. These accounts are interspersed, however, with short essays and introductions written by Bourdieu and a few colleagues that bring out the "objective" conditions being described in the personal stories. This is the method of "participant objectivation" whereby the analyst must objectify the interviewee's points of view, but without so distancing a gaze that they become objects. At the same time, the analyst must internalize sociological reflexivity, so that it becomes "natural" and like the "feel for the game" during interviews. For the most part, Bourdieu contrasts this method to the sociological use of the survey, highlighting its virtues of sensitivity to the situation and informant, rather than to more intensive ethnographic methods of anthropology. Rather than spending time in a milieu and developing contacts with persons to interview (which is the conventional method of anthropological fieldwork), Bourdieu and his team worked through either people they already knew or who were led to them by people they knew. Bourdieu made a "virtue out of necessity" (to use his own vocabulary), in this mode of access to acquaintances as informants, by claiming in his chapter on methodology ("Understanding") that whenever possible interviews were carried out by people who knew their interviewees, in order to minimize the social distance between the two.

The concept of "point of view" was employed by Bourdieu in this context as a key phrase to both justify the methods used (showing that they are not overly subjective or ethnomethodological) and convey the feelings of the interviewees. Bourdieu claimed to have borrowed his method of juxtaposing the interviews not from social science, but from the novels of Virginia Woolf and James Joyce ("modernist" novelists, I might add), in which there was no omniscient narrator who adopted the "lofty" gaze (part of his critique of the "scholastic point of view"). Rather, various points of view were juxtaposed in order to provide a plurality of perspectives. Bourdieu cautioned that this was not "subjectivist relativism," however, but was "in the very reality of the social world," and is a method that explains suffering that results from 'colliding interests, different dispositions and lifestyles' (1993: 15; my translation) in work or living situations where people of different backgrounds are thrown together.

Four examples that I have selected from interviews undertaken by Bourdieu himself, and his commentary on them, usefully demonstrate Bourdieu's methods and aims. These are: (1) three youths—two from North Africa, and one "native" French youth; (2) two French farmers in Béarn; (3) a French scientist who is the child of two schoolteachers; and (4) a young social worker. The first two and the fourth are interviews undertaken by Bourdieu himself; the other by his son. In the cases of the farmers and the scientist, the interviewers knew the interviewees fairly well prior to the interview.

In the set of interviews titled "The Order of Things," Bourdieu first gave details on his interview with a twenty-year-old Beur youth, whose parents were from Algeria, and who had gone further in school than most of his peers in the housing project on the outskirts of a northern French town where he lives. His parents encouraged him in school, and his father earned a decent wage, so the boy did not live in the worst conditions. Bourdieu commented on this boy's fears that he would not be permitted to advance to the next level of schooling, and on his sense of teetering between being a failure and being a "miracle." He characterized this youth as being quite aware of the disconnection between high school and the neighborhood. The transcript of that interview is not reproduced in the text, but Bourdieu's summary of it is followed by an interview with two youths who dropped out of school and were characterized as "delinquents"—one whose parents were Moroccan and the other from a poor French family. Bourdieu noted that he was able to gain their trust just by being interested in them and that they allowed him to use the familiar form of "*tu*" with them. Their failures in school are, in Bourdieu's mind, connected to their class habitus. The Moroccan boy entered school without sufficient French skills, and was doomed from the start. Bourdieu suggested that the Moroccan boy's situation was just an extreme case of that of the French one who dropped out of school before getting his diploma (BEP). They made statements to Bourdieu such as "Oh, the teachers don't give a shit" and "In our project no one goes to school" (66). Their rejection of school was viewed by Bourdieu in terms of their having made a "virtue out of necessity." The title of the interview declares the fatalistic worldview of these youths, who seemingly accepted "the order of things" and their place in it. This case illustrates Bourdieu's view that the dominated come to "choose" their destiny, and thereby participate in their domination.

Another interview conducted by Bourdieu, and previously published elsewhere (Bourdieu 1991d), was with two middle-aged farmers who were interviewed in the 1980s and who were acquaintances of Bourdieu's in his native region of Béarn. In this case, Bourdieu stressed the authenticity of the interview by noting that the farmers were glad to have the opportunity to voice their opinions ("they jumped at the opportunity to say the things that were closest to their hearts") so that they might shape public opinion. He wrote that his intention with this interview was political as well as scientific: "I wanted to try and give to people whom I'd known for a long time—farmers, workers, artisans, small-time employees—the chance to express their profound malaise and discontent" (1999: 390). This interview was titled "A Life Lost," and returns to issues of succession in farm households that interested Bourdieu throughout his career. These are men who escaped the fate of remaining unmarried that Bourdieu described in some earlier work. The tone of this interview is that of disappointment and depression, and the title underscores these emotions. Bourdieu described them as living in a double bind of heavy dependence on the state in today's economy, yet having been inculcated in the habitus of the traditionally "independent" farmer. One of the men spoke of his son who worked with him on the farm, but had remained a bachelor. The other man's son had left farming, and there was no heir. The habitus of these farmers was close to a rupture, Bourdieu claimed, because the social and economic conditions of their lives were out of harmony with their habitus. They were forced to consciously think about inheritance issues in ways that were automatic before and to consider factors that may lead to the end of the family farm. The farmer without an heir remarked that "Young people today have become very hard; they don't give a damn that you've lost your whole life," and Bourdieu interpreted this to signify that the man was really telling Bourdieu that his son had "killed him"—something that Bourdieu felt the man could not admit to himself in such frank terms. The end of the farm was "social death."

A third example comes from a middle-class person, who suffers the malaise of knowing that his success in school and his life trajectory were predetermined by his background. He describes the feeling of having followed a "program." This interview does not appear in the English translation, and is called "The Family Dream." Although Bourdieu himself provided the commentary on this interview, it was conducted by his son, Jérome. Bourdieu wrote of Henri that he "succeeded in all that he wanted, but he was not sure that he wanted all that he accomplished" (1993: 1221; my translation). Torn between two choices for his higher education, Henri became aware of the dispositions that denied him certain choices. He said in his interview that "I have the feeling of having always been programmed to be a scientist" (1993: 1236; my translation). Bourdieu prefaced this interview and a few others with an essay on "The Contradictions of Inheritance" in which he wrote of the family's role in social suffering, even "the paradoxical form of suffering based on privilege" (1999: 511; my translation). With the example of this young scientist, Bourdieu attempted to demonstrate that the constraints of habitus affected those from the middle classes who succeed in school, because of their docility in the face of the system, as well as those from the most dominated classes.

The final example comes from an interview, "An Impossible Mission," that Bourdieu conducted with a social worker, Pascale. He interpreted her plight as that of a struggle between the logic of social work (benevolence and militancy on behalf of the poor) and that of the state bureaucracy (rigid and conservative in its actions). It was because of the maneuverings and initiative of people like Pascale, who are "practical analysts," inhabit contradictory social spaces, and are thus not "imprisoned" in their function, that bureaucracies are able to work at all, according to Bourdieu. People like Pascale keep bureaucracies from reproducing their own logic and becoming paralyzed, he argued. Pascale left her first position because she came to be viewed by the authorities as (as she put it [with prompting of the word by Bourdieu]) "Yes, subversive. Bad temper. Not bending to authority" (1999: 194).

Apart from the first set of interviews with the youth in housing projects, who demonstrate some harmony between their habitus and their destiny (which they more or less accept or at least to which they have resigned themselves), Bourdieu's other interviewees are individuals who suffer a malaise of being aware of the contradictions in their lives—and this is the social suffering that Bourdieu wanted to show in the book. Even if they cannot, thus, change their futures, and perhaps because they cannot, they are more aware of their objective circumstances than people in circumstances of harmony between habitus and structures (such as traditional peasants in a traditional economy). Bourdieu seems to have been able to make use, therefore, of these "native theories" because he saw the interlocutors as "practical analysts." Bourdieu noted in *Homo Academicus* that "Marx suggested that, every now and then, some individuals managed to liberate themselves so completely from the positions assigned to them in social space that they could comprehend that space as a whole, and transmit their vision to those who were still prisoners of the structure" (1988: 31). Although he went on to qualify this by saying that a totalizing view was not possible, he did feel that sociologists produce studies that transcend "ordinary visions" and in his analysis of narrative, that some "spontaneous sociologists" or "practical analysts" could achieve this as well.

NEOLIBERALISM, INDIVIDUALISM, AND THE "NEW" EUROPE

In the 1990s, Bourdieu began to get more involved in social issues in France related to the economy and to the growth of the European Union. For Bourdieu, the policies of neoliberalism reinforced and constructed notions of individualism and rational action that were creating Darwinian struggles, and undermining conditions for collective struggle among those suffering from those policies.[7] Bourdieu's theory of habitus thus came to intersect with his politics, as he saw the concept of the individual not just as a "modern" notion related to the modern economy as opposed to a precapitalist economy (that is, in terms of theory), but he saw the concept of "the autonomous individual" as dangerous and prohibitive of political actions that could protect the poor and working class. Bourdieu's criticisms of neoliberalism were mainly that it was breaking down collective structures. The economic world it had created was one that was becoming self-evident (*doxic*) to people. The policies of the IMF (International Monetary Fund) and the OECD (Organization for Economic Cooperation and Development) were "reducing labor costs, reducing public expenditures and making work more flexible" (1998e: 1). Bourdieu pointed out the symbolic and structural violence inherent in management practices whereby "organizational discourse has never talked as much of trust, cooperation, loyalty, and organizational culture as in an era when adherence to the organization is obtained at each moment by eliminating all temporal guarantee of employment" (4). Bourdieu further cautioned that "the market" had become more powerful than the nation-state and that any intervention by the state was being discredited. He suggested the bleak prospect that whatever mechanisms were keeping chaos at bay, by what little survival of state intervention existed, would soon be dismantled. The solution was to appear to support the disintegrating state while working to construct a new social order, the "supranational state" of Europe: "One that will not have as its only law the pursuit of egoistic interest and the individual passion for profit and that will make room for collectives oriented toward the rational pursuit of ends collectively arrived at and collectively ratified" (6).

Bourdieu was concerned that the media had painted the European question in terms that portrayed those in favor of the EU as progressive and modern, and those against it as archaic or even anti-Semitic. This was too clear-cut a division, according to Bourdieu. He felt that the Social Democrats who were the most visible leaders in the EU were undermining collective struggles of the past. He feared that their neoliberal policies would contribute

> In the name of monetary stability and budgetary rigor, to the liquidation of the most admirable profits of the social struggles of the last two centuries: universalism, egalitarianism . . . or internationalism; and to the destruction of the very essence of the idea or socialist ideal, that is to say, broadly, the ambition to protect solidarities menaced by economic forces through collective action. (1999a: 2)

Although he had concerns about the EU, Bourdieu also felt that Europe had to come together collectively in order to keep the United States from dictating much of the global economic and diplomatic policy. He suggested that those who want to promote a "social Europe" that will protect workers in opposition to what he called a "Europe of banks and money," a "police and prison Europe," and a "military Europe," needed to find ways of mobilization. One model he suggested was worker unions organized at the European level, and he wrote that syndicalism in Europe could be "the motor of a social Europe" that broke with the nationalism associated with nationally organized unions, the discourse on the inevitability of globalization of the economy, neoliberalism, and "social liberalism" that supports deregulation favoring corporations while appearing to be social policies (1999: 4). Bourdieu painted a utopia that included hopes of an "internationale" of immigrants in Europe, but also admitted that creating a social Europe would entail changing the dispositions of millions of people. Appealing to E. P. Thompson's *The Making of the English Working-Class,* Bourdieu suggested that the nineteenth-century model of a worker's movement could be a model for the present, as the conditions facing workers today are comparable. This movement, he suggested would be one of contestation and negotiation. Bourdieu's emphasis on personal narrative, which he employed to show collective histories (either those of privilege or struggle), was closely connected to his visions of a sociology that could potentially liberate thought and counter the *doxa* associated with capitalism and neoliberalism. With his use of the concept of "intellectual love" to describe the relationship between informants and interviewers in *The Weight of the World,* Bourdieu was moving toward a fuller integration of his political activism and his methods of research. It is also possible that his attention to the notion of love in *Masculine Domination* was part of this convergence in terms of theory. Later in his career, we can see Bourdieu shifting from his initial concerns with domination and social reproduction to a stronger sense of urgency to not only reveal the mystification of dominant ideologies (which he continued to stress in *Pascalian Meditations*) but to intensify efforts toward solutions through political action (Bourdieu 2002h).

MARGIN AND CENTER

Bourdieu viewed subjectivity or point of view as embedded in social and spatial positions within social and spatial fields. In this, his work has implications for theories of space and power in anthropology and also in fields of urban planning (i.e., Low and Lawrence-Zúñiga 2003; Hillier and Rooksby 2002). That he should privilege the point of view of someone like the Algerian cook, who is linked to both margin and center, is undoubtedly connected to his own sensibilities and the French context. In France, more so than in the United States, geographies of center and periphery are more explicit and their hierarchies of value are also more explicit. There is Paris (the only "true" center) and its provinces, France the metropole and its former colonies (such as Algeria), and the city and *banlieue*—a French term that can be translated as "suburb" but connotes more "the projects" or spaces of poverty rather than the manicured lawns and nice houses of a middle-class suburbia. *Banlieue* is, literally, the "banned" or "banished place."

Bourdieu was himself a person with ties to margin and center, and his insider and outsider, familiar and distant positions within academia and his research sites, have been a theme in his writing. He was from the margins (the provinces) but managed to penetrate the core of French academia in Paris, and he traveled back and forth between that center and its two peripheries of the French provinces and the former French colony of Algeria both literally and figuratively through his writing and research. The ideal informant for Bourdieu was, thus, someone like himself—a "marginal man" or "man between two worlds" who can adopt both the objective and subjective perspective that is not available to all people. The "native theories" of that sort of person are not dangerous, according to Bourdieu, because they are able to reflect the objective structures.

Conclusion

While writing this book, I have been well aware of the dangers in interpreting Bourdieu's work in terms of his autobiography. It is, however, tempting to do so, and Bourdieu himself has encouraged this reading of his work through his autobiographical and self-reflexive writings. It is easy to understand his preoccupations with education and social class in terms of his own social origins and education; his interest in Algerian social change in terms of his own rural roots in France; and his interest in marriage strategies both in Algeria and in rural France in terms of his own parents' "misalliance" between the son of sharecroppers and the daughter of wealthy peasants. Even the prolific and wide-ranging scope of his work could be understood in terms of Bourdieu's own admission (2004: 93–94) that his tendency toward melancholy and depression pushed him to keep busy and to be a workaholic. Bourdieu's theory of habitus relies upon an understanding of social origins, and he applied this in his own explanations of his life trajectory. But, in writing this book, I have not taken on the role of Bourdieu's biographer, searching for evidence about his life in order to write about it in ways that might contradict his own autobiography. I have relied on his writings—including those that are and are not explicitly autobiographical—and on other secondary literature related to an understanding of the circumstances in which he lived and worked. My aim has not been to create a realistic portrait of Bourdieu the man but to critically engage with his work in ways that might lead us to fuller appreciations of it. In so doing, I have attempted to balance what he tells us about himself and what we might understand about the contributions of his work to scholarship in the humanities and social sciences.

The legacy of Pierre Bourdieu is still to be determined as scholars sift through his writings and assess the ways in which his thought shaped social science disciplines in the late twentieth century and will continue to influence new forms of scholarship into the twenty-first century. There are still many questions to be addressed in Bourdieu's work—texts to be discovered and rediscovered, work to be juxtaposed with other work by Bourdieu and with that of other scholars. In this book, I have revisited certain themes already considered central to Bourdieu's work, such as education, and tried to shed new light on them. I also, however, have sought to uncover some potential areas for further attention that have been marginal in previous discussions or uses of his work—such as personal narrative, the connections between the early French and Algerian research, and emotion. My approach was one that worked to uncover the autoethnography in Bourdieu's work—piecing together from the scattered fragments in which he presented this an understanding of the uses he made of his life trajectory, balancing Bourdieu's own reflections on his life and career with a consideration of the wider institutional and national frameworks in which he worked. I spent many months working on this book not because I necessarily feel that Bourdieu had all the answers or even because I agree with all that he said or wrote. Rather, I think his ideas are "good to think with."

This book was not intended as a primer on Bourdieu's thought, as many previous volumes on his work have attempted to be, although I hope that it has helped readers to better understand his work. I have included an appendix that suggests further reading on Bourdieu that may further elucidate his thought for those for whom this book may have served as an introduction. My goal was, rather, to place Bourdieu within the particular social locations in which his work was positioned—primarily that of France and its former colony of Algeria, in order to discuss its implications for anthropology—itself largely a product of Enlightenment Europe and colonialism.

While working on the final stages of this book, I visited an exhibit on Edouard Manet at the Art Institute of Chicago, while attending The American Anthropological Association Meetings in Chicago. I was struck by the ironies of going to see this display of works by an artist about whom Bourdieu was writing a book at the end of his life,[1] while I had in turn just finished a book about Bourdieu. Apart from the art itself, with the theme of "Manet and the Sea," I was struck by two aspects of the exhibit. First, the curators had interestingly traced not only the precursors to Manet's work and influences on it but also had attempted to demonstrate that Manet continued to develop his style over his career in response to his contemporaries, various aspects of modern life, the Japanese style that was popular at the time, and most cogently for me, new artists such as Monet. We could see therefore, how his style was shaped in response to these influences. I saw parallels in the analysis of the work of a social scientist and theorist like Bourdieu, and was reminded that his work evolved over the course of a long career in response to various developments. The second aspect of the exhibit that I found compelling was a room in which several paintings of waves, by different artists, were placed side-by-side along a wall, showing their highly nuanced distinctions in style, use of color, and so on. This prompts me to think of a fictive wall of social theorists who were concerned with issues of the relationship between individuals, power, and society—figures such as Weber, Elias, Giddens, Foucault, Williams, and Bourdieu, their ideas juxtaposed to show the commonalities and distinctions of their approaches. The exhibit thus cautions the reader of Bourdieu to not fossilize his thought at any one period of time but to look at the total oeuvre over the course of his career; at the same time, it underscores the need to keep in mind the wider issues he addressed in social theory even as we seek to understand the subtle and not-so-subtle differences among theorists working on similar issues of power, structure, and agency.

If I were to distill Pierre Bourdieu's thought, I would say that his two main intellectual goals were to combat what he called "the denial of the social" and the "scholastic point of view." In the first case, Bourdieu argued that there was no "natural" human self or behavior that was not constrained to some degree by society, and he was critical of those (particularly philosophers) who argued otherwise. In the second case, he criticized intellectuals for imputing their own point of view, which was a product of inculcation in the academy, to subjects of research. Instead, he argued, scholars should try to determine not the "native point of view," but the "the logic of practice," or the habitus and dispositions of a social agent and the social field of possibilities in which their habitus operated. Bourdieu felt that freedom from forms of symbolic domination would only be possible through research that avoided these two traps.

Bourdieu also must be seen as keeping an eye on domination and inequality in society throughout his life, and as having a strong moral sense about the role and responsibilities of the intellectual. We can see a change in Bourdieu's perspective on the causes of suffering and inequality in France. In an earlier period Bourdieu was, I believe, swayed by the strongly Republican ideology of France (and by his ambivalence about that ideology) in a way that caused him to always *chercher l'école* as a way of explaining "modern" societies. Education, the scholastic point of view, and academia were unpacked by Bourdieu in order to unmask their role in perpetuating systems of domination in society while presenting themselves as based on reason, equality, and democratic ideals. Later, in the final decade or so of his life, Bourdieu came to see neoliberalism as the culprit, turning not entirely away from education but seeking to critique the state itself more directly. This became the major paradigm in Bourdieu's life, and caused him to be criticized in France by many, often quite vehemently, who felt his political engagements were extreme.

BOURDIEU AS PUBLIC INTELLECTUAL

In the many obituaries and commentaries on his life that followed Bourdieu's death, the theme of his public political engagement in the last few years of his life dominated these discussions (Goussault 2002; Müller 2002). Although Bourdieu is associated with the May 1968 protests and movements as a result of his critical writings on the educational system, he did not take an active role in those struggles. He remained somewhat apart from public political stances, and was vilified by many on the left for his support of the presidential candidacy of the French comedian Coluche during the campaign that eventually resulted in the victory of socialist François Mitterrand in 1981. Many of Bourdieu's writings from the late 1990s on were critical of what he viewed as the close association between intellectuals and journalists, so that the autonomy of scholarship in France was called into question. Nevertheless, Bourdieu became actively involved as a spokesperson for populist movements against certain reforms of the social security system in France in 1995 and, from that time on, was very much in the public eye and in the press. As a result, he became a controversial political figure, criticized on many fronts. He wrote in *Esquisse pour une auto-analyse* (2004) that he was wounded by the misunderstandings associated with the criticism applied to him charging that he fancied himself somewhat divine (both through the pun on his name and the label of his thought as *bourdivine;* "Dieu," of course, meaning God in French).[2]

Bourdieu's engagement with politics continued with his increasing attacks on neoliberalism (which I discussed in Chapter 5), and he became a spokesperson for peasant protests, protests among Algerian intellectuals, and against the WTO. In some ways, this involvement in politics contradicts his own criticisms of intellectuals such as Sartre—whom he called "total intellectuals"—who felt authorized to speak on any subject and take a position on any topic. Bourdieu associated this with a certain type of bourgeois privilege that he repudiated, and with the "lofty" position adopted by philosophers at the time of his initial training at ENS, which he also rejected. There is scant mention of Bourdieu's political involvement in his later reflexive writings. In *Esquisse pour une auto-analyse* (2004), the most recent publication that serves as an intellectual memoir, Bourdieu makes no explicit reference to his involvement other than to mention, somewhat in passing, the ways in which he angered colleagues when he supported Coluche at around the same time that he was elected to the Collège de France. In that essay, he makes what can only be surmised as veiled references to his public political roles in his admissions about his stubborn and somewhat contrary personality. In light of Bourdieu's other stances in his research, it is likely that he distinguished his own political activism from the behaviors of "total intellectuals" by virtue of his modest social origins that authorized him to speak out for the disenfranchised.

HABITUS

Bourdieu's major theoretical contribution has been his theory of habitus and its associated concepts of dispositions, point of view, social field, symbolic or cultural capital, and symbolic violence. Given the breadth of writing and uses of examples that Bourdieu employed to articulate this concept, there is much room for interpretation of what it meant and about how much social agency it afforded to individuals. From an earlier theory that saw it primarily in terms of bodily habitus, Bourdieu moved to a consideration of the habitus as inculcated domination in his work on social class reproduction in education. He later, however, expanded the concept of habitus with his growing use of social field as a way to articulate the expression of inculcated dispositions in social contexts, the struggle over symbolic meaning and capital in which agents engage within a field, and the ways in which one agent can express his or her habitus differently in different fields. The concept of structure in his work began to transform into the idea of social fields. This became a more flexible notion of habitus, and also allowed for the acquisition of a secondary habitus beyond the initial one based on family origins. Bourdieu's notion of habitus was developed in fieldwork situations in Algeria and Béarn in which people were undergoing social change and a lack of fit between their understandings of the world and the societal structures in which they lived. Bourdieu thus articulated a sort of "ideal type" of society in which there was harmony between one's dispositions and one's world, a society he described as the traditional Kabyles. Most of Bourdieu's theorizing about habitus took place in situations of discordance between habitus and structure.

Does habitus refer to a concept akin to "culture," as some have suggested, or, is it best thought of as a form of "identity"? The collective and shared nature of habitus, which also has qualities unique to each person, presents a challenge to either construction. Bourdieu rarely evoked the notion of culture in the standard anthropological sense of a holistic system of shared meanings, cultural distinctiveness, worldview, and so on. He argued that this notion, aligned with nationalism, was an artifact of power and a construction that diverted attention away from the more universal principles of social life—such as forms of classification themselves and relations of power and domination. Here he distinguished between French universalism (a cultural artifact) and the scientific search for universal principles. He wrote, "in the case of France, the nationalist dimension of culture is masked under a universalist façade. The propensity to conceive the annexation to one's national culture as a means of acceding to universality is at the basis of both the brutally integrative vision of the republican tradition (nourished by the founding myth of the universal revolution) and the very perverse forms of universalist imperialism and of internationalist nationalism" (1998c: 46). Despite Bourdieu's reservations about the concept of culture, habitus has important implications for the ways in which we think of culture, both in its emphasis on embodiment and emotion, and in its inextricable links to a theory of power.

As a theory of identity, habitus also has implications for understanding subjectivity and the person. For Bourdieu we are each a habitus, a product of collective history, and not an autonomous individual. One of the major potential drawbacks to this concept is that it maintains a unitary view of the person as social agent (if not "individual") who has one habitus or maybe two. Newer forms of hybrid identities, shifting forms of subjectivity related to either geographical mobility or rapid social change, cannot easily be accommodated with this view of habitus as something inculcated in early childhood and then providing a set of dispositions that guide a person's life trajectory. Bernard Lahire (1998) has been instrumental in working to explore ways to make the concept of habitus more flexible in order to take these facets of contemporary experience into account. Bourdieu's own later work on habitus pointed toward an admission of a nonunitary habitus. His work on the personal narratives of those who were situated in border spaces in society and during times of swift social change, like the Algerian worker about whom he wrote, opens up the possibility of a habitus that is split. Bourdieu made reference to his own habitus as being split or divided as a result of his upward mobility. I believe it is worth continuing to see the implications of habitus for identity (moving beyond individualism but accommodating change) as well as for understandings of what is commonly called "culture."

FIELDS OF POWER

Bourdieu's ethnographic research in Kabylia and Béarn, because it stands outside of mainstream anthropological approaches, offers some useful research questions if not answers. Bourdieu never conducted a conventional "community study" and so he cannot be accused of the structural-functionalist biases associated with some of the earlier studies in Europe and the Mediterranean. His *Outline of a Theory of Practice* looks nothing like a conventional realist ethnography, and he never wrote a community-study ethnography based on his research in Béarn. He primarily worked through extended open-ended interviews with some ethnographic observation, and I discussed these methods in Chapter 5. That he worked on both shores of the Mediterranean, and as both insider and outsider ethnographer, provides a model for comparative work of the type advocated by Driessen

(2001). He was in some ways a pioneer of "multi-sited ethnography," and as anthropologists are currently interrogating constructions of the "field" (Marcus and Clifford 1986; Gupta and Ferguson 1997) and critiquing the standard community-study or localized method (Albera et al. 2001), this is an aspect of his work that has been underexamined. At the same time, as Goodman (2002), Addi (2002), and I (1995) have pointed out, much of Bourdieu's work in rural France and Algeria was based on distinctions between differentiated and undifferentiated societies, "ideal types," and the occulting of factors in his field sites (particularly in Kabylia) that would undermine the portrait of tradition he presented. Béarn and Kabyle were parallel worlds in Bourdieu's work, used to present a mirror to a modern society (France) that believed itself to be bureaucratic and rational, and that was highly stratified and full of contradictions.

Bourdieu's preference for his Béarnais and Kabyle informants and lower-class French informants over the subjects of his research among the bourgeoisie in France (in the work on taste and on education) is quite obvious. He provided more nuanced interview data from them, lent their subjectivity more voice, and seemed to foster a common "cultural intimacy" (Herzfeld 1997a) with those informants. This is a decided bias in his work, reflecting the longstanding ethnographic concern with subordinate peoples but not seriously taking the call to "study up" (Nader) and carefully understand the "practical logics" of the dominant. Although Bourdieu did study institutions and power in French society, those studies, with the exception of *The State Nobility,* lack the ethnographic detail and nuance of his work among subordinate populations.

Bourdieu's work has implications for our understandings of anthropology as a form of travel. Bourdieu went to Algeria first as part of the colonial project of France, sent as a result of the mandatory military service at that time in place, to defend the nation's interests in its resistant colony. He stayed there not in order to continue that project of nationalism, but because he opposed it and supported Algerian independence. Nevertheless, his research in Algeria is intricately tied to colonialism and to the assumptions of a dichotomy between Europe and its others that is deeply embedded in history and in anthropology (Bhabha 1994). Bourdieu's own mobility across the Mediterranean and within France, both in terms of his own life trajectory and his research topics (which were so closely aligned, as I have tried to show), displays a particular point of view associated with travel. As many excellent historians of anthropology (Stocking, Kuper) have alerted us, anthropology as a discipline and a point of view has its origins in European imperialism and colonialism. It goes without saying that I do not believe that invalidates the entire enterprise today, which has in many ways, tried to overcome that legacy. Nevertheless, what Bourdieu called the "scholastic point of view" and attributed to the educational institution and its modes of inculcation, that "lofty gaze," is just as much if not more so a product of the colonial or imperial gaze.

The entire construction of travel, the ability to do it and the reasons for doing it, are connected historically to imperialism—if differently through tourism, commerce, or militarism. Bourdieu did not admit this in his work, nor did he seriously engage with his own implication in that "gaze" in any of his autobiographical reflections. His self-reflexive method centered mainly on the specifically French context of philosophy and the academic milieu in which Bourdieu operated. For the most part, his reflexivity was a defensive posture, aimed at defending him against critiques in French academia and helping to position him within the social field of positionings and strategies within that particular milieu. He did not seriously engage with the broader questions that have concerned anthropology since the 1960s about the issue of representation of others and of oneself in the fields of power that constitute the "field" of fieldwork. And yet, we can see Bourdieu's emphasis on insider/outsider research, on subjectivity and objectivity, as forms of addressing this—if in a different register from that of engaged anthropological discussions.

WRITING AS A FORM OF SOCIAL THEORY

In works such as *Distinction* and the *State Nobility*—both forms of ethnography that blur the boundaries between cultural studies, anthropology, and sociology—there are also interesting models of composing a text.[3] These books are eclectic in sources used, in the combination of statistical and subjective material included, and in the use of popular culture and everyday documents such as employment ads or obituaries. Although as an anthropologist, I would like to have seen more "ethnography" in all of Bourdieu's work—descriptions of lived practices, everyday behaviors, and so on; there is no reason why that could not be combined with the type of other materials he often includes. Part of this is because of the collaborative approach he took, working with a team of associates to produce portions of the books, even though he usually appeared as sole author on the cover page—with indications of collaboration in material in appendices or in various co-authored chapters within books. The model of the single anthropologist going to one place to do participant-observation was rarely adopted by Bourdieu. Even in Béarn, he collaborated—with his wife and with a demographer.

Bourdieu's form of writing is also of interest for the study of auto-ethnography, in that he drew upon his own experiences quite often, if in veiled form. His approach to self-reflexivity, which he wanted to distance from narcissism, was one that required the writer to be conscious of his or her assumptions, position-takings, and point of view. Although, as I have pointed out repeatedly in this book, there were silences in and limits to Bourdieu's autobiographical reflections, his work underscores the biographical element in writing and urges us to theorize our practice. Because of Bourdieu's very social view of the individual (as social agent), he encourages writers to see their experience in terms of collective histories rather than unique or autonomous choices.

In his discussions of objectivity and subjectivity, and the logic of practice or practical logics in relationship to the scholastic point of view, Bourdieu tackled the issue of how anthropologists or sociologists can understand anything of their own cultural experiences or social systems. It was through the reflexive methods of socioanalysis and auto-analysis that he felt this could be accomplished. He wrote in an early essay: "The ethnologist is on terms of intimacy with his culture and therefore finds it difficult to think objectively about the patterns governing his own thought" (1967a: 339). Bourdieu's work entails a cautionary note to Euroamerican ethnologists studying Europe to be on guard against succumbing to their own taken-for-granted, commonsense understandings. Although at times Bourdieu seemed to infer that intellectuals (especially sociologists) could transcend everyday *doxa* in order to demystify the ideologies in our lives, we can see from his own struggles to be aware of the role of his own social origins and life trajectory, and from his attention to the (albeit limited) possibilities that other social actors can be "practical analysts," that Bourdieu felt it was vital to be aware of our own "locations" in the fields of possibilities as well as those of our subjects of research.

APPENDIX I

REMEMBERING PIERRE BOURDIEU, 1930–2002

Pierre Bourdieu died in Paris of cancer on January 23, 2002. He is survived by his wife of 40 years, Marie-Claire, and their three children Jerome, Emmanuel, and Laurent. Bourdieu was a prolific writer and significant post-war intellectual whose influence on contemporary thought in the social sciences and humanities has been immense. His key concepts of habitus, field, and symbolic capital continue to shape research and theory in many disciplines. The author of over 25 books, his *Outline of a Theory of Practice* is the best known of his works among American anthropologists.[1]

Given the wide breadth of his writings, and the uneven timing of translations of his work, knowledge of Bourdieu's many contributions is scattered in the United States according to disciplinary interests, and there are relatively few scholars who are familiar with the total oeuvre. His social activism and political position in France are also not well known among his readers outside of France. During the 1990s, Bourdieu became firmly established, along with Derrida and Foucault, as a major French intellectual presence in American academia. He was at this time, already, one of the leading intellectuals in France, widely known and controversial among the public as well as among scholars. His outspoken criticism of the social class structure provoked a range of critics in France.

For English-speaking audiences, Bourdieu's work has been the subject of several book-length treatments[2] and edited collections.[3] A two and one-half hour documentary film on Bourdieu, "Sociology is a Combat Sport" (with the title based on a quote from Bourdieu), was widely shown in France in 2001. Bourdieu felt that much of his work was misunderstood by readers, and he tried to clarify the meaning of his work through several published interviews and essays (*In Other Words* [1990]; *An Invitation to Reflexive Sociology* [1992]).

Originally published as Reed-Danahay, Deborah. 2002. Remembering Pierre Bourdieu. *Anthropological Quarterly*. 75(2): 375–81. Reprinted with permission.

Bourdieu was born to a rural family in the region of Béarn, in south-western France, near the Pyrenees. His family had peasant roots and spoke the regional dialect of Gasgogne as well as French. His father, who never finished high school, was a postal worker. Bourdieu's modest origins made him particularly sensitive to issues of power and prestige in France, shaping his research interests, social activism, and defense of the underprivileged. He was a "scholarship boy" who attended lycée in the regional city of Pau and then went on to lycée Louis-le-Grand in Paris, before eventually entering the Ecole Normale Supérieure (one of the elite institutions of higher learning in France.) There he studied with Louis Althusser and received a degree in philosophy. He started his teaching career in 1955 in a high school in Moulins. From there, he took teaching positions in Algiers (1958–60), Paris, and then in the industrial northern French city of Lille.

Bourdieu became Director of Studies at EHESS (Ecole des Hautes Etudes en Sciences Sociales) in Paris in 1964, where he edited the journal *Actes de la Recherches en Sciences Sociales* and founded the Center for the Sociology of Education and Culture. In his early years at EHESS, he worked with Raymond Aron. He was elected to the prestigious Chair of Sociology at Collège de France in 1981. His inaugural lecture at the Collège de France (reprinted in *In Other Words* as "A Lecture on the Lecture") is now famous for its self-reflexive commentary on the giving of such lectures. Bourdieu gave his last lecture there on March 28, 2001, as he prepared to retire after 20 years. In 1993, Bourdieu received the highest honor from CNRS (the French National Scientific Research Center), the "Medaille d'Or" (Gold Medal).

Bourdieu studied philosophy, anthropology and sociology. He came of age in a French academic climate dominated by Sartre and Lévi-Strauss, amid the backdrop of the Algerian war for independence from French colonial rule. Influences on Bourdieu's work include, in addition to those thinkers already cited, Marx, Durkheim, Weber, Mauss, Elias, and Goffman. His early work is characterized by a split between ethnographic peasant studies in Algeria and southwestern France on the one hand, and statistical sociological studies of education and social class in urban France on the other. Because of his interest in the situation in Algeria, he took a university post early in his career at the University of Algiers, and undertook ethnographic research while there. This work resulted in *Sociologie de l'Algérie* (1958), *Travail et Travailleurs en Algérie* (1963), and several essays, including the classic essays published in English as "The Attitude of the Algerian Peasant Toward Time" (1964), "The Sentiment of Honour in Kabyle Society" (1965), and "The Berber House" (1973). At around the same time, Bourdieu conducted ethnographic research on marriage strategies in his natal region of Béarn in southwestern France. Although Bourdieu never published a book on his rural French research, he wrote several articles, including "Célibat et Condition Paysanne" (1962) and "Marriage Strategies as Strategies of Social Reproduction" (1976). Bourdieu's work engaged with structuralism from the outset, analyzing structure while also arguing for a more nuanced version of it that could better capture the role of individual social actors.

Bourdieu first gained wide notoriety not for his ethnological work, but as a sociological critic of the French educational system. Soon after his return to France from Algeria, Bourdieu began a series of statistical studies of education and social class reproduction. This resulted in two volumes co-authored with Jean-Claude Passeron: *Les Héritiers, Les Etudiants et la Culture* (1964) and *La Reproduction: Eléments pour Une Théorie du Système d'Enseignement* (1970). The work was published just before and after the May 1968 student/worker uprisings in Paris, during which time the entire social fabric of France was being questioned. These books demonstrated that success in education depends upon symbolic or cultural capital—a complex of values, linguistic skills, and worldviews that is unevenly distributed among the population. Exclusion from the system results not only from judgments and exams in the school, but also through internalized (largely unconscious) attitudes among students that support the system of exclusion. Bourdieu made extensive use of the concepts of habitus and symbolic violence in this research, themes that characterized much of his later work on a variety of topics.

Along with *Reproduction* (1977), Bourdieu's best known books are *Outline of a Theory of Practice* (1977), *Distinction* (1984), and *The Logic of Practice* (1990). These three books synthesize Bourdieu's sociological and ethnographic research and formulate his theoretical approach. His notion of practice seeks to reconcile structuralist and methodological individualist approaches. It draws from concepts of social actors' "common sense" to understand how noticeable patterns emerge from human behavior. As he has written, he wanted to move from the study of "rules to strategies." Nevertheless, Bourdieu retained a limited view of the possibilities for human agency, and focused on the constraints of the habitus and of systems of symbolic domination. Bourdieu made use of these concepts in his writings in the fields of art, literature, and language, among others.

In two recent books, *Masculine Domination* (2001) and *The Weight of the World* (1999), Bourdieu addressed social problems of sexism and poverty in his own society through trenchant critiques relying upon the concept of symbolic domination. He also wrote books attacking television (1999) and neoliberalism (1999). Bourdieu was increasingly in the French public eye in the years immediately preceding his death as an outspoken critic of globalization. Bourdieu supported the controversial peasant-hero

José Bové, who led French farmers to attack a McDonald's restaurant. He also supported Algerian causes at home in France and in North Africa.

Bourdieu was not comfortable with labels of his work, and avoided easy characterizations in large part by leaving such a huge legacy of work that crosses disciplinary boundaries. He also avoided facile political labels, often alienating members of left-wing groups in France with which he, for the most part, identified. Bourdieu offered criticisms of the centers of power in France, including his own academic colleagues, with the publication of *Homo Academicus* (1988). His contributions to the study of power in modern society have moved social theory in new directions, helping shape arguments about social agency and structure. His premature death came as he continued up until the end to offer a critical voice in human affairs. Despite his powerful position in French academic circles and the extraordinary influence of his work throughout the world, Bourdieu's demeanor in person could be surprisingly understated and modest. Those who were privileged enough to get to know Pierre Bourdieu attest to his warmth and gentle sense of humor.

NOTES

1. The most extensive bibliography of Bourdieu's work and critical analyses of it can be found at the website HyperBourdieu http://www.iwp.uni-linz.ac.at/lxe/sektktf/bb/HyperBourdieu.html.

2. Examples include Robbins 1991; Jenkins 1991; Lane 2000; Swartz 1997.

3. Examples include Brown and Szeman 2000; Harker et al. 1990; Calhoun et al. 1993; Grenfell and James 1998; Shusterman 1999.

SUGGESTED READINGS

There have been several other book-length treatments of Bourdieu's work published in English. I recommend Lane 2000, in particular, for an excellent overview of Bourdieu in terms of French intellectual history and French society. Other general overviews or primers on his work include Jenkins 1992; Swartz 1997; Fowler 1997; Robbins 1991 and 2000; and Webb, Schirato, and Danaher 2002. Books that are highly critical of Bourdieu include Kauppi 2000 and Verdès-Leroux 2001.

Numerous edited collections on Bourdieu's work are also available, and some of these include essays or introductions by Bourdieu. Among those, I recommend that the reader first look at Harker et al. 1990, because it deals most specifically with anthropology and ethnography, and Calhoun et al. 1993 for key discussions of Bourdieu's major concepts. Other edited collections include Fowler 2000 and Brown and Szeman 1999 for a cultural studies approach, Shusterman 1999 on Bourdieu's applications in philosophy, Grenfell and James 1998, and Grenfell and Kelly 1999 for essays dealing with Bourdieu's contribution to education studies. Robbins (2000) has edited a four-volume collection of previously published works on Bourdieu that concern mainly social science approaches in anthropology and sociology, and philosophy. Extensive bibliographies include Delsant and Rivière (2002) and the online sources *HyperBourdieu* (Mörth and Fröhlich) and the *Bourdieu Bibliography* (Barnard) that lists secondary literature but, unfortunately, was last updated in 1999.

Many before me have compiled suggested reading lists for Bourdieu's writings. Richard Jenkins (1992) included a list at the end of his book, and Loïc Wacquant wrote an essay, "How to Read Bourdieu," that is included in Bourdieu and Wacquant 1992. My own brief list of recommended readings in English, particularly for anthropologists, includes the following books, which I list in terms of my suggested order of reading: *Logic of Practice, Distinction, Pascalian Meditations, The State Nobility, Language and Symbolic Power, Photography: A Middle-Brow Art,* and *The Weight of the World.* Also indispensable are *In Other Words* and *Toward a Reflexive Sociology.* I also suggest the following key articles: "The Sentiment of Honor in Kabyle Society" (1965), "Marriage Strategies as Strategies of Social Reproduction" (1976), "Men and Machines" (1981b), "The Forms of Capital"

(1986b), "Flaubert's Point of View" (1988), "Rites as Acts of Institution" (1992b), "On the Family as a Realized Category" (1996d), "Making the Economic Habitus" (2000c), and "Participant Objectivation" (2003c). Because many of Bourdieu's writings were reprinted in other texts, if often in reworked form, this list tries to avoid that duplication and represents a broad base in his thought without that duplication. For instance, his article on "Rethinking the State" (1994) is important, but much of that appears at the end of *Pascalian Meditations,* so I did not include it in my list as that book was listed.

NOTES

INTRODUCTION

1. Most of these criticisms, while appearing in various other texts by Bourdieu, are present in *Pascalian Meditations*. For a spirited rebuttal of Bourdieu's attacks on postmodernism, see Marcus (1994).

2. See Gaulejac (1995). Emmanuel Poncet (2002) applied this term to Bourdieu in an obituary published in *Libération*. The animosity felt by some French intellectuals to Bourdieu is clearly illustrated in Poncet's comment that Bourdieu's death represented "finally the disappearance of a superbly bad class consciousness in French society. And when a bad collective consciousness disappears, with the problems that it entailed, that is always a type of good news for those who remain." See also Ferry and Renault (1990).

3. This statement should not be taken at face value or out of context. From an American perspective, particularly that shared by many graduate students reading him for the first time, Bourdieu represents the epitome of the Parisian intellectual, whose breadth of knowledge is overwhelming. His style of writing, which has been much criticized, displays a knowledge and facility with ideas drawing from a wide range of disciplines. Bourdieu operated in a French academic context in which rhetoric and academic discourse are part of the "game," and he had to play that game in order to gain respect in that field. He also operated in a context in which intellectuals are more highly respected than they are in the United States, and in which higher education still emphasizes argumentative writing, the classics, and elitism. Although Bourdieu may have made claims that his humble peasant background, and experience "in the field" in Algeria, caused him to have a better feel for "practical reason" than most academics, and although he may have been ambivalent about the dual identity that his social trajectory had created, it seems somewhat disingenuous of him to disown any ambitions regarding intellectualism given his scholarly output. But this is also part of the contradictions in Bourdieu's persona.

4. As reported by Swartz (1997: 22).

5. In this, Bourdieu was in some ways like American presidential candidates who want to position themselves as "outsiders" to Washington.

6. Reed-Danahay (1997a). I have characterized autoethnography as an emergent approach that "synthesizes both a postmodern ethnography, in which the realist conventions and objective observer position of standard ethnography have been called into question, and a postmodern autobiography, in which the notion of the coherent, individual self has been similarly called into question. The term has a double sense—referring either to the ethnography of one's own group or to autobiographical writing that has ethnographic interest" (2). I should say at the outset that I am fully aware that Bourdieu distanced himself from postmodernism, and in using this term in reference to this book and his work, do not mean to imply that he viewed himself as a postmodernist. He called for a scientific study of sociology, and was highly critical of postmodernism. Nevertheless, his approach does the things I mention in this quote, if not in the service of a relativism that he associated with

postmodernism but, rather, a more universal search for truth and freedom that he associated with science.

7. When I gave one of my first presentations on this research at the American Anthropological Association (AAA) meetings in a session on French Anthropology organized by Susan Carol Rogers, and later edited by me into a special issue of *Anthropological Quarterly*, one of the session discussants was a French cultural attaché. She vehemently opposed my attempt to study French schools ethnographically because, she claimed, this was a futile exercise: everyone knew that education was exactly the same in every French primary school! I knew I was "on" to something by her reaction, and her unquestioning acceptance of the centralization and homogeneity of the educational system, a view long promoted by the Republican ideals associated with state education in France. The various crises in French education that have taken place since that panel in the early 1980s have caused fewer people in France to espouse such a dogmatic view of homogeneity in schools.

8. I must be clear here in absolving both Suzanne Lallemand and Jeanne-Françoise Vincent, both of whom were very supportive of my work in rural Auvergne, from that charge.

9. In a different register, the anthropologist Marc Augé (1987) has written of a distinction between "anthropology of the familiar" and "anthropology of the remote" to reflect the location of fieldwork as either "at home" or "away." See also Segalen (1989).

10. Bourdieu's (1981b: 309–10) analysis of the café waiter, and his critique of Sartre's description, while not using the vocabulary of "scholastic point of view," is a good example of what he had in mind.

11. I refer the reader to Appendix I, suggested readings for major texts that discuss Bourdieu in these terms. See also Free (1996) and Wacquant (2002).

12. This phrase comes from the title of the English version of the documentary film about Bourdieu, *Sociologie est un sport de combat* (Carles 2001).

13. Other French ethnographers have worked in and outside of France, applying perspectives from afar as they work in their own cultural context. A prime example is Marc Abélès, who started out as a political anthropologist in Ethiopia but subsequently turned his attention first to politics in Burgundy (1991) and then to formal political institutions in France and Europe (2000). Because Abélès is a Parisian, provincial Burgundy was not a familiar world to him ("how different it was from Paris!"; 1991: xii), as Béarn was for Bourdieu. Another anthropologist and colleague of Abélès, Irène Bellier, worked in the Amazon before undertaking a study of one of the elite Grandes Écoles (1993) in France and eventually the institutions of the European Union.

14. For an insightful review of that book, paired with Bourdieu's own book *Masculine Domination*, see Lane (1998).

1. BOURDIEU'S POINT OF VIEW

1. Bourdieu frequently used the term "social agent" in the place of individual or person or subject. This was to foreground the collective nature of identity in a shared habitus, instead of the idea of the autonomous individual.

2. There is controversy surrounding this as the memoir was viewed as unauthorized by his family and had been given to the press by the journalist Didier Eribon without their permission. Because of the legal battle and subsequent retraction of the memoir excerpts by the magazine, I will not quote from it here. I did, however, read the published version when it first appeared on line in early 2002. It is still online (Bourdieu 2002c).

3. It should be noted that Bourdieu was responsible for bringing translations of Hoggart's work (as well as that of others including Bateson and Goffman) to French audiences through his work as series editor at the press Minuit (Harker, Mahar, and Wilkes 1990: xiii)

4. France is very much a nation of immigrants, but has only recently recognized this aspect of its national identity. Six percent of the population in 1991 were foreign-born noncitizens, and many immigrants in France have become incorporated into the citizenry from nations such as Portugal and Italy, Eastern Europe, and North Africa. Noiriel (1996 [1988]) and Grillo (1995) provide good introductions to the issues of education and immigration in France. See also Reed-Danahay and Anderson-Levitt (1991) for a discussion of teacher attitudes toward "difference" in urban and rural contexts.

5. This revelation is intriguing on several points. It shows that not all funding for his research came from the national government, which, as I will discuss in Chapters 2 and 3, funds most ethnographic research in France and employs all academics. It is also interesting because it reveals (in a very small way) some of his strategizing to obtain resources, something he left out of other discussions of his career trajectory. It is, moreover, interesting to see the combination of corporate interest and research that took place in that study, given Bourdieu's more recent criticisms of corporations and neoliberalism. He does not indicate how (or if) Kodak used his study results.

2. EDUCATION

1. Pivot is most famously known for hosting *Apostrophes,* a now-defunct talk show featuring what Bourdieu derisively called "fast thinking" intellectuals. Bourdieu was highly critical of intellectuals who appeared on television, willing to address any subject at all, spouting what he called "fast thinking" and promoting "fast-food culture" (1996a).

2. See Kelly and Kelly (2001); Leon (1991).

3. Sources for this overview include Prost (1968); Halls (1976); Vincent (1980); Weber (1976); Furet and Ozouf (1982); Hobsbawm (1983); Grew and Harrigan (1991); Green (1990). I offer, here, however, my own narrative synthesis of this history, which may depart from the interpretations of any particular historian cited above. See also the historian André Burguière's essay on French education and French culture (1995).

4. The mass education and world culture approach of John Meyer, Francesco Ramirez, and John Boli argues this point with several in-depth studies. See, for example, Boli, Ramirez, and Meyers (1985); see also Green (1997). Anderson-Levitt (2003) provides ethnographic examples and anthropological responses to mass education theory.

5. France is frequently referred by shorthand in France and among French scholars as "the hexagon" because of its shape.

6. See Prost (1968) and Baudelot and Establet (1971).

7. Two very different perspectives on this series of events can be read in Ferry and Renault (1990) and Ross (2002).

8. Examples include Durkheim (1922; 1925; and 1969 [1928]).

9. Bourdieu wrote an important essay on religion and "the religious field" (1991d) that traced the growth of the power of organized religion and its connection to the rise of bourgeois dominance in societies. He addressed both Christianity and Islam, opposing in both cases the spiritual beliefs of peasants and the "legitimate" religious knowledge (a form of cultural capital) of the dominant religion. Bourdieu did not, however, discuss educational institutions or the relationship between education and religion in that essay.

10. Continuing controversies over female practices of wearing the Muslim scarf or veil in French schools is an indication of the new issues confronting religion and state relationships in France.

11. A concise overview of Bourdieu's academic career can be found in Wacquant (2002). See also Mahar (1990: 26–57) on interpretations by both Bourdieu and his translator Richard Nice on Bourdieu's career.

12. See Bowen and Bentaboulet (2002) for an overview of the institutional structure of human and social sciences in France, which is critical of Bourdieu's "star" position within it.

13. Bourdieu claimed that students entering the social sciences tend, therefore, to be "bourgeois children with fair-to-middling [test] results" (1988 [1984]: 121) since the higher status disciplines attract better students.

14. Interestingly, however, Bourdieu never completed the Thèse d'état in France, the highest doctoral degree. This degree is no longer given in France but was the mark of highest academic achievement in previous generations, and awarded in mid-career, after the preliminary doctorate and after several additional years of research and study.

15. See Bourdieu (1984a); Bourdieu, Passeron, and Eliard (1964); Bourdieu, Passeron, and Saint Martin (1965); Bourdieu, Boltanski, and Saint Martin (1973).

16. It is common for the French to discuss educational success in terms of the child being naturally gifted in various subjects (*doué*), with the opposite implication that children who do not succeed in school are not "gifted" in this sense. I came across this discourse in my own fieldwork in a rural French school, as it was used by both teachers and parents, and all those familiar with French education would recognize this construction.

17. Bourdieu's thinking at this time resembled the work of Basil Bernstein (1977) on restricted and elaborated codes.

18. Bourdieu focused more closely on changes in the types of capital needed for domination in an earlier study (Bourdieu, Boltanski, and Saint-Martin 1973).

19. One example of the continued use of this dialectic between the two paradigms is the study of social destinations in France by Goux and Maurin (1997).

20. Critiques and discussions of Bourdieu in terms of the agency, resistance, reproduction, and structure controversy during the 1980s also include Fernandes (1988); Harker (1984); Lakomski (1984); and Shirley (1986). That social reproduction continues to be a debated topic in the sociology of education is evidenced in a recent encyclopedia entry that discusses the differences between Bowles and Gintis, Bourdieu and Passeron, and Willis (Swartz 2002).

21. Loïc Wacquant refutes the construction of an opposition between Willis and Bourdieu (Bourdieu and Wacquant 1992: 80–81, fn. 24) stressing the complementarity of theoretical approaches and collaborations.

22. See Anderson-Levitt (2002).

23. Other recent critical ethnographies of education include Yon (2000) and Hayward (2000).

24. LeWita (1988) provides an ethnographic approach to the socialization at home and at school of bourgeois girls in France that helps to show how habitus is inculcated. She, however, focuses on young women and not only early childhood. It is also worth noting that in France, research on early childhood has generally been carried out by psychologists, and even though ethnographic studies of schooling have begun to flourish in France (since the 1980s), there is still this division between pedagogical studies of education in schools, and psychological studies at home or prior to schooling.

25. The following section is adapted from a paper entitled "Elias and Critical Ethnography of Schooling" that I delivered at the International Conference on "Norbert Elias et l'ethnologie" sponsored by the Societé d'Ethnologie Française and the Norbert Elias Foundation. Université de Metz, September 21–22, 2000.

26. There are parallels between the work of Foucault and Erving Goffman (1961) in the usage of the term "inmates," in Goffman's case, to describe any inhabitant of what he called a "total institution," including mental hospitals and boarding schools. The internalization of social control into cultural control, in Nader's sense, and the implications of this for the sense of self, was of interest to both theorists.

3. INSIDER/OUTSIDER ETHNOGRAPHY IN ALGERIA AND FRANCE

1. For a much condensed discussion of Bourdieu's ethnographic work in Béarn and Kabylia, which also draws from Bourdieu's self-reflexive writings, see Reed-Danahay (2004).

2. One could also interpret this in terms of his immersion in the urban, academic world in which he also felt apart because of his provincial and rural background and that led him out of the peasant milieu. But I think he was primarily referring to the Algerian context in these remarks.

3. Susan Carol Rogers (1999 and 2001) has noted that French anthropologists, particularly those who study French society, tend to employ a temporal (modern) rather than spatial (Western) frame of reference when locating contemporary Europe. Bourdieu, who was influenced by both Elias and Weber, both of whom wrote in terms of the West, used this construction perhaps more than his anthropological colleagues. He also was working in a North African context in which the division between occident and orient was highly charged, and in which the spatial and temporal dimensions were frequently merged (in Fabian's terms). It was this that Bourdieu sought to resist in his reluctance to compare Kabylia and the West. Although Bourdieu did not frequently use the terms West or Western (in French, *occident*), I maintain that his references to literate, state societies invariably referred to such "places."

4. Robert Lafont's (1967 and 1971) critique of internal colonialism in France's regions has influenced regionalist movements in Corsica, Brittany and the Basque region. Eugen Weber also noted that French territory (the hexagon) was itself "a colonial empire shaped over the centuries" (1976: 485). Colonna (1975) drew some parallels along these lines between schooling and colonialism in Algeria and provincial France. See also Caroline Ford on Brittany (1993).

5. Bové is the French farmer most famous for driving his tractor into a McDonald's in order to protest globalization and American imperialism. See Bové and Luneau 2000. Bourdieu attended Bové's trial and at least one demonstration at which Bové spoke.

6. Examples include Dyer (1978); Fuchs and Moch (1990); Ogden and White (1989).

7. The landscape of French academia is confusing for American scholars to comprehend because of its complexity. All institutions are funded by the national government, but there are many different types of them. There are research institutes, museums, universities and Grandes Écoles where teaching is done and degrees are conferred, and the CNRS (the scientific research arm of the government)—which is technically apart from the academic milieu, although it's research labs may be housed in universities. Most anthropologists have multiple affiliations, and may teach at a university while also being affiliated with a research institute. The Collège de France is itself a special case, and although lectures are given by its members to an interested public of students and others, it does not confer degrees. Bourdieu held the Chair in Sociology at the Collège de France but also had a research center at the École des Hautes Études en Sciences Sociales. See Rogers (2001) for a more extensive overview of French anthropology and Bowen and Bentaboulet (2002) for a more general overview of the human and social sciences in France.

8. See Goodman (2003) for an insightful critique of Bourdieu's use of proverbs in his work among the Kabyle. He also made extensive use of proverbs in his work among the Béarnaise peasants. Mark (1987) links Bourdieu's work in rural France (especially his use of Gascon proverbs) to folklore studies, and to the role that they have played in the production of regionalist ideologies. See also Segalen (1992) on folklore and on proverbs as ideology in gender power relations.

9. For an overview of the study of France by French anthropologists, especially since the 1970s, see Rogers (1999 and 2001).

10. See also Varenne (1984).

11. An important exception to this is Anthony Free (1996) who notes Bourdieu's Mediterranean approach and critiques his assumptions about homogeneous community life among the Kabyle. Unfortunately, Free depended only on *Outline* and *The Logic of Practice* in his critique of Bourdieu, neglecting the work coauthored with Sayad and the French rural research he conducted. Addi (2002) has more recently undertaken a major evaluation of Bourdieu's work that he frames as anthropological (concerned with "tradition") and sociological (concerned with "modernity") in Algeria.

12. It is particularly noteworthy that Gilmore does not discuss Bourdieu in this article because Gilmore explicitly argues for an anthropology *of* the Mediterranean "which includes both Christian and Muslim sides" and which he argues is "both new and controversial" (1982: 175). He distinguishes this from anthropological work simply done in the region. Since Bourdieu worked in both southwestern France and Algeria, he clearly was working on both "sides" and whether explicitly or not, recognized the affinities between peasant societies in the two regions. However, as the English translation of *The Logic of Practice,* Bourdieu's first book to include material from his work in both rural France and Algeria, did not appear until 1990, much of his French work was seemingly unknown to scholars working outside of France in the 1980s. It remains so for the most part.

4. HABITUS AND EMOTION

1. An example of this is Marcus and Fischer (1986), in which they have an entire chapter devoted to issues of personhood and emotion in anthropology but place references to Bourdieu's work in a chapter on political economy, with a focus on his contributions to scholarship on agency and structure.

2. In France, the editor of the journal *Terrain* has reported (Langlois 1999: 414) that as she was organizing a special issue on emotions (*Terrain* 1994), she had to search high and low for studies by French anthropologists, ignoring the work of Bourdieu. Seeing this as a "classic topic in the United States," she turned to Vincent Crapanzano to write an overview of the field (Crapanzano 1994). In her landmark ethnographic study of emotions on Ifaluk, which confronts Western theories of emotion and advances the anthropology of emotion in numerous ways, Catherine Lutz (1998 [1988]) cites Bourdieu only briefly and in a limited context, positioning him (misguidedly, I think) as someone who rejects an objective, "outsider" perspective in fieldwork. She does not acknowledge his work on the habitus as embodiment or draw out its implications for emotion in any way. Only a brief mention of his early work on honor is cited in Lutz and White's (1986) review of the literature.

3. Bourdieu and his bibliographer Yvette Delsaut (Bourdieu and Delsaut 2002: 191) also cited this in a footnote in their joint interview, with the comment that it was unfinished (*il n'a pas connu de suite*). Bourdieu objected, however, to the citation of it in HyperBourdieu.

4. Lane has interpreted this statement by Bourdieu to indicate that it refers to his early essays on Algerian peasants and subproletariats (Lane 2000: 24), but I think it is clear from the context of the interview that Bourdieu is referring to his much earlier work on the philosophy of Merleau-Ponty, before he was conscripted to the Army and left for Algeria. This is not to say, however, that this work did not influence his eventual approach in Algeria, as I argue in this chapter.

5. I will not elaborate here on the deep history of sociological and anthropological approaches to emotion but will focus on relationships between Bourdieu's thought and contemporary approaches. Good sources for those histories and for broader discussions of

emotion in social thought include Lutz and White (1986); Williams (2001); Schweder and Levine (1984); Fisher and Chon (1989); Scherer and Ekman (1984): Lynch (1990); Leavitt (1996).

6. For an overview of the literature on the sociology of emotions, and a call for what she terms "emotional sociology," see Ellis (1991).

7. For just a few examples, see Briggs (1970) among the Eskimo; Crapanzano's (1985 [1980]) study of a Moroccan man; Abu-Lughod's (1986) work among Bedouin women; Owen Lynch's (1990) edited volume on emotion in India; Lutz's (1998) work in Micronesia; Michelle (1980) and Renato Rosaldo's (1989) work in the Philippines; Geertz in Indonesia and Morocco (1973; 1995); Morton's (1996) study in Tonga; Behar's (1993) work a Mexican peasant woman; etc. In keeping with Fabian's (1983) observation that alterity is accomplished with distance in time as well as in space, one can also mention the work of Harkin (2003) on ethnohistory and emotion in the Northwest Coast, and the volume by Medick and Sabean (1982) on the history of the family and emotion.

8. See Morton (1996: 215–16) for a brief overview of these alternative views. She maintains that the ethnopsychological and social constructivist positions on emotion do not rule out the biological basis for emotion even while they focus on the subjective experience and social meanings of it.

9. Genealogies of the terms habit and habitus can be found in Kauppi (2000). Bourdieu never claimed to have invented this term, and was critical of those who accused him of either doing so or misusing the term in light of previous incarnations. See Bourdieu (1990b: 12–13 and 1996a: 181 and 375, fn. 5).

10. The parallels between Bourdieu's concept of habitus and Anthony Gidden's (1984) concept of "structuration," as well as Raymond Williams's (1961) concept of "structure of feeling," have been noted by other scholars. I am not going to discuss these here, but will point out that Bourdieu's concept departs from the other two in its emphasis on the internalization of the habitus and its preconscious dispositions. Both Giddens and Williams see social action as more emergent and consciously taken than does Bourdieu.

11. Barnard (1990) has drawn attention to parallels between Bourdieu's concept of dispositions and that proposed by Cifford Geertz in some of his earlier writings. Barnard writes that habitus corresponds to Geertz's concept of culture, and that Geertz sought to bridge the Cartesian dualism of body and mind with the concept of dispositions, as did Bourdieu. He defined these as "tendencies, capacities, propensities, skills, habits, liabilities, proneness" (1973: 95; cited in Barnard 1990: 64). Barnard argues that significant differences between the work of these two theorists overshadow any similarity (the semiotics of Geertz, the Marxism of Bourdieu), however, and that Geertz never systematically developed the concept of dispositions as did Bourdieu.

12. In this passage, there are echoes of Elias's comment on the fear of death, "a collective destruction," quoted earlier in this chapter. Whereas Bourdieu is talking about the individual's fear, however, Elias is referring to a group dynamic.

13. Alain Touraine, along with Raymond Boudon, were in opposite camps to that of Bourdieu in France, both espousing more individual-centered approaches associated with "methodological individualism." For a discussion of the rivalries among these leading figures in French sociology, circa the 1970s, see Lemert (1981). The animosity continued up until Bourdieu's death.

14. Here Bourdieu is suggesting that "authenticity" is more present in his view of social action guided by habitus (in a situation in which there is harmony between habitus and structure) than in Sartre's position that this constitutes a form of "alienation" and "bad faith," so that "authenticity" is located only in acts that are freely and consciously chosen.

15. These properties are well enacted through the portrayal, bordering on parody, of

the bourgeois diplomat played by the French actor Thierry L'Hermitte in the recent Merchant-Ivory movie *Le Divorce,* based on Diane Johnson's novel. This character is, interestingly, a combination of British (filmmakers), American (novelist), and French (actor) input.

16. This work first appeared in English translation in Bourdieu 1976. The 1972 article on bachelors was recently reprinted in Bourdieu's collection of essays on his rural French ethnography (2002a).

17. In their study of a village in Normandy, carried out a few years earlier than Bourdieu's in southwestern France, Bernot and Blanchard also discuss courtship behavior and the fact that "good matches" are often achieved. They write that "in reality, the two partners are more 'found' than chosen" (1953: 188; my translation). Their explanation for this lies more in gentle parental steering of the youth, however, whereas Bourdieu posits the internalized dispositions that lead to the right "choice." See also Zonabend (1984) on changing strategies of courtship associated with village dances in Burgundy, and changing roles of sentiment and coercion in marriage decisions. We can see the influence of Bourdieu's work on Zonabend's analysis, whereas the Nouville study predates Bourdieu's research.

18. See, for example, discussions in Bertilsson (1986); Luhman (1986); Langford (1999); Evans (2003).

19. Two other works that connect dances to bodily habitus are Cowan (1990) and Elias (1984). Jane Cowan argues in her ethnography on gender, power, and dance in Greece that the body can be an "agent of practice" and she employs Bourdieu's more nuanced theory of habitus dating from *Outline,* rather than his earlier work in Béarn, which she does not cite. Norbert Elias used a metaphor of dance to describe the relations between habitus and configuration, with the dance being a somewhat stable setting, in which individuals expressed their habitus (in a more structural-functionalist approach than that taken by Bourdieu).

20. Bernot and Blanchard (1953) similarly point to the village dance as the main setting for encounters between couples in Nouville, but describe the setting without pointing to the dilemmas of bachelors. Their analysis does not focus on a problem of bachelorhood in the village but on the influences of mass media and cinema on youth.

21. See Reed-Danahay (2001b) for an overview of autobiographical approaches in ethnography.

22. See also Kleinman and Copp (1993), on emotions and fieldwork from a sociological perspective.

5. SITUATED SUBJECTIVITIES

1. Augé uses this term to describe places where a diverse collection of people are in transit and not obviously connected to each other, such as supermarkets and airports. Some of these have higher status than others. He connects this to the postmodern condition. I have made use of both Augé's *non-lieu* (nonplace) and Bourdieu's *lieu* (location) in an analysis of concepts of "home" in an American nursing home (Reed-Danahay 2000).

2. The study of the real estate market was a topic of research for Bourdieu and collaborators in the 1990s, much of which was published in *Les structures sociales de l'économie* (2000a).

3. Bourdieu was aware that these two would be confused by readers, and took pains to explain the difference. He tried to preempt criticisms of his methodology of using real names of scholars (not only Lévi-Strauss, but also Foucault, Althusser, et al.) in his introductory chapter called "A Book for Burning?"

4. The French version of this article (Bourdieu 2003d) appeared in print after the English version (Bourdieu 2000c). In it, Bourdieu uses the term *économiste spontané* (spontaneous economist).

5. In my remarks about this text, I will quote passages from both the translated version (1999) and the original French version (1993), indicating when I have translated a passage myself. In the few instances when I have done this, it is for consistency in terminology. For example, the translator turns the French "dispositions" into "orientations," ignoring the theoretical history in Bourdieu's work of that term. Also, she translated "objectivation" in the French to "objectification." As Bourdieu uses both terms ("objectification" in French), it is obvious that he wished to distinguish between them. See also Bourdieu (2003).

6. Bourdieu set out his critique of that methodology in the chapter on "Understanding" in *The Weight of the World* and in the earlier essay on "L'Opinion publique n'existe pas" published in *Questions de Sociologie* (Bourdieu 1980b).

7. Bourdieu increasingly came to critique neoliberalism in the last decade of his life. An article that appeared in *Le Monde Diplomatique* (Bourdieu 1998d) and the short book *Acts of Resistance: Against the Tyranny of the Market* (Bourdieu 1998c), are good sources for his thinking on this.

CONCLUSION

1. I assume this book may eventually be published posthumously. Bourdieu published shorter pieces on Manet, one of which was reprinted in *The Field of Cultural Production* (1993a).

2. A posthumously published collection (Bourdieu 2002h) of Bourdieu's political writings spanning his career demonstrates his long-standing commitment to political issues, starting with the Algerian war. As the two editors of the collection indicate in their introduction, this volume was published, in part, as a response to the critics of Bourdieu who vilified him for using his high academic position to engage in political struggles from the 1990s on.

3. Anthropological concerns with representations of fieldwork and other research in writing provoked interesting discussions following Clifford and Marcus's (1986) *Writing Culture*. See especially Spencer (1989), Behar and Gordon (1995), and Okely and Callaway (1992).

BIBLIOGRAPHY

BOURDIEU, PIERRE

1958   *Sociologie de l'Algérie.* Paris: Presses Universitaires de France.

1962a   *The Algerians.* Alan C. M. Ross, trans. Boston: Beacon Press.

1962b   Les relations entre les sexes dans la societé paysanne. *Les Temps Modernes* 195: 307–331.

1962c   Célibat et condition paysanne. *Études Rurales* (Paris) 5/6: 32–136.

1963a   (and Alain Darbel, Jean-Paul Rivet, and Claude Seibel) *Travail et travailleurs en Algérie.* Paris and The Hague: Mouton.

1963b   The Attitude of the Algerian Peasant toward Time. Gerald E. Williams, trans. In *Mediterranean Countrymen: Essays in the Social Anthropology of the Mediterranean.* Julian A. Pitt-Rivers, ed. Pp. 55–72. Paris and The Hague: Mouton.

1964a   (and Abdelmalek Sayad) *Le déracinement: La crise de l'agriculture traditionelle en Algérie.* Paris: Les Éditions de Minuit.

1964b   (and Abdelmalek Sayad) Paysans déracinés: Bouleversements morphologiques et changements culturels en Algérie. *Études rurales* (Paris) 12: 56–94.

1964c   (and Jean-Claude Passeron) *Les héritiers: Les étudiants et la culture.* Paris: Les Éditions de Minuit.

1964d   (and Jean-Claude Passeron and Michel Eliard) *Les étudiants et leurs études.* Paris and The Hague: Mouton.

1965a   (and Marie Claire Bourdieu) Le paysan et la photographie. *Revue Française de Sociologie* 6(2): 164–174.

1965b   (and Luc Boltanski, Robert Castel, Jean-Claude Chamboredon, Gérard Lagneau, and Dominique Schnapper) *Un art moyen: Essais sur les usages sociaux de la photographie.* Paris: Les Éditions de Minuit.

1965c   (and Jean-Claude Passeron, and Monique de Saint Martin, with Christian Baudelot and Guy Vincent) *Rapport pédagogique et communication.* Paris and The Hague: Mouton.

1966a   The Sentiment of Honour in Kabyle Society. In *Honour and Shame: The Values of Mediterranean Society.* John G. Peristiany, ed. Pp. 191–241. London: Weidenfeld and Nicholson.

1966b Condition de classe et position de classe. *Archives Européennes de Sociologie* (Paris). 7(2): 201–223.

1966c (and Alain Darbel and Dominique Schnapper) *L'amour de l'art: Les musées d'art et leur public.* Paris: Les Éditions de Minuit.

1967a Systems of Education and Systems of Thought. *International Social Science Journal* (Paris) 19(3): 338–358.

1967b Postface. In *Architecture gothique et pensée scholastique.* Erwin Panofsky. Pp. 133–67. Paris: Minuit.

1967c (and Jean-Claude Passeron) Sociology and Philosophy in France since 1945. Death and Resurrection of a Philosophy Without Subject. *Social Research* 34(1): 162–212.

1968   (and Jean-Claude Chamboredon and Jean-Claude Passeron) *Le métier de sociologue: Préalables épistémologiques.* Paris: Mouton and Bordas.

1970   (and Jean-Claude Passeron) *La reproduction: Eléments pour une théorie du système d'enseignement.* Paris: Les Éditions de Minuit.

1971   Genèse et structure du champ religieux. *Revue Française de Sociologie* 12(3): 295–334.

1972a *Esquisse d'une théorie de la pratique: Précédé de trois études d'ethnologie Kabyle.* Genéve: Librairie Droz.

1972b Les stratégies matrimoniales dans le système de reproduction. *Annales: Économies, Sociétés, Civilisations* 27(4/5): 1105–1127.

1973   (and Luc Boltanski and Monique de Saint Martin) Les stratégies de reconversion. Les classes sociales et le système d'enseignement. *Information sur les sciences sociales* (Paris) 12(5): 61–113.

1976   Marriage Strategies as Strategies of Social Reproduction. In *Family and Society.* Robert Forster and Orest Ranum, eds. Pp. 117–144. Baltimore and London: Johns Hopkins University Press.

1977a *Outline of a Theory of Practice.* Richard Nice, trans. Cambridge: Cambridge University Press.

1977b Afterword. Mia Fuller, trans. In *Reflections on Fieldwork in Morocco.* Paul Rabinow. Pp. 163–167. Berkeley: University of California Press.

1977c Cultural Reproduction and Social Reproduction. In *Power and Ideology in Education.* Jerome Karabel and A.H. Halsey, eds. Pp. 487–510. New York: Oxford University Press.

1977d Une classe objet. *Actes de la Recherche en Sciences Sociales* 17/18: 2–5.

1978   (and Luc Boltanski) Changes in Social Structure and Changes in the Demand for Education. In *Contemporary Europe: Social Structures and Cultural Patterns.* Salvador Giner and Margaret S. Archer, eds. Pp. 197–227. London: Routledge and Kegan Paul.

1979a *La distinction: Critique sociale du jugement.* Paris: Les Éditions de Minuit.

1979b Les trois états du capital culturel. *Actes de la Recherche en Sciences Sociales* 30: 3–6.

1979c (and Jean-Claude Passeron) *The Inheritors. French Students and their Relation to Culture.* Richard Nice, trans. Chicago and London: University of Chicago Press.

1980a *Le sens pratique.* Paris: Les Éditions de Minuit.

1980b *Questions de sociologie.* Paris: Les Éditions de Minuit.

1980c L'identité et la représentation. Eléments pour une réflexion critique sur l'idée de région. *Actes de la Recherche en Sciences Sociales* 35: 62–72.

1981a Structures, Strategies and the Habitus. In *French Sociology. Rupture and Renewal since 1968.* Charles C. Lemert, ed. Pp. 86–96. New York: Columbia University Press.

1981b Men and Machines. In *Advances in Social Theory and Methodology: Toward an Integration of Micro-and Macro-sociologies.* Karin Knorr-Cetina and Aron V. Cicourel, eds. Pp. 304–317. Boston and London: Routledge and Kegan Paul.

1982a *Ce que parler veut dire: L'économie des échanges linguistiques.* Paris: Librairie Arthème Fayard.

1982b Les rites d'institution. *Actes de la Recherche en Sciences Sociales* 43: 58–63.

1982c *Leçon sur la leçon.* Paris: Editions de Minuit.

1984a *Homo academicus.* Paris: Les Éditions de Minuit.

1984b *Distinction: A Social Critique of the Judgement of Taste.* Richard Nice, trans. Cambridge, Mass.: Harvard University Press.

1985a The Genesis of the Concepts of Habitus and Field. *Sociocriticism* 2(2): 11–24.

1985b Du bon usage de l'ethnologie (Interview with Mouloud Mammeri). *Awal. Cahiers d'études berbéres* (Paris) 1: 7–29.

1986a L'illusion biographique. *Actes de la Recherche en Sciences Sociales* 62/63: 69–72.

1986b The Forms of Capital. In *Handbook of Theory and Research in the Sociology of Education.* John G. Richardson, ed. Pp. 241–258. New York and London: Greenwood Press.

1987 *Choses dites.* Paris: Les Éditions de Minuit.

1988a *L'ontologie politique de Martin Heidegger.* Paris: Les Éditions de Minuit.

1988b *Homo Academicus.* Peter Collier, trans. Stanford, Calif.: Stanford University Press.

1988c Flaubert's Point of View. *Critical Inquiry* 14(3): 539–562.

1989a *La noblesse d'état: Grandes écoles et esprit de corps.* Paris: Les Éditions de Minuit.

1989b Reproduction interdite. La dimension symbolique de la domination économique. *Études rurales* (Paris) 113/114: 15–36.

1990a *The Logic of Practice.* Richard Nice, trans. Stanford, Calif.: Stanford University Press.

1990b *In Other Words: Essays Towards a Reflexive Sociology.* Matthew Adamson, trans. Stanford, Calif.: Stanford University Press.

1990c The Scholastic Point of View. *Cultural Anthropology* 5 (4): 380–391.

1990d (and Luc Boltanski, Robert Castel, Jean-Claude Chamboredon, Gérard Lagneau, and Dominique Schnapper) *Photography: A Middle-Brow Art.* Shaun Whiteside, trans. Stanford, Calif.: Stanford University Press.

1990e (and Alain Darbel, and Dominique Schnapper) *The Love of Art. European Art Museums and Their Public.* Caroline Beattie and Nick Merriman, trans. Stanford, Calif.: Stanford University Press.

1990f [1977] (and Jean-Claude Passron) *Reproduction in Education, Society and Culture.* 2nd ed. Tom Bottomore, trans. London: Sage Publications.

1991a *The Political Ontology of Martin Heidegger.* Peter Collier, trans. Stanford, Calif.: Stanford University Press.

1991b (and James S. Coleman, eds.) *Social Theory for a Changing Society.* Boulder, Colo.: Westview Press.

1991c *Language and Symbolic Power.* John B. Thompson, trans. Cambridge, Mass.: Harvard University Press.

1991d Genesis and Structure of the Religious Field. *Comparative Social Research* 13: 1–44.

1991e Une vie perdue. Entretien avec deux agriculteurs béarnais. *Actes de la Recherche en Sciences Sociales* 90: 29–36.

1991f *"Meanwhile, I have come to know all the diseases of sociological understanding"* (an interview with Beate Krais). In *The Craft of Sociology.* Pierre Bourdieu, Jean-Claude Chamboredon, and Jean-Claude Passeron. Pp. 247–259. Berlin and New York: Walter de Gruyter.

1992a *Les règles de l'art. Genèse et structure du champ littéraire.* Paris: Éditions du Seuil.

1992b Rites as Acts of Institution. In *Honor and Grace in Anthropology.* J. G. Peristiany and J. Pitt-Rivers, eds. Pp. 79–89. Peter Just, trans. Cambridge: Cambridge University Press.

1992c (and Jean-Claude Passeron and Monique de Saint Martin, with Christian Baudelot and Guy Vincent) *Academic Discourse: Linguistic Misunderstanding and Professional Power.* Richard Teese, trans. Stanford, Calif.: Stanford University Press.

1992d (and Loïc J. D. Wacquant) *An Invitation to Reflexive Sociology.* Chicago: University of Chicago Press.

1993a   *The Field of Cultural Production. Essays on Art and Literature.* Randall Johnson, trans. New York: Columbia University Press.

1993b   À propos de la famille comme catégorie réalisée. *Actes de la Recherche en Sciences Sociales* 100: 32–36.

1993c   (and A. Accardo, G. Balazs, S. Beaud, et al.) *La misère du monde.* Paris: Éditions du Seuil.

1994a   *Raisons pratiques: Sur la théorie de l'action.* Paris: Éditions du Seuil.

1994b   Stratégies de reproduction et modes de domination. *Actes de la Recherche en Sciences Sociale*s 105: 3–12.

1994c   Rethinking the State: Genesis and Structure of the Bureaucratic Field. Loïc J. D. Wacquant and Samar Farage, trans. *Sociological Theory* 12(1): 1–18.

1996a   *The State Nobility: Elite Schools in the Field of Power.* Lauretta C. Clough, trans. Stanford, Calif.: Stanford University Press.

1996b   *Sur la télévision.* Paris: Éditions Liber.

1996c   *The Rules of Art: Genesis and Structure of the Literary Field.* Susan Emanuel, trans. Stanford, Calif.: Stanford University Press.

1996d   On the Family as a Realized Category. *Theory, Culture & Society* 13(1): 19–26.

1998a   *Contre-feux: Propos pour servir à la résistance contre l'invasion néo-libérale.* Paris: Liber.

1998b   *La domination masculine.* Paris: Éditions du Seuil.

1998c   *Practical Reason: On the Theory of Action.* Stanford, Calif.: Stanford University Press.

1998d   *Acts of Resistance: Against the New Myths of Our Time.* Oxford: Polity Press.

1998e   The Essence of Neoliberalism. Jeremy J. Shapiro, trans. *Le Monde Diplomatique* (Paris). December: 1–7. http://mondediplo.com/1998/12/08bourdieu, accessed November 6, 2003.

1999a   Pour un mouvement social européen. *Le Monde Diplomatique* (Paris). June: 1–8. http://www.monde-diplomatique.fr/1999/06/BOURDIEU/12158.html, accessed July 18, 2003.

1999b   (and Alain Accardo, Gabrielle Balazs, Stephane Beaud, et al.) *The Weight of the World: Social Suffering in Contemporary Society.* Priscilla Parkhurst Ferguson, Susan Emanuel, Joe Johnson, and Shoggy T. Waryn, trans. Stanford, Calif.: Stanford University Press.

2000a   *Les structures sociales de l'économie.* Paris: Éditions du Seuil.

2000b   [1997] Pascalian Meditations. Richard Nice, trans. Stanford, Calif.: Stanford University Press.

2000c   Making the Economic Habitus. Algerian Workers Revisited. Richard Nice and Loïc J. D. Wacquant, trans. *Ethnography* 1(1): 17–41.

2000d (and Loïc J. D. Wacquant) The Organic Ethnologist of Algerian Migration. *Ethnography* 1(2): 173–182.

2001a *Science de la science et réflexivité: Cours du Collège de France, 2000–2001.* Paris: Raison d'Agir.

2001b *Masculine Domination.* Richard Nice, trans. Stanford, Calif.: Stanford University Press.

2002a *Le bal des célibataires: Crise de la société paysanne en Béarn.* Paris: Points Seuil.

2002b The Role of Intellectuals Today. *Theoria* 99: 1–6.

2002c Inédit: "J'avais 15 ans . . .": Pierre par Bourdieu. *Le Nouvel Observateur:* L'Hebdo on line (Paris). No. 1943. January 31. http://www.nouvelobs.com/dossiers/p1943/a10243.html, accessed December 6, 2003.

2002d Habitus. In *Habitus: A Sense of Place.* Jean Hillier and E. Rooksby, eds. Pp. 27–34. Aldershot, U.K.: Ashgate.

2002e Les conditions sociales de la circulation internationale des idées. *Actes de la Recherche en Sciences Sociales* 145: 3–8.

2002f (and Yvette Delsaut) Entretien entre Pierre Bourdieu et Yvette Delsaut sur l'esprit de la recherche. In *Bibliographie des Travaux de Pierre Bourdieu.* Yvette Delsaut and Marie-Christine Rivière. Pp. 177–239. Paris: Les Temps des Cerises.

2002g *Ein Soziologischer Selbstversuch.* Frankfurt: Suhrcamp.

2002h (and Franck Poupeau and Thierry Discepolo) *Interventions, 1961–2001: Science sociale et action politique.* Marseille: Agone.

2003a *Images d'Algérie: Une affinité élective.* Edited by Franz Schultheis. Arles: Actes Sud.

2003b *The Social Structures of the Economy.* Cambridge, U.K.: Polity Press.

2003c Participant Objectivation. *Journal of the Royal Anthropological Institute* 9: 281–294.

2003d La fabrique de l'habitus économique. *Actes de la Recherche en Sciences Sociales* 150: 79–90.

2004 *Esquisse pour une auto-analyse.* Paris: Éditions Raisons d'Agir.

PUBLICATIONS BY OTHER AUTHORS

Abélès, Marc
1991 [1989] Quiet Days in Burgundy: A Study of Local Politics. Annella McDermott, trans. Cambridge: Cambridge University Press.
2000 *L'ethnologie à l'assemblée.* Paris: Editions Odile Jacob.

Abu-Lughod, Lila
1989 Zones of Theory in the Anthropology of the Arab World. *Annual Review of Anthropology* 18: 267–306.

1993   *Writing Women's Worlds: Bedouin Stories.* Berkeley: University of California Press.

Accardo, Alain
1983   *Initiation à la sociologie de l'illusionisme social: Invitation à la lecture des oeuvres de Pierre Bourdieu.* Éditions le Mascaret.

Addi, Lahouari
2002   *Sociologie et anthropologie chez Pierre Bourdieu: Le paradigme anthropologique Kabyle et ses conséquences théoriques.* Paris: Éditions La Découverte.

Agar, Michael
1980   *The Professional Stranger: An Informal Introduction to Ethnography.* New York: Academic Press.

Albera, Dionigi, Anton Blok, and Christian Bromberger, eds.
2001   *L'Anthropologie de la Méditerranée/Anthropology of the Mediterranean.* Paris: Maisonneuve et Larose.

Althusser, Louis
1970   Ideologie et appareils ideologiques d'état. *La Pensée* 151: 3–38.
1971   Ideology and Ideological State Apparatuses: Notes Toward an Investigation. In *Lenin and Philosophy.* Pp. 127–186. B. Brewster, trans. New York: Monthly Review Press.

Anderson, Benedict
1991 [1983]   *Imagined Communities: Reflections on the Origin and Spread of Nationalism.* Revised ed. London: Verso.

Anderson-Levitt, Kathryn M.
2002   *Teaching Cultures: Knowledge for Teaching First Grade in France and the United States.* Cresskill, N.J.: Hampton Press.

Anderson-Levitt, Kathryn M., ed.
2003   *Local Meanings, Global Schooling: Anthropology and World Culture Theory.* New York: Palgrave Macmillan.

Apple, Michael
1982   *Education and Power.* Boston: Routledge and Kegan Paul.

Augé, Marc
1987   Qui est l'autre? Un itinéraire anthropologique. *L'Homme* 27 (103): 7–26.
1995 [1992]   *Non-Places: Introduction to an Anthropology of Supermodernity.* J. Howe, trans. New York: Verso.

Bahloul, Joëlle
1991   France-USA: Ethnographie d'une migration intellectuelle. *Ethnologie Française* 21: 49–55.

Bailey, F. G.
1983   *The Tactical Uses of Passion: An Essay on Power, Reason, and Reality.* Ithaca, N.Y., and London: Cornell University Press.

Ball, Stephen J.
1990   Introducing Monsieur Foucault. In *Foucault and Education: Discipline and Knowledge*. Stephen J. Ball, ed. Pp. 1–8. London and New York: Routledge.

Barnard, Henry, ed.
1999   Bourdieu Bibliography. Massey University. http://www.massey.ac.nz/~nzsrda/bourdieu/home.htm, accessed April 9, 2004.

Bateson, Gregory
1958 [1936]   *Naven*. 2nd ed. Stanford, Calif.: Stanford University Press.

Baudelot, Christian, and Roger Establet
1971   *L'école capitaliste en France*. Paris: Maspero.

Behar, Ruth
1993   *Translated Woman: Crossing the Border with Esperanza's Story*. Boston: Beacon Press.
1996   *The Vulnerable Observer: Anthropology That Breaks Your Heart*. Boston: Beacon Press.

Bellah, Robert N.
1999   Max Weber and World-Denying Love: A Look at the Historical Sociology of Religion. *Journal of the American Academy of Religion* 67(2): 277–304.

Bellier, Irène
1993   *L'ENA comme si vous y étiez*. Paris: Editions Seuil.

Belmont, Nicole
1974   *Arnold Van Gennep: Le Créateur de l'Ethnographie Française*. Paris: Payot.

Benedict, Ruth
1989 [1934]   *Patterns of Culture*. Boston: Houghton Mifflin.

Bennoune, Mafhoud
1985   What Does It Mean to Be a Third World Anthropologist? *Dialectical Anthropology* 9: 357–364.

Bernot, Lucien, and René Blanchard
1953   *Nouville: Un village français*. Paris: Institute d'Ethnologie.

Bertaux, Daniel, ed.
1981   *Biography and Society: The Life History Approach in the Social Sciences*. Beverly Hills, Calif.: Sage.

Bertaux, Daniel, and Martin Kohli
1984   *The Life Story Approach: A Continental View*. Annual Review of Anthropology 10: 215–237.

Berthelot, J-M.
1982   Réflexions sur les théories de la scolarisation. *Revue Française de Sociologie* 23: 585–604.

Berthelot, J.-M., ed.
2000   *La sociologie française contemporain*. Paris: Presses Universitaires de France.

Bertilsson, Margareta
1986   Love's Labour Lost? A Sociological View. *Theory, Culture and Society* 3(2): 19–35.

Bhabha, Homi K.
1994   *The Location of Culture.* London and New York: Routledge.

Boli, John, Francisco O. Ramirez and John W. Meyer
1985   Explaining the Origins and Expansion of Mass Education. *Comparative Education Review* 29(2): 145–170.

Bologh, Roslyn W.
1990   *Love or Greatness: Max Weber and Masculine Thinking—A Feminist Inquiry.* London and Boston: Unwin Hyman.

Boudon, Raymond
1973   *L'inégalité des chances: La mobilité sociale dans les societés industrielles.* Paris: Armand Colin.

Bourdieu, Emmanuel
2004   *Le vert paradis.* Feature film. Paris: Haut et Court.

Bourdieu, Jérome, Patrick Champagne, and Franck Poupeau, eds.
2003   Regards croisés sur l'anthropolgie de Pierre Bourdieu. Special issue. *Actes de la Recherche en Sciences Sociale* 150 (Dec).

Bové, José, and Gilles Luneau
2000   *Nous, paysans.* Paris: Hazan.

Bowen, John R., and Martine Bentaboulet
2002   On the Institutionalization of the "Human and Social Sciences" in France. *Anthropological Quarterly* 75(3): 537–556.

Bowles, Samuel, and Herbert Gintis
1976   *Schooling in Capitalist America.* New York: Basic Books.

Brandes, Stanley
1980   *Metaphors of Masculinity: Sex and Status in Andalusian Folklore.* Philadelphia: University of Pennsylvania Press.

Briggs, Jean
1970   *Never in Anger: Portrait of an Eskimo Family.* Cambridge, Mass.: Harvard University Press.

Bromberger, Christian
2001   Aux trois sources de l'ethnologie du monde méditerranéen dans la tradition française. In *L'Anthropologie de la Méditerranée/Anthropology of the Mediterranean.* Dionigi Albera, Anton Blok and Christian Bromberger, eds. Pp. 65–83. Paris: Maisonneuve et Larose.

Brown, Nicholas, and Imre Szumen, eds.
1999   *Pierre Bourdieu: Fieldwork in Culture.* Lanham, Md.: Rowman and Littlefield, Publishers.

Brubaker, Rogers
1983 Rethinking Classical Theory: The Sociological Vision of Pierre Bourdieu. *Theory and Society* 14: 745–775.
1993 Social Theory as Habitus. In *Bourdieu: Critical Perspectives.* Craig Calhoun, Edward LiPuma, and Moishe Postone, eds. Chicago: University of Chicago Press.

Calhoun, Craig, Edward LiPuma, and Moishe Postone, eds.
1993 *Bourdieu: Critical Perspectives.* Chicago: University of Chicago Press.

Carles, Pierre
2001 *La sociologie est un sport de combat.* Documentary film. Paris: C-P Productions and VF Films. [Released in English as *Sociology is a Martial Art.* New York: First Run/Icarus Films.

Certeau, Michel de
1988 [1984] *The Practice of Everyday Life.* S. Randall, trans. Berkeley: University of California Press.

Chamoiseau, Patrick
1997[1994] *School Days.* Linda Coverdale, trans. Lincoln: University of Nebraska Press.

Chiva, Isac
1992 Entre livre et musée: Emergence d'une ethnologie de la France. In *Ethnologies en miroir: La France et les pays allemandes.* Isas Chiva and Utz Jeggle, eds. Pp. 9–33. Paris: Editions de la Maison des Sciences de l'Homme.

Chiva, Isac, and Utz Jeggle, eds.
1992 *Ethnologies en miroir: La France et les pays allemandes.* Paris: Editions de la Maison des Sciences de l'Homme.

Chombart de Lauwe, P.
1956 *La vie quotidienne des familles ouvrières.* Paris: Centre National de la Recherche Scientifique.

Coffey, Amanda
1999 *The Ethnographic Self: Fieldwork and the Representation of Identity.* London, Thousand Oaks, Calif., and New Delhi: Sage Publications.

Collier, Jane Fishburne
1997 *From Duty to Desire: Remaking Families in a Spanish Village.* Princeton, N.J.: Princeton University Press.

Colonna, Fanny
1975 *Instituteurs algériens, 1883–1939.* Paris: Presses de la Fondation Nationale des Sciences Politiques.
1997 Educating Conformity in French Colonial Algeria. In *Tensions of Empire: Colonial Cultures in a Bourgeois World.* Frederick Cooper and Ann Laura Stoler, eds. Pp. 346–370. Berkeley: University of California Press.

Comité Interministériel sur l'Education Nationale
2003   Le Debat National sur l'Avenir de l'Ecole. Press Release. Paris. http://
        www.premier-ministre.gouv.fr (7/28/03) [date press release was posted to
        this website].

Connell, R. W.
1983   *Which Way Is Up? Essays on Sex, Class, and Culture.* Sydney: George Allen
        and Unwin.

Cowan, Jane
1990   *Dance and the Body Politic in Northern Greece.* Princeton, N.J.: Princeton
        University Press.

Crapanzano, Vincent
1994   Réflexions sur un anthropologie des émotions. *Terrain* 22: 109–117.
1985 [1980]   *Tuhami: Portrait of a Moroccan.* Chicago: University of Chicago
        Press.

Csordas, Thomas J.
1990   Embodiment as a Paradigm for Anthropology. *Ethos* 18(1): 5–47.

Davies, Charlotte Aull
1999   *Reflexive Ethnography: A Guide to Researching Selves and Others.* London:
        Routledge.

Décheaux, Jean-Hughes
1993   N. Elias et P. Bourdieu: Analyse conceptuelle comparée. *Archives Européene
        de Sociologie* 34: 364–385.

Delsaut, Yvette, and Marie-Christine Rivière
2002   *Bibliographie des travaux de Pierre Bourdieu.* Paris: Les Temps des Cerises.

Denzin, Norman
1989   *Interpretive Biography.* Newbury Park, Calif.: Sage Publications.

Dianteill, Erwan
2002   Pierre Bourdieu et la religion: Synthèse critique d'une synthèse critique.
        Archives de Science Sociales des Religions 118 (April–June): 5–19.

Driessen, Henk
2001   Divisions in Mediterranean Ethnography: A View from Both Shores. In
        L'anthropologie de la Méditerranée/Anthropology of the Mediterranean.
        Dionigi Albera, Anton Blok and Christian Bromberger, eds. Pp. 625–644.
        Paris: Maisonneuve et Larose.
1983   Male Sociability and Rituals of Masculinity in Rural Andalusia. *Anthro-
        pological Quarterly* 56: 125–133.

Dubisch, Jill, ed.
1986   *Gender and Power in Rural Greece.* Princeton, N.J.: Princeton University Press.

Dumont, Jean-Paul
1992 [1978]   *The Headman and I: Ambiguity and Ambivalence in the Field-
        working Experience.* 2nd ed. Prospect Heights, Ill.: Waveland Press.

Dumont, Louis
1951   La Tarasque: Essai de description d'un fait local d'un point de vue ethno-
        graphique. Paris: Gallimard.

Durkheim, Emile
1922   Éducation et sociologie. Paris: Alcan.
1925   L'éducation morale. Paris: Alcan.
1951   Suicide: A Study in Sociology. J. A. Spaulding and G. Simpson, trans. New
        York: Free Press.
1961   The Elementary Forms of Religious Life. J. W. Swain, trans. New York: Collier.
1969 [1928]   L'évolution pédagogique en France. Paris: Presses Universitaires de
        France.
1984   The Division of Labor in Society. W. D. Halls, trans. New York: Free Press.

Duru-Bellat, Marie
2000   L'analyse des inégalités de carrières scolaires: Pertinence et résistance des
        paradigmes des années soixante-dix. Education et Societés 1(5): 25–41.

Duru-Bellat, Marie, and Agnès Henriot-van Zanten
1992   Sociologie de l'école. Paris: Armand Colin.

Elias, Norbert
1978   The Civilizing Process. Edmund Jephcott, trans. New York: Urizen Books.
1991 [1987]   The Society of Individuals. Edmund Jephcott, trans. Oxford and
        Cambridge, Mass.: Basil Blackwell.
1998 [1980]   The Civilizing of Parents. In The Norbert Elias Reader. Johan
        Goudsblom and Stephen Mennell, eds. Pp. 189–211. Oxford: Blackwell.

Ellis, Carolyn
1991   Emotional Sociology. Studies in Symbolic Interaction 12: 123–145.
2003   The Ethnographic I: A Methodological Novel about Autoethnography. Wal-
        nut Creek, Calif.: AltaMira Press.

Encrevé, Pierre, and Rose-Marie Lagrave, eds.
2003   Travailler avec Bourdieu. Paris: Flammarion.

Evans, Mary
2003   Love: An Unromantic Discussion. Cambridge, U.K.: Polity Press.

Fabian, Johannes
1983   Time and the Other: How Anthropology Makes Its Object. New York: Co-
        lumbia University Press.

Favret-Saada, Jeanne
1980 [1977]   Deadly Words: Witchcraft in the Bocage. Catherine Cullen, trans.
        Cambridge: Cambridge University Press.

Fernandes, João Viegas
1988   From the Theories of Social and Cultural Reproduction to the Theory
        of Resistance. British Journal of Sociology of Education 9(2): 169–180.

Ferry, Luc, and Alain Renault
1990   French Philosophy of the Sixties: An Essay on Antihumanism. Mary H. S.

Cattani, trans. Amherst: University of Massachusetts Press. [Orig. *La Pensée 68: Essai sur l'anti-humanisme contemporain.* Paris: Gallimard, 1895.]

Fisher, Gene A., and Kyum Koo Chon
1989 Durkheim and the Social Construction of Emotions. *Social Psychology Quarterly* 52(1): 1–9.

Foley, Douglas E.
1990 *Learning Capitalist Culture: Deep in the Heart of Tejas.* Philadelphia: University of Pennsylvania Press.

Ford, Caroline
1993 *Creating the Nation in Provincial France: Religion and Political Identity in Brittany.* Princeton, N.J.: Princeton University Press.

Foucault, Michel
1975 *Surveiller et punir: La naissance de la prison.* Paris: Editions Gallimard.

Fowler, Bridget
1997 *Pierre Bourdieu and Cultural Theory: Critical Investigations.* London and Thousand Oaks, Calif.: Sage.

Fowler, Bridget, ed.
2000 *Reading Bourdieu on Society and Culture.* Oxford and Malden, Mass.: Blackwell Publishers.

Free, Anthony
1996 The Anthropology of Pierre Bourdieu: A Reconsideration. *Critique of Anthropology* 16(4): 395–416.

Frémont, Armand
1997 La terre. In *Les lieux de mémoire.* Pierre Nora, ed. Pp. 3047–3080. Paris: Gallimard.

Furet, François, and Jacques Ozouf
1982 *Reading and Writing: Literacy from Calvin to Jules Ferry.* La Maison des Sciences de l'Homme and Cambridge University Press, trans. Cambridge: Cambridge University Press; Paris: Editions de la Maison des Sciences de l'Homme.

Gaillard, Gérald
2003 Then and Now: Teaching Anthropology in France. In *Educational Histories of European Social Anthropology.* Learning Fields. Vol. 1. Dorle Dracklé, Iain Edgar and Thomas K. Schippers, eds. Pp. 156–168. New York and Oxford: Berghan Books.

Gaulejac, Vincent de
1995 [1987] *La névrose de classe: Trajectoire sociale et conflits d'identité.* 3rd ed. Paris: Hommes and Groupes.

Geertz, Clifford
1973 *The Interpretation of Cultures.* New York: Basic Books.
1995 *After the Fact: Two Countries, Four Decades, and One Anthropologist.* Cambridge, Mass.: Harvard University Press.

2000   *Available Light: Anthropological Reflections on Philosophical Topics.* Prince-
        ton, N.J.: Princeton University Press.

Giddens, Anthony
1984   *The Constitution of Society.* Berkeley: University of California Press.
1992   *The Transformation of Intimacy.* Cambridge, U.K.: Polity Press.

Giroux, Henry
1983   Rationality, Reproduction and Resistance: Toward a Critical Theory of
        Schooling. *Current Perspectives in Social Theory* 4: 85–117.
2001 [1983]   *Theory and Resistance in Education.* 2nd ed. Westport, Conn., and
        London: Bergin and Garvey Publishers.

Godelier, Maurice
1997   American Anthropology as Seen from France. *Anthropology Today* 13(1):
        3–5.

Goffman, Erving
1961   *Asylums: Essays on the Situation of Mental Patients.* New York: Anchor
        Books.

Goodman, Jane
2003   The Proverbial Bourdieu: Habitus and the Politics of Representation in
        the Ethnography of Kabylia. *American Anthropologist* 105(4): 782–93.

Goussault, Benedicte
2002   La mort de Pierre Bourdieu dans la presse. *EspacesTemps.net.* http://
        espacetemps.revues.org, accessed October 15, 2002.

Goux, Dominique, and Eric Maurin
1997   Meritocracy and Social Heredity in France: Some Aspects and Trends.
        European Sociological Review 13(2): 159–177.

Green, Andy
1997   *Education, Globalization and the Nation State.* New York: St. Martin's
        Press.
1990   *Education and State Formation: The Rise of Education Systems in England,
        France, and the USA.* London: Macmillan.

Grenfell, Michael, and Michael Kelly, eds.
1999   *Pierre Bourdieu: Language, Culture, and Education—Theory into Practice.*
        Bern and New York: Peter Lang.

Grenfell, Michael, and David James, eds.
1998   *Bourdieu and Education: Acts of Practical Theory.* London and Bristol, Pa.:
        Falmer Press.

Grew, Raymond, and Patrick Harrigan
1988   *School, State and Society: The Growth of Elementary Schooling in 19th Cen-
        tury France.* Ann Arbor: University of Michigan Press.

Grignon, Claude
1988   Presentation. In *33 Newport Street: Autobiographie d'un intellectuel issue*

des classes populaires anglaises. Richard Hoggart. Pp. 7–21. Christiane and Claude Grignon, trans. Paris: Gallimard Le Seuil.

Guillais, Joëlle
2002   *La teinturerie.* Trouville-sur-Mer: Editions le Reflet.

Gupta, Akhil and James Ferguson, eds.
1997   *Anthropological Locations: Boundaries and Grounds of a Field Science.* Berkeley: University of California Press.

Halbwachs, Maurice
1969   Introduction. In *L'évolution pédagogique en France.* Emile Durkheim. Pp. 1–5. Paris: Presses Universitaires de France.

Halls, W. D.
1976   *Education, Culture and Politics in Modern France.* Oxford: Pergamon Press.

Harker, Richard
1984   Reproduction, Habitus and Education. *British Journal of Sociology of Education* 5(2): 117–127.
1990   Bourdieu—Education and Reproduction. In *An Introduction to the Work of Pierre Bourdieu: The Practice of Theory.* Richard Harker, Cheleen Mahar, and Chris Wilkes, eds. Pp. 86–108. London: Macmillan Press.

Harker, Richard, Cheleen Mahar, and Chris Wilkes, eds.
1990   *An Introduction to the Work of Pierre Bourdieu: The Practice of Theory.* Richard Harker, Cheleen Mahar, and Chris Wilkes, eds. London: Macmillan Press.

Hayward, Clarissa Rile
2000   *De-Facing Power.* Cambridge and New York: Cambridge University Press

Hebdige, Dick
1979   *Subcultures: The Meaning of Style.* London: Methuen.

Hechter, Michael
1975   *Internal Colonialism: The Celtic Fringe in British National Development, 1536–1966.* Berkeley: University of California Press.

Hélias, Pierre-Jakèz
1978   *The Horse of Pride: Life in a Breton Village.* J. Guicharnaud, trans. New Haven, Conn.: Yale University Press.

Henry, Jean-Robert
1993   Introduction. In *French and Algerian Identities from Colonial Times to the Present.* Alec G. Hargreaves and Michael J. Heffernan, eds. Pp. 1–20. Lewiston, U.K.: The Edwin Mellen Press.

Henry, Jules
1936   The Linguistic Expression of Emotion. *American Anthropologist* 38(2): 250–256.

Hertz, Robert
1913   *Saint Besse, étude d'une culte alpèstre.* Paris: Armand Colin.

Herzfeld, Michael

1985   *The Poetics of Manhood.* Princeton, N.J.: Princeton University Press.

1987   *Anthropology through the Looking-Glass: Critical Ethnography in the Margins of Europe.* Cambridge: Cambridge University Press.

1997a *Cultural Intimacy: Social Poetics in the Nation-State.* New York and London: Routledge.

1997b *Portrait of a Greek Imagination: An Ethnographic Biography of Andreas Nenedakis.* Chicago: University of Chicago Press.

2001   Ethnographic and Epistemological Refractions of Mediterranean Identity. In *L'anthropologie de la Méditerranée/Anthropology of the Mediterranean.* Dionigi Albera, Anton Blok and Christian Bromberger, eds. Pp. 663–683. Paris: Maisonneuve et Larose.

2003   *The Body Impolitic: Artisans and Artifice in the Global Hierarchy of Value.* Chicago and London: University of Chicago Press.

Hillier, Jean, and E. Rooksby, eds.

2002   *Habitus: A Sense of Place.* Aldershot, U.K.: Ashgate.

Hind, Robert J.

1984   The Internal Colonialism Concept. *Comparative Studies in Society and History* 26(3): 543–68.

Hobsbawm, Eric

1988 [1983]   Mass-Producing Traditions: Europe 1870–1914. In *The Invention of Tradition.* Eric Hobsbawm and Terence Ranger, eds. Pp. 263–307. Cambridge: Cambridge University Press.

Hochschild, Arlie

1983   *The Managed Heart.* Berkeley: University of California Press.

Hoggart, Richard

1992 [1957]   *The Uses of Literacy.* New Brunswick, N.J., and London: Transaction Publishers.

1994   *A Measured Life: The Times and Places of an Orphaned Intellectual.* New Brunswick, N.J.: Transaction Publishers.

Holland, Dorothy C. and Margaret A. Eisenhart

1990   *Educated in Romance: Women, Achievement, and College Culture.* Chicago and London: University of Chicago Press.

hooks, bell

2000   *All About Love: New Visions.* New York: Perennial.

Irigaray, Luce

2002   *The Way of Love.* Heidi Bostic and Stephen Pluhácek, trans. London and New York: Continuum.

Jackson, Michael

1983   Knowledge of the Body. *Man* 18(2): 327–345.

Jenkins, Richard

1992   *Pierre Bourdieu.* London and New York: Routledge.

Jenkins, Timothy
1994 Fieldwork and the Perception of Everyday Life. *Man* 29: 433–455.

Kauppi, Niilo
1999 *The Politics of Embodiment: Habits, Power, and Bourdieu's Theory.* Bern and New York: Peter Lang.

Kelly, Gail Paradise, and David H. Kelly, eds.
1999 *French Colonial Education: Essays on Vietnam and West Africa.* New York: AMS Press.

Kleinman, Sherryl, and Martha A. Copp
1993 *Emotions and Fieldwork.* Newbury Park, Calif., London, and New Delhi: Sage Publications.

Lafont, Robert
1967 *La révolution régionaliste.* Paris: Gallimard.
1971 *Décoloniser en France: Les régions face à l'Europe.* Paris: Gallimard.

La Grave, Rose-Marie
1980 *Le village romanesque.* Le Paradou: Actes Sud.

Lahire, Bernard
1998 *L'homme pluriel.* Paris: Nathan.

Lakomski, Gabriele
1982 On Agency and Structure: Pierre Bourdieu and Jean-Claude Passeron's Theory of Symbolic Violence. *Curriculum Inquiry* 14(2): 151–163.

Lane, Jeremy
1997 "Domestiquer l'exotique . . . Exotiser le domestique": The Symbiosis of Ethnology and Sociology in the Work of Pierre Bourdieu. *Modern & Contemporary France* 5(4): 445–456.
1998 La bourdieumania fait des ravages dans les médias. *Modern and Contemporary France* 7(1): 105–108.
1999 "Un étrange retournement"? Pierre Bourdieu and the French Republican Tradition. *Modern & Contemporary France* 7(4): 457–470.
2000 *Pierre Bourdieu: A Critical Introduction.* London and Sterling, Va.: Pluto Press.

Langford, Wendy
1999 *Revolutions of the Heart: Gender, Power and the Delusions of Love.* London: Routledge.

Leavitt, John
1996 Meaning and Feeling in the Anthropology of the Emotions. *American Ethnologist* 23: 514–39.

Leiris, Michel
1950 L'ethnographe devant le colonialisme. *Temps Moderne* (August): 359.

Lemert, Charles
1981 *French Sociology: Rupture and Renewal Since 1968.* New York: Columbia University Press.

1986   French Sociology: After the Patrons, What? *Contemporary Sociology* 15: 689–719.

Léon, Antoine
1991   *Colonisation, enseignement et éducation: Étude historique et comparative.* Paris: L'Harmattan.

Le Sueur, James D.
2001   *Uncivil War: Intellectuals and Identity Politics during the Decolonization of Algeria.* Philadelphia: University of Pennsylvania Press.

Levinson, Bradley A. U.
2001   *We Are All Equal: Student Culture and Identity at a Mexican Secondary School, 1988–1998.* Durham, N.C.: Duke University Press.

Levinson, Bradley, Douglas E. Foley, and Dorothy C. Holland, eds.
1996   *The Cultural Production of the Educated Person: Critical Ethnographies of Schooling and Local Practice.* Albany: State University of New York Press.

Lévi-Strauss, Claude
1988 [1955]   *Tristes Tropiques.* John and Doreen Weightman, trans. New York: Penguin Books. [Orig. Paris: Libraire Plon, 1955.]

Lévi-Srauss, Claude, and Didier Eribon
1991 [1988]   *Conversations with Claude Lévi-Strauss.* Paula Wissing, trans. Chicago and London: University of Chicago Press. [Orig. French *De près et de loin.* Paris: Editions Odile Jabob, 1988.]

LeWita, Beatrix
1988   *Ni vue ni connue: Approche ethnographique de la culture bourgeoise.* Paris: Editions de la Maison des Sciences de l'Homme.

Lorcin, Patricia M. E.
1995   *Imperial Identities: Stereotyping, Prejudice and Race in Colonial Algeria.* London and New York: I. B. Tauris Publishers.

Low, Setha M., and Denise Lawrence-Zúñiga eds.
2003   *The Anthropology of Space and Place: Locating Culture.* Malden, Mass.: Blackwell Publishers.

Luhmann, Niklas
1986   *Love as Passion: The Codification of Intimacy.* Jeremy Gaines and Doris L. Jones, trans. Cambridge, Mass.: Harvard University Press.

Lutz, Catherine
1988   *Unnatural Emotions: Everyday Sentiments on a Micronesian Atoll and Their Challenge to Western Theory.* Chicago: University of Chicago Press.

Lutz, Catherine, and Geoffrey M. White
1986   The Anthropology of Emotions. *Annual Review of Anthropology* 15: 406–436.

Lynch, Owen
1990   The Social Construction of Emotion in India. In *Divine Passions: The*

Social Construction of Emotion in India. Owen Lynch, ed. Pp. 3–34. Berkeley: University of California Press.

Lyon, Margot L.
1988 Missing Emotion: The Limitations of Cultural Constructionism in the Study of Emotion. *Cultural Anthropology* 10(2): 244–263.

Maget, M.
1955 Remarques sur le village comme cadre de recherches anthropologiques. *Bulletin de Psychologie.* 375–382.
1962 *Guide practique d'étude directe des comportements culturels.* Paris: CNRS.

Mahar, Cheleen
1990 Pierre Bourdieu: The Intellectual Project. In *An Introduction to the Work of Pierre Bourdieu: In The Practice of Theory.* Richard Harker, Cheleen Mahar and Chris Wilkes, eds. Pp. 26–57. London: Macmillan.

Marcus, George E.
1994 On Ideologies of Reflexivity in Contemporary Efforts to Remake the Human Sciences. *Poetics Today* 15(3): 383–404.

Marcus, George, and Michael M. J. Fischer.
1986 *Anthropology as Cultural Critique.* Chicago: University of Chicago Press.

Mark, Vera
1987 In Search of the Occitan Village: Regionalist Ideologies and the Ethnography of Southern France. *Anthropological Quarterly* 60(02): 64–70.

Marshall, James D.
1990 Foucault and Educational Knowledge. In *Foucault and Education: Discipline and Knowledge.* S. J. Ball, ed. London and New York: Routledge.

Mauss, Marcel
1979 [1950] Body Techniques. *Sociology and Psychology: Essays.* Ben Brewster, trans. Pp. 97–123. London, Boston, and Henley: Routledge and Kegan Paul.

Medick, Hans, and David Warren Sabean
1982 Interest and Emotion in Family and Kinship Studies: A Critique of Social History and Anthropology. In *Interest and Emotion: Essays on the Study of Family and Kinship.* Hans Medick and David Warren Sabean, eds. Pp. 9–27. Cambridge: Cambridge University Press and Paris: Editions de la Maison des Sciences de l'Homme.

Mendelson, E. Michael
1958 Some Present Trends of Social Anthropology in France. *British Journal of Sociology* 9(3): 251–270.

Mendras, Henri, and Alistair Cole
1991 *Social Change in Modern France: Towards a Cultural Anthropology of the Fifth Republic.* London: Cambridge University Press.

Minge-Kalman, Wanda
1978 The Industrial Revolution and the European Family: The Institutional-

ization of "Childhood" as a Market for Family Labor. *Comparative Studies in Society and History* 29(3): 454–467.

Mitchell, Jon P.
1997   A Moment with Christ: The Importance of Feelings in the Analysis of Belief. *Journal of the Royal Anthropological Institute* 3(1): 79–94.

Morton, Helen
1996   *Becoming Tongan: An Ethnography of Childhood.* Honolulu: University of Hawaii Press.

Mörth, Ingo, and Gerhard Fröhlich, compilers
2003   *HyperBourdieu World Catalogue.* Online Bibliography. http://www.iwp.uni-linz.ac.at/lxe/sektktf/bb/HyperBourdieu.html, accessed December 6, 2003.

Müller, Anne Friederike
2002   Sociology as a Combat Sport. *Anthropology Today* 18(2): 5–9.

Nader, L.
1997   Controlling Processes: Tracing the Dynamic Components of Power. *Current Anthropology* 38(5): 711–37.

Noiriel, Gérard
1996 [1988]   *The French Melting Pot: Immigration, Citizenship and National Identity.* Geoffrey de LaForcade, trans. Minneapolis and London: University of Minnesota Press.

Okely, Judith
1975   The Self and Scientism. *Journal of the Social Anthropology Society* 6(3): 171–88.
1992   Anthropology and Autobiography: Participatory Experience and Embodied Knowledge. In *Anthropology and Autobiography.* Judith Okely and Helen Callaway, eds. Pp. 1–28. London: Routledge.

Okely, Judith, and Helen Callaway, eds.
1992   *Anthropology and Autobiography.* London: Routledge.

Ortner, Sherry
1984   Theory in Anthropology Since the Sixties. *Comparative Studies in Society and History* 26: 126–166.

Ottaway, A. K. C.
1955   The Educational Sociology of Emile Durkheim. *The British Journal of Sociology* 6(3): 213–227.

Ozouf, Mona
1963   *L'école, l'église, et la république, 1871–1914.* Paris: Armand Colin.

Pelissier, Catherine
1991   The Anthropology of Teaching and Learning. *Annual Review of Anthropology* 20: 75–95.

Peneff, Jean
1990   *La méthode biographique.* Paris: Armand Colin.

Peristiany, J. G., ed.
1966   *Honour and Shame: The Values of Mediterranean Society.* Chicago: University of Chicago Press.

Peristiany, J. G., and Julian Pitt-Rivers, eds.
1992   *Honor and Grace in Anthropology.* Cambridge: Cambridge University Press.

Peyrefitte, Alain
1963   *Rue d'Ulm: Chroniques de la vie normalienne.* 2nd ed. Paris: Paris: Flammarion.

Pitt-Rivers, Julian, ed.
1963   *Mediterranean Countrymen.* Paris and La Haye: Mouton and Co.

Pompougnac, J. C.
1984   L'école et l'enfance de la sociologie. In *L'Empire du sociologie.* Jacques Rancière, ed. Pp. 37–50. Paris: Éditions de la Decouverte.

Poncet, Emmanuel
2002   "La névrose de classe" de Bourdieu. *Libération.* February 7. http://www.liberation.com, accessed March 15, 2002.

Prost, Antoine
1968   *Histoire de l'enseignement en France, 1800–1967.* Paris: Libraire Armand Colin.

Reddy, William
1997   Against Constructionism: The Historical Ethnography of Emotions. *Current Anthropology* 38(3): 327–351.

Reed-Danahay, Deborah
1986   "Educational Strategies and Social Change in Rural France." Ph.D. dissertation, Brandeis University.
1987   Farm Children at School: Educational Strategies in Rural France. *Anthropological Quarterly* 60(2): 83–89.
1993   Talking about Resistance: Ethnography and Theory in Rural France. *Anthropological Quarterly* 66(4): 221–246.
1995   The Kabyle and the French: Occidentalism in Bourdieu's Theory of Practice. In *Occidentalism: Images of the West.* James Carrier, ed. Pp. 61–84. Oxford and New York: Oxford University Press.
1996a   *Education and Identity in Rural France: The Politics of Schooling.* Cambridge: Cambridge University Press.
1996b   Champagne and Chocolate: Taste and Inversion in a French Wedding Ritual. *American Anthropologist* 98(4): 750–761.
1997a   Introduction. In *Auto/Ethnography: Rewriting the Self and the Social.* Deborah Reed-Danahay, ed. Pp. 1–20. Oxford and New York: Berg Publishers.
1997b   Leaving Home: Schooling Stories and the Ethnography of Autoethnography in Rural France. In *Auto/Ethnography: Rewriting the Self and the Social.* Deborah Reed-Danahay, ed. Pp. 123–144. Oxford and New York: Berg Publishers.

1999   Friendship, Kinship and The Life Course in Rural Auvergne. In *The Anthropology of Friendship.* Sandra Bell and Simon Coleman, eds. Pp. 137–154. Oxford and New York: Berg Publishers.

2000   Habitus and Cultural Identity: Home/School Relationships in Rural France. In *Schooling the Symbolic Animal.* Bradley Levinson, ed. Pp. 223–236. Lanham, Md.: Rowman and Littlefield.

2001a   This Is Your Home Now! Conceptualizing Location and Dislocation in a Dementia Unit. *Qualitative Research* 1(1): 47–63.

2001b   Autobiography, Intimacy and Ethnography. In *Handbook of Ethnography.* Paul Atkinson et al., eds. Pp. 407–425. London: Sage.

2002   Sites of Memory: Women's Autoethnographies from Rural France. *Biography* 25(1): 95–109.

2003   Europeanization and French Primary Education: Local Implications of Supranational Policies. In *Local Meanings, Global Schooling: Anthropology and World Culture Theory.* Kathryn Anderson-Levitt, ed. Pp. 201–218. New York: Palgrave Macmillan.

2004   *Tristes Paysans:* Bourdieu's Early Ethnography in Béarn and Kabylia. *Anthropological Quarterly* 77(1): 87–106.

Reed-Danahay, Deborah E., ed.
1997   *Auto/Ethnography: Rewriting the Self and the Social.* Oxford and New York: Berg.

Reed-Danahay, Deborah, and Kathryn M. Anderson-Levitt
1991   Backward Countryside, Troubled City: French Teachers' Images of Rural and Working-Class Families. *American Ethnologist* 18(3): 546–564.

Robbins, Derek
1991   *The Work of Pierre Bourdieu: Recognizing Society.* Boulder, Colo.: Westview Press.

2000   *Bourdieu and Culture.* London and Thousand Oaks, Calif.: Sage.

2003   The Responsibility of the Ethnographer: An Introduction to Pierre Bourdieu on "Colonialism and Ethnography." *Anthropology Today* 19(2): 11–12.

Robbins, Derek, ed.
2000   *Pierre Bourdieu.* 4 vols. London and Thousand Oaks, Calif.: Sage.

Rogers, Susan Carol
1985   Gender in Southwestern France: The Myth of Male Dominance Revisited. *Anthropology* 9: 65–86.

1987   Good to Think: The "Peasant" in Contemporary France. *Anthropological Quarterly* 60(2): 56–63.

1991   *Shaping Modern Times in Rural France.* Princeton, N.J.: Princeton University Press.

1999   Interesting Friends and *Faux Amis:* An Introduction to New Directions in French Anthropology. *Cultural Anthropology* 14(3): 396–422.

2001   Anthropology in France. *Annual Review of Anthropology* 30: 481–504.

Rosaldo, Michelle Z.
1980   *Knowledge and Passion: Ilongot Notions of Self and Social Life.* Cambridge: Cambridge University Press.
1983   The Shame of Headhunters and the Autonomy of Self. *Ethos* 11(3): 135–151.
1984   Toward an Anthropology of Self and Feeling. In *Culture Theory: Essays on Mind, Self and Emotion.* Richard A. Shweder and Robert A. LeVine, eds. Pp. 137–157. Cambridge: Cambridge University Press.

Rosaldo, Renato
1986   From the Door of His Tent: The Fieldworker and the Inquisitor. In *Writing Culture: The Poetics and Politics of Ethnography.* James Clifford and George E. Marcus, eds. Pp. 77–97. Berkeley: University of California Press.
1989   *Culture and Truth: The Remaking of Social Analysis.* Boston: Beacon Press.

Ross, Kristin
2002   *May '68 and Its Afterlives.* Chicago: University of Chicago Press.

Rousmaniere, K., K. Delhi, and N. de Coninck-Smith
1997   Moral Regularion and Schooling: An Introduction. In *Discipline, Moral Regulation, and Schooling: A Social History.* K. Rousmaniere, K. Delhi, and N. de Coninck-Smith, eds. Pp. 3–18. New York and London: Garland Press.

Scherer, Klaus, and Paul Ekman, eds.
1984   *Approaches to Emotion.* Hillsdale, N.J.: Lawrence Erlbaum Associates.

Sciences Humaines
2002   L'œuvre de Pierre Bourdieu. *Sciences Humaines.* Numéro Special Pierre Bourdieu—2002. Auxerre: Sciences Humaines.

Scott, James C.
1985   *Weapons of the Weak: Everyday Forms of Peasant Resistance.* New Haven, Conn.: Yale University Press.

Segalen, Martine
1983 [1980]   *Love and Power in the Peasant Family: Rural France in the Nineteenth Century.* Sarah Matthews, trans. Chicago: University of Chicago Press.
1984   "Avoir sa part": Sibling Relations in Partible Inheritance in Brittany. In *Interest and Emotion: Essays on the Study of Family and Kinship.* Hans Medick and David Warren Sabean, eds. Pp. 129–144. Cambridge: Cambridge University Press and Paris: Editions de la Maison des Sciences de l'Homme.
1989   *L'autre et le semblable: Regards sur l'ethnologie des sociétés contemporaines.* Paris: Presses Universitaires de France.

Shirley, Dennis
1986   A Critical Review and Appropriation of Pierre Bourdieu's Analysis of Social and Cultural Reproduction. *Journal of Education* 168(2): 96–112.

Shusterman, Richard, ed.
1999   *Bourdieu: A Critical Reader.* Oxford and Malden, Mass.: Blackwell Publishers.

Shweder, Richard, and Robert Levine, eds.
1984   *Culture Theory: Essays on Mind, Self, and Emotion.* Cambridge: Cambridge University Press.

Silverstein, Paul
2002   *A Crisis in Time: Kabyle Habitus, Uprooting, and Historical Consciousness.* Paper presented at the American Anthropological Association Meetings, New Orleans, November.
2003   De l'enracinement et du déracinement. *Actes de la Recherche en Sciences Sociales* 150: 27–34.

Sirota, Régine
1988   *L'école primaire au quotidien.* Paris: Presses Universitaires de France.

Stora, Benjamin
2001   *Algeria 1830–2000: A Short History.* Jane Marie Todd, trans. Ithaca, N.Y., and London: Cornell University Press.

Swartz, David
1997   *Culture and Power: The Sociology of Pierre Bourdieu.* Chicago: University of Chicago Press.
2002   Social Reproduction. In *Education and Sociology: An Encyclopedia.* D. L. Levinson, ed. Pp. 551–557. New York and London: Routledge Falmer.

Touraine, Alain
2002   Le sociologue du peuple. *Sciences Humaines.* Numéro Special Pierre Bourdieu—2002. Pp. 101–103. Auxerre: Sciences Humaines.

Van Gennep, Arnold
1937–58. *Manuel de folklore français contemporain.* 3 vols. Paris: Picard.

Van Krieken, Robert
1998   *Norbert Elias.* New York and London: Routledge.

Varenne, Hervé
1984   Collective Representation in American Anthropological Conversations: Individual and Culture. *Current Anthropology* 25(3): 281–300.

Verdès-Leroux, Jeannine
2001   *Deconstructing Pierre Bourdieu: Against Sociological Terrorism from the Left.* New York: Algora.

Vincent, Guy
1980   *L'école primaire française: Etude sociologique.* Lyon: Presses Universitaire de Lyon.

Wacquant, Loïc
2002   The Sociological Life of Pierre Bourdieu. *International Sociology* 17(4): 549–556.
2003   *Body and Soul: Notebooks of an Apprentice Boxer.* Oxford and New York: Oxford University Press.

Webb, Jen, Tony Schirato, and Geoff Danaher
2002   *Understanding Bourdieu.* London: Sage.

Webber, Sabra
1980   Review of Outline of a Theory of Practice. *Mera Forum* 4(3): 12–14.

Weber, Eugen
1976   *Peasants into Frenchmen: The Modernization of Rural France, 1870–1914.* Stanford, Calif.: Stanford University Press.

Weber, Florence
1989a Les études rurales dans la France des années trente: Un apogee oublié. *Recherches Sociologiques* 20(3): 367–381.
1989b *La travail à-côté: Étude d'ethnographie ouvrière.* Paris: Institute National de la Recherche Agronomique and Éditions de l'École des Hautes Études en Sciences Sociales.

Weber, Max
1946   *Max Weber: Essays in Sociology.* H. H. Gerth and C. Wright Mills, trans. New York: Oxford University Press.

Williams, Raymond
1961   *The Long Revolution.* New York: Columbia University Press.

Williams, Simon
2001   *Emotion and Social Theory.* London, Thousand Oaks, Calif., and New Delhi: Sage Publications.

Willis, Paul
1981 [1977]   *Learning to Labor: How Working Class Kids Get Working Class Jobs.* New York: Columbia University Press.
1981   Cultural Production is Different from Cultural Reproduction is Different from Social Reproduction Is Different from Reproduction. *Interchange* 12(2/3): 48–67.

Wylie, Laurence
1975 [1957]   *Village in the Vaucluse.* 3rd ed. Cambridge, Mass.: Harvard University Press.

Yacine, Tassadit.
2003   L'Algérie, matrice d'une oeuvre. In *Travailler avec Bourdieu.* Pierre Encrevé and Rose-Marie Lagrave, eds. Pp. 333–345. Paris: Flammarion.

Yon, Daniel A.
2000   *Elusive Culture: Schooling, Race, and Identity in Global Times.* Albany: State University of New York Press.

Zonabend, Françoise
1979   Anthropologie de la France et de l'Europe. In *L'Anthropologie en France: Situation Actuelle et Avenir.* Paris: Editions du Centre National de la Recherche Scientifique (CNRS).
1984 [1980]   *The Enduring Memory: Time and History in a French Village.* Anthony Forster, trans. Manchester: Manchester University Press.

INDEX

NEW ANTHROPOLOGIES OF EUROPE

EDITORS
Daphne Berdahl, Matti Bunzl, and Michael Herzfeld

PUBLICATIONS
Algeria in France: Transpolitics, Race, and Nation
Paul A. Silverstein

Locating Bourdieu
Deborah Reed-Danahay

DEBORAH REED-DANAHAY is Professor of Anthropology at the University of Texas at Arlington. She is the editor of *Auto/Ethnography: Rewriting the Self and the Social*, and author of *Education and Identity in Rural France: The Politics of Schooling*, as well as several key articles drawing on the work of Pierre Bourdieu.